W9-AXH-599

James F. Gilsinan, Criminal Justice Coordinator at Saint Louis University and an Associate Professor of Urban Affairs and Criminology, has served as a consultant to a variety of law enforcement agencies and has trained police officers in both crisis intervention and management techniques. He has worked with the Denver, Colorado, and St. Louis, Missouri, Police Academies.

1/10/83

Bill —

Happy Birthday

I knew you'd like this
better than a bottle of
Chivas. The effect is the
same, however. If you read
too much at one time, you'll
fall asleep!

Jim or Bill
or whatever

P.S. Leave this in a prominent
place in your office

DOING JUSTICE

How the System Works —As Seen by the Participants

James F. Gilsinan, Ph.D.

A SPECTRUM BOOK

Prentice-Hall, Inc., Englewood Cliffs, New Jersey 07632

Library of Congress Cataloging in Publication Data

Gilsinan, James F.
  Doing justice.

  A Spectrum Book
  Includes bibliographical references and index.
  1. Criminal justice, Administration of—United States.
  I. Title
  KF9223.G5   345.73'05   81-17950
                 347.3055   AACR2

ISBN 0-13-217315-8

ISBN 0-13-217307-7 {PBK.}

Editorial/production supervision and interior design by Suse Cioffi
Cover illustration by Jeannette Jacobs
Manufacturing buyer: Barbara Frick

This Spectrum Book can be made available to businesses
and organizations at a special discount
when ordered in large quantities. For more information contact:

Prentice-Hall, Inc.
General Publishing Division
Special Sales
Englewood Cliffs, New Jersey 07632

10 9 8 7 6 5 4 3 2 1

Printed in the United States of America

PRENTICE-HALL INTERNATIONAL, INC., *London*
PRENTICE-HALL OF AUSTRALIA PTY. LIMITED, *Sydney*
PRENTICE-HALL OF CANADA, LTD., *Toronto*
PRENTICE-HALL OF INDIA PRIVATE LIMITED, *New Delhi*
PRENTICE-HALL OF JAPAN, INC., *Tokyo*
PRENTICE-HALL OF SOUTHEAST ASIA PTE. LTD., *Singapore*
WHITEHALL BOOKS LIMITED, WELLINGTON, *New Zealand*

To James Francis the Second and James Francis the Fourth.
Life continues, hidden from a part of itself.

Contents

Preface

When I told a colleague that I was writing this book, her response was, "What could possibly be said about crime and criminal justice that has not already been said?" After that, I quit telling my colleagues what I was doing.

Still, the question is a valid one. What has not been said, at least not in any one place, is how those who do justice day in and day out see the world. The police officer, the attorneys (both defense and prosecution), the judge, the probation/parole officer, the prison guard, and citizens involved as victims or jurors all have different stories to tell about crime and what it means to them. Of course, the story they each tell about crime helps shape that phenomenon and the image people hold about criminal acts and criminal perpetrators. By revealing these stories and analyzing the rules criminal justice people use to construct them, a greater understanding of what we call the crime problem can emerge. The terms *crime* and *criminal* are not viewed, therefore, as simply empirical descriptions of events, but rather as evaluations of events made in response to the cross-pressures and tensions of daily living.

The intellectual debt I owe to people like Erving Goffman, Donald Black, Howard Becker, Harold Garfinkel, David Sudnow, and others will be evident to many. A very real debt is also owed to the police officers, attorneys, and corrections people who let me share their lives. Hopefully, by telling their stories, the good as well as the bad, citizens will be more understanding of the impossible tasks society expects these individuals to perform. This understanding in turn can be the first step toward realistic expectations and policy in the area of criminal justice.

I would also like to thank those directly involved in helping bring this book about. I was fortunate to have colleagues at St. Louis University's Center for Urban Programs who were supportive both with intellectual stimulation and social camaraderie, particularly Henry Schmandt, George Wendel, Brian Nedwek, Donald Sprengel, John Manns, and E. Allan Tomey. I was also fortunate to have three excellent student assistants, Mary Domihidy, Bridget Flood, and Hilda Besand, who read drafts, did research, and cut and pasted when editing so required. My typist, Donna McBride-Braun did more than just type. She helped clarify ideas and cheerfully typed and retyped from handwritten copy that sometimes looked more like a treasure map with arrows and "x's" pointing to where the next word was. Finally, my wife, Christine Gilsinan, gave far more than just moral support. Her legal expertise, her keen editing, and her insistence on intellectual rigour and clarity made the book far better than it would have been.

If I still did not get it right after all of this help, I deserve and accept responsibility for any errors and mistakes remaining.

chapter one

Do You Believe in Witches?

The Really Real

This book argues a rather strange thesis for a work on criminal justice. The thesis is that crime and criminals are not empirical realities. What is really "real" are the accounts or descriptions people give about their world. For some, the categories *crime* and *criminal* are meaningful ways to organize and make sense out of certain events and the people involved in them. Factors that have little relationship to an actual empirical occurrence influence such accounting and describing practices. This suggests that to understand the problem of crime in our society, one must look at the individuals charged with identifying, processing, and treating those persons categorized as criminals. What values motivate them, what beliefs help them structure their social reality, what strategies do they use to reaffirm their view of the world? In the following pages, you are invited to observe and participate in the building of a social world by various actors on the criminal justice scene. Seeing the world through their eyes can lead to policy suggestions that will lessen the likelihood of our being victimized by an uncritical acceptance of the prevailing beliefs and practices concerning crime and deviance.

Who Are the Deviants, and How Do We Recognize Them?

Kai T. Erikson, in his book *Wayward Puritans,* has shown the importance of values and beliefs in the creation and perpetuation of deviance.[1] Erikson examines three crime waves of Puritan colonial America. The crime waves consisted of outbreaks of witchcraft, heresy, and the satanic manifestations of Quakerism. These three crime waves coincided with periods of rapid social change and upheaval in the colonies. The witchcraft hysteria in Salem, for example, was preceded by shifts in the social, political, and religious climate of Massachusetts. The Puritan settlers saw their carefully structured theocracy being swept away by the winds of historical circumstance. The Puritan island of sanctity in the midst of the wilderness was in danger of again becoming swallowed up by the surrounding wilds. At this point in the Puritans' history, the wilderness that threatened was no longer the harsh physical surroundings. Rather, the Puritans saw a dark, dangerous, demon-infested spiritual swamp that was about to engulf them as punishment for moving away from God's divine plan. There was a need to reestablish community boundaries and to stake out the path the community was to tread in the midst of continuing flux. A new map was essential if the Puritans were to find their way to renewed spirituality and to avoid the ever-threatening demons of change. It was within the framework of this interpretation of history that, as Erikson says, "the witches decided to strike."

Twenty-two persons died in a four-month period during the height of the witchcraft hysteria. Nineteen people had been adjudicated as witches and had been promptly executed. One was pressed to death under a rock pile in an effort to overcome the person's reluctance to testify at his trial. Two died in prison.[2] The first hearing, conducted to deal with one witch in a quiet, efficient way, rather than bringing a speedy end to the affair led to other trials and accusations engulfing hundreds of people. The figures testify to the power of beliefs and the mechanisms beliefs inspire for creating and perpetuating deviance. Witches were now seen everywhere. Indeed, it was the very efficiency of the witch-defining mechanism and the identification processes it wrought that eventually brought about the abatement of witchcraft hysteria. Soon witchcraft and witches were uncovered not only in the fringe groups of the society (among servants, old women, etc.) but also in the upper echelons. When this shift in labeling occurred and allowed the inclusion of community influentials in the category of potential deviant, the whole process was challenged and eventually halted.

Erikson's discussion of witchcraft hysteria in colonial America illustrates a number of factors concerning deviance. The definition of deviance is related to the beliefs and values of the community at a given historical moment. Also, societies may experience a greater need to produce deviants at particular times in their history. Thus, when a society's social boundaries shift or become blurred because of rapid social change, the identification of deviants helps to articulate the society's concerns and gives it a means of reestablishing an image of itself and its future goals. People find out who they are by pinpointing who they are not. The "others" or the "are nots" provide a comparison for what we ourselves are or want to become.

The process of identifying these others is, of course, also heavily influenced by currently held beliefs. Witches were "discovered" by numerous "legitimate" procedures. Uncovering witch's marks, which were simply body moles, scars, or abrasions interpreted by experts to be signs of Satan, was one legitimate procedure of identification. Failure to repeat the Lord's Prayer without a mistake was another legitimate index of witchcraft. If a person afflicted by a witch saw another's image, that provided evidence that the second individual had allowed Satan to use his or her form for his malevolent deeds. Other similarly valid criteria were developed in the hunt for Satan's minions. Some people confessed. In Salem, at any rate, this was a smart tactic. No one who confessed was executed.

There was one procedure that was not used in Salem. That was the seventeenth-century European custom of ordeal by water. A person, bound hand and foot with a rope, was "dunked" in a body of water. If the person floated, this meant that Satan was coming to his or her rescue, and the individual was promptly executed. If, on the other hand, the individual sank, this provided proof of innocence. Unfortunately, there were times when the now-proven innocent subject could not be pulled out in time to prevent drowning. There were other times when the rope broke, with the same result. This apparently happened with enough frequency so that it became necessary to outlaw the ordeal by water.[3] Nevertheless, some people justified the procedure and the unintentional drownings by claiming that the person's death was inconsequential because he or she died in the state of innocence and went to heaven. The officials had really done the individual a favor.[4]

What barbarians, we say. If they had only critically examined some of their beliefs and procedures, they might have avoided inflicting untold instances of human suffering and pain. But the dynamics of deviance discovery, processing, and treatment may not have changed all that much. I once asked a group of students if they believed in witches. Most did not. I then asked if they believed in criminals, psychotics, and sociopaths. All believed, even though few had ever seen any. They accepted the words of the experts as being true, valid descriptions of social reality. Their sacred book may no longer be a Bible, but there is still a divine text, be it a psychology book or a sociology book. These books say there are particular kinds of people out there, and even though very few have seen them, if the authorities and experts say they are there, they must be there. All of this illustrates the power of beliefs. I suspect that this class of students is really a microcosm. There is a group that will reject any challenge to the currently held sacred truths. There is also a group that is perhaps more analytical, but in the end this second group, too, bases its arguments on what the experts say. And finally, there are those, perhaps in fact the majority, who do not want to hassle and will accept the prevailing standard in order to get by.

For citizens interested in the process of justice, none of these three alternatives is really acceptable. After all, some of you will be the ones to administer the "truth," and unless you are willing to challenge the prevailing beliefs you may well end up being the inquisitors and witch hunters of today. Perhaps you are reading this book only because you want to be a better informed citizen. Your responsibility, then, will be just as great. Because you will share the burden of supporting or challenging suggested reforms in the system, you, too, must be able to analyze the current trends critically. Otherwise, suggested reforms will not work. They will simply operate to perpetuate the existing system and solidify the prevailing beliefs. For example, suggesting to the Salem witch hunters that they should require a college education before admission to their ranks does little to bring about basic reform in their beliefs and the system created to bolster such beliefs. This would be particularly true if future witch hunters were required to take most of their courses in witch-hunting techniques and laws dealing with witches. By analogy, the current emphasis on law enforcement courses in colleges and the requirement of a college degree for police officers needs to be critically examined in light of currently held beliefs about crime and the modern organizational structure of police departments. Will increased education increase humane treatment of offenders? There is certainly room for doubt. The need to validate the self and society as good or normal by invalidating the other as evil will not be seriously challenged by simply requiring more education of criminal justice functionaries. If a belief in "otherness" helps to create and perpetuate deviance, then what is needed is a thorough examination of such beliefs to discover the extent of their validity. Such an examination can help us avoid treatment that merely reaffirms existing societal images while doing little for those who are subject to it, except degrading them to the point at which further deviance becomes likely.

Altruism need not be the only motive for critically examining our beliefs regarding crime and the criminal. After all, it is difficult to be philosophical if one is faced with an immediate threat of harm. Confronting someone about to do us bodily injury calls for practical action. The problem is with our perception of who is about to do us harm. Most Americans fear harm from strangers, and yet if we are to be victimized, the chances are it will be by someone we know. What form will the victimization take? Here again, most fear being victims of street crime. The kinds of crime that appear in official police statistics, like assault, robbery, homicide, rape, and so forth, raise the most fear among the population. And yet, victimization can come about in situations where it is least expected. Recent data gathered by medical societies underscore the point. Of the 320,000 practicing physicians, 16,000 (or 5 percent) are unfit to practice. A 5 percent incompetency rate is perhaps no worse a rate than in any other profession. Unfortunately, however, there are 7.5 million people treated by this 5 percent.[5] That is a lot of people risking victimization. Most are probably unaware of the threat to life and limb that they face and, if anything, are more worried by so-called street crime. The real danger they face, however, is not on the street. There are "nearly 2.4 million unnecessary operations each year in which 11,900 patients die as a result of complications."[6] The debilitating effects of drugs are also an area of concern, exemplified by recurrent governmental programs to eliminate pushers and suppliers. But again, this danger is not only present on the street. Yearly, "at least 30,000 Americans accept the drugs their doctors prescribe for them and die as a direct result." According to a recent report on the matter, "perhaps ten times as many patients suffer life-threatening and sometimes permanent side effects." Further, it has been estimated "that 22 percent of the antibiotics prescribed in hospitals are unnecessary." Eliminating these would save ten thousand or more patients from untold pain, suffering, and, in some instances, premature death.

When American physicians are compared to physicians in countries with similar health profiles, "United States doctors write twice as many prescriptions" as their foreign colleagues.[7] In part, physicians' prescribing habits are due to consumer demands.

But consumer demands are themselves culturally influenced. Advertising has gone to great lengths to convince people that drugs are the answer to a variety of problems, from getting up in the morning through going to bed at night. Any problems that arise in between, from an upset stomach to a tension headache, are all easily remedied. Thus, physicians may overprescribe, but they do so in response to societal beliefs. Street pushers and suppliers also respond to the same cultural beliefs. Yet, overprescribing physicians are not processed, identified, and treated in the same way as the street-level dealer. Victimization risk may be as great to the public, but reaction is generally only directed toward the latter group. Our views of who is likely to be deviant prevent us from being aware of the bodily threat posed by respectables. From a practical standpoint, then, reviewing cultural beliefs about deviance can help us avoid victimization from others in our environment who may present just as serious a threat as those normally identified as criminal.

Certainly, this is the case with respect to traffic violators. Hartjen notes that in the United States there is a 1:20,000 risk of being killed by an assaultist. There is a 1:4,000 chance of being killed in a traffic accident.[8] Fifty thousand people are killed annually in traffic accidents. Over half of these involve the drunk driver. Very few people, though, talk about the need for drastic action regarding the drunk driver. Nobody would argue that capital punishment is a fitting remedy for this problem. Why? Probably because most of us can put ourselves in the place of the individual who drives while intoxicated. He or she is not an "other." He or she is an "us." Besides, traffic violations are not crimes. Patterned evasions of traffic laws are an American way of life. Now, with C.B. radios and "fuzz busters," such evasions have been raised to a sophisticated level, and all in the name of good, clean fun. But the fun costs millions of dollars in property loss and immeasurable anguish to those who are injured and to the survivors of those who are killed. Deviance is in the eye of the beholder. Unless it is a critical eye, however, we risk becoming victims of our own blindness.

Now That We've Caught Them, What Will We Do?

The field of corrections is one that seems vulnerable to whatever the current fad happens to be. If criminals are seen as devils, we impose suffering on them to help expiate their sins. If they are viewed as hopeless wretches, we isolate them. If they are seen as sick, we treat them. The fad is spawned by the belief. Despite views to the contrary, however, all of these approaches contain a heavy dose of punishment. Punishment is seen as necessary in order to deter future crime. It will deter others, as well as the individual himself, or so the popular belief has it. At present, though, the issue remains in doubt. While many studies have found some evidence for a deterrent effect, others seem to cast doubt on the efficacy of punishment for deterrence. As one authoritative panel has noted, the state of both available data and current research methods makes it difficult to show conclusively whether or not punishment deters.[9] Our discussion of Salem witchcraft hysteria, however, suggested that the more institutions one creates for the purposes of punishment, the more people there seem to be to punish.

Research by William G. Nagel "has shown that the fifteen states with the most prison construction in the 1955–75 period had a combined increase in cell space of 56 percent, a figure closely matched by their 57 percent increase in prison populations. In contrast, the fifteen states with the least prison construction . . . experienced a 9 percent drop in prison populations."[10]

Some students might object to the notion that treatment, a term borrowed from the medical paradigm, contains as one of its major facets, punishment. Punishment curtails a person's freedom to a greater or lesser extent. A person confined to prison for five years has his freedom curtailed. A person fined twenty-five dollars for littering also has his freedom curtailed, at least insofar as he was going to spend that money on something else. When the treatment or therapeutic model is compared with the penal model, it can be argued that the assault on human freedom is as great or possibly greater in the former. Nicholas N. Kittrie, in his book *The Right to Be Different*, compares the two approaches and notes that in some ways the therapeutic model is less humane than the penal model it sought to replace.[11] One reason for this is that the treatment or medical approach, when taken from medicine and applied to corrections, has an important element added to it. This is the element of compulsion. When an individual is sick, he theoretically has the option of whether or not to choose treatment. In the framework of a correctional approach, however, the person has no authority in determining if he is to be given treatment.

The Supreme Court has recognized the need to protect people, particularly juveniles, from treatment. In *In re Gault* the Supreme Court said that the juvenile court must provide for those that come before it the same legal safeguards that are provided in adult proceedings. The juvenile courts had, prior to that decision, acted primarily as dispensers of treatment. Gault, a fifteen-year-old, was brought before the court for making obscene phone calls. The court sentenced him to a state treatment facility until the end of his twenty-first year. Hence, this juvenile was to be incarcerated for seven years for an offense that an adult would probably be admonished about or at worst fined for.

Further implications for the dignity and protection of the individual contained in the medical model have been noted by Erving Goffman.[12] When a person is subject to treatment, one indication of his progress is his willingness to admit that he was sick or in error. The same approach, when carried over into criminology, means that an individual would have to admit that he was wrong or criminal before he could be considered successfully "treated" and therefore no longer in need of continued treatment. This presents shades of the Salem witchcraft hysteria. Confession to being a witch was a way of avoiding further "treatment." If the term *criminal* is as nebulous as the term *witch*, forcing a person to accept this self-definition perpetrates an added assault on individual dignity. Sickness and punishment also have different social implications. For example, a youngster sent to a disciplinarian by his grammar school teacher is reprimanded and that is the end of the incident, assuming that the teacher and the disciplinarian do not conspire to hang the label "troublemaker" on the defendant. But to treat discipline problems as matters for the school psychologist means that our same young man is now seen as sick and relentlessly pursued in the quest to give him treatment. The psychologist gains much more control over the life of the young lad than did the disciplinarian. The boy's background, his family, his dreams all become possible subjects to be discussed and dissected. Rather than punishment swiftly given and perhaps swiftly forgotten, treatment which is not swift and not easily forgotten is substituted, and personal integrity is seriously challenged.

The potential for the lessening of human dignity and freedom is also illustrated by noting that with the development of predictive instruments, the medical model allows for intervention before any given act is committed. The legal criterion of proving guilt or innocence before interfering in a person's life is not required in a treatment paradigm. While the notion of preventive medicine may be beneficial, preventive treatment in the area of crime has frightening social implications. But unless those interested in criminal justice, both liberal and conservative, begin to examine some of the assumptions inherent in their theoretical approaches more critically, they may be instrumental in ushering in the Orwellian nightmare which they are supposedly on guard against. A treatment approach, as much as a penal one, must avoid the tendency to put people in categories that make normal interactions with others less and less likely. Both must also avoid the fallacy of the inquisitors of the Middle Ages—namely, we can do what we want to you, because we seek the salvation of your soul (or psyche).

What Is Law?

The suggestion that we need to critically examine the beliefs that underlie our view of the world is particularly germane to a discussion of criminal justice. One of the major symbols manipulated in our society is law, particularly criminal law. Law embodies beliefs and values about the society and how that society should function. The study of law, then, raises numerous questions. Whose beliefs and values does it purport to represent? All of society's, or those of a select few? In its application, who possesses the most power? Is it the legislature who creates the laws, the police officer who enforces them, the judge who decides the case by making his own application, or perhaps the society generally which demands certain laws be made by its representatives? Are the values of all these groups the same? Do they all possess a common set of beliefs about the world? If they do, what are these beliefs and what are their effects on the administration of justice? If they do not possess a common set of beliefs, are laws applied and manipulated differently at each stage of the process so that they symbolize a different set of concerns depending on whether you are a police officer, an attorney, a judge, or a defendant? All of these questions can of course be subsumed under the more general question, "What is law?" The definitions of law are perhaps as numerous as the actual number of statutes in existence. Law is different things to different people. Some of these definitions can be noted by describing the various theories that have been postulated to explain the development of law. One school of thought holds that criminal law developed from an attempt to regulate the adjudication of private wrongs. Thus criminal law is seen as developing from matters of tort. Torts are private wrongs, settled primarily by the participants themselves. However, it was not always clear when sufficient justice was rendered to one person by another. If someone kills my brother, is sufficient justice extracted by killing him or his brother? Are the two lives equal? If, in the view of the family whose brother I killed to make up for my own brother's death, the former's life is worth more than the latter's, they may feel it incumbent upon them to do away with a member of equal status in my family. Of course, I may not agree with their assessment, thus necessitating another killing of one of their own. And so a vicious circle ensues, the end result of which is a blood feud, with a lot of people getting killed and nobody being really sure when justice has been achieved. Hence a need to introduce a third party, represented by law. Limits are now put on the extent to which a person can be expected to be compensated for an injury. Today tort law, or civil law, is primarily concerned with private injuries and the adjudication of just settlements between two parties. The tort model, however, never quite answers the question of why certain laws become criminal, that is, of concern to the state, and others remain a matter of civil litigation with the parties themselves being the prime initiators of an action. After all, if a robbery occurs, the victim does not pursue the individual with a piece of paper that says he will sue him to recover his lost revenue. Instead the state takes over, and pursues the individual on its own, regardless of what the victim thinks. The state's interest in the matter is underscored by noting that in a criminal procedure, the case is described as *The State of Illinois vs. Escobedo*, not *John Jones vs. Escobedo* as it would appear in a civil matter. What, then, distinguishes criminal law from civil law?

Some theorists argue that only the most sacred values of a society are embodied in its criminal law.[13] This value consensus theory sees law as developing from the mores of a society. Those values and norms of behavior that everybody agrees are important are given over to the state to enforce. This view assumes that there are a common set of values in society and that everybody agrees on them. While it is true that most people would agree that burglary is wrong, clearly not all criminal laws are of this type. For example, not all people would agree that the current criminal regulation of certain drugs is necessary or desirable. Further, while most people could agree with the general statement that taking something belonging to another is wrong, it is not at all clear that everyone agrees as to when this action should be governed by law. Should a child who takes a dime from her mother's dresser be processed by the legal system? At what point should the behavior in question become a public concern? It is not even certain that everyone would agree about what constitutes taking something from another. In one family, the little girl in question might be seen as having taken her mother's dime. In another family, however, the same action can be viewed as merely sharing common resources, with the dime seen as belonging to the family rather than to the mother for her exclusive use. Taking something from another clearly involves a concept of property rights and what constitutes possession. Even the simple statement that "everybody agrees that taking something belonging to another is wrong," on further examination seems much more complex. Agreement or disagreement depends on how a host of other factors are seen and defined. The value consensus theory, even though it may contain some truth, seems a bit oversimplified.

Perhaps law is a rational response to the problems of social order. Legislators pass laws as a rational way of dealing with disruptions that impede the smooth functioning of society. This theory, too, may contain an element of truth. Traffic laws, for example, are a rational way to deal with the problems created by a multitude of cars. Again, however, not all laws appear rational, and indeed some may be passed in the heat of the moment, later to be rescinded as unenforceable or unworkable. Prohibition might be an example of this. Moreover, it is certain that laws, even good laws, may not ensure the smooth functioning of society, and in fact may accelerate social discord. Law and order are not the same thing. Enforcing the law may create large scale social disorder, as happened in some of the urban riots of the 1960s. Finally, as we begin to explore the workings of the criminal justice system, it is doubtful that we will find that it is rational all or even most of the time. As we have already seen, a variety of emotions and beliefs shape the law, and rationality has to compete for its influence with a number of not-so-rational values.

Law must be distinguished from other social norms. As the previous discussion implies, law gives some the power to levy sanctions against law violators. If individuals do not accept the constraints of law in seeking justice, if they violate sacred mores, or if they are disruptive, law contains a mechanism to bring the errant back in line. Thus, one definition of law that attempts to distinguish it from other social norms is that offered by Hoebel:

A social norm is legal if its neglect or infraction is regularly met, in threat or in fact, by the application of physical force by an individual or group possessing the socially recognized privilege of so acting.[14]

This definition, while it distinguishes law from other social norms, still does not give us an insight into the question, "In whose interest is such power exercised?" A final theory of how criminal law develops attempts to answer this question by saying that the power is exercised in the interests of a few to help them maintain their positions. Law is power, and those who have power pass laws that will help them maintain it. This interest group theory of law would hold that law symbolizes the interests of the haves as opposed to those of the have nots. This theory, too, contains elements of truth. Many laws represent the efforts of vocal groups to get their values enshrined in the legal codes in order to obtain a variety of rewards. To go back to Prohibition, this law might be viewed as an attempt on the part of white rural Protestants to symbolize their dominance over the large number of Eastern European Catholic immigrants that were entering the country during the early part of this century. Once the law was passed it could be used as a means of controlling these urban masses. Even if the law was violated, it was clear whose law it was.[15] The current controversy over decriminalization of abortion represents a similar kind of interest group conflict. Clayton Hartjen, in his book *Crime and Criminalization,* notes that even the principle of double jeopardy resulted from a conflict between the Church and the State about who should have the power to punish. England during the eleventh century was plagued with a multiple court system, with both the Church and the King claiming the right of punishment. By enunciating the principle that a person could only be tried once for an offense, the State was claiming the prerogative of punishment, a prerogative which it eventually won. Thus, the result of double jeopardy was to give the State more power, the Church less.[16]

If law and power go together, we can answer the question of what law symbolizes most of the time by examining the applications of the law made by those who are recognized as having the authority to enforce and administer the tenets of our legal system.

A Note on Theory and Method

The theoretical perspective underlying this book is ethnomethodology. While the word itself seems a bit foreboding, its meaning is relatively simple. *Ethno* means group. *Methodology* is the science or study of arrangement, literally the study (logy) of methods or the ways people systematically order things. Putting that all together, ethnomethodology seeks to understand the process by which groups construct order or make sense out of their social activity. In this book, we will observe the patterning created by certain criminal justice personnel as they attempt to weave from the threads of daily activity a whole cloth of order and social meaning. Thus, we cannot take the existence of any preconceived pattern for granted. For our purposes, terms like criminal justice system, crime, criminal, and so on are like the term witch. We suspend belief in their empirical reality, and instead, approach them simply as constructs used by others to make sense out of their world. Given our previous socialization, it will not be easy to abandon our belief in the reality of the categories typically used to construct an explanation for certain types of deviance in our society. Perhaps not easy, but of extreme importance. Imagine an investigator who wanted to learn and understand the dynamics of colonial Puritan society. If such an investigator were to approach the subject without critically examining the constructs used at that time to define social reality, the understanding gained would certainly be limited. An outbreak of witchcraft in Salem, for example, would be fully explained by noting that there was an increase in the number of witches!

The above discussion helps explain what may seem an obvious omission from the previous pages. There are no statistical tables reporting the rates of crime. While some may breathe a sigh of relief at this omission, the question of crime rate statistics and their meaning will be addressed throughout the following chapters. But it is the producers of such rates, those who actually do the counting or categorizing, who will be examined. Traditional theory has assumed that by explaining the behaviors of people that are defined as criminal, one also explains the rates of deviant behavior. There are a number of problems with this assumption, however. First, in terms of theory building, the categories used in official crime indices are said to be irrelevant to a sociological definition of crime or deviance. Thus, Merton cautions investigators against the use of official definitions of deviant behavior, since such classification schemes may confuse actual behavior patterns with legal or bureaucratic formulations. A second problem, also noted by Merton, is the unreliability of such statistics due to "successive layers of error" which are introduced between the event and the recording of the event by various agencies within the criminal justice system.[17] Following from this, a third problem appears in the attempt to validate certain theories by linking them to official rates of deviance. The fit between the two is always imperfect. For example, theories that postulate poverty as a cause of delinquency have a difficult time explaining why, in areas where poverty is present, not everyone shows up in the official records of control agencies. As this chapter has tried to point out, the behavior of an individual defined as deviant is a different phenomenon than the defining process itself. One person acts in a particular way, and another person or group categorizes and defines that behavior. Therefore, to explain crime rates we need to broaden our perspective to include an examination of the social agencies and the behavior of their personnel that produce the rates. The F.B.I. publishes the Uniform Crime Report, not the group of people whose behavior is supposedly represented in these reports. Crime tables and crime statistics are a social production, sometimes used merely to reinforce a current world view. They do not tell us why people see what they see out there, nor do they tell us the factors that influence the scorekeeping methods of those who categorize and record events. We want to know why people now count criminals and not witches. To further aid in this understanding, statistical categories other than crime rates will be discussed, as for example the number of people *not* victimized by activity defined as criminal. Such an examination will allow us to compare our typical understanding of the crime problem, one often formed by reliance on typical crime rates, with that gained by using other, not-so-typical, counting categories.

Since a major focus of this work is on how criminal justice personnel construct meaning and order, the data presented are for the most part ethnographic descriptions. Thus, the theoretical perspective is ethnomethodology, while the method used to discover order construction processes is ethnography.

Ethnography contains its own set of methodological problems. Some of these will be specifically addressed in Chapter 7. Ethnography also runs into certain problems at the level of social acceptance. It is viewed as a product of earlier social science, no longer in vogue because of the rapid advancement of statistical knowledge and computer technology. While participant observation and the collection of ethnographies were necessary tools for anthropologists studying primitive tribes, these techniques are viewed by some as having little utility for examining modern-day institutions. *Ethno* means group, just as it did a few pages back, and *graphy* means a description of. Thus, ethnography is literally a written description of a group of people. There was good reason for anthropologists to collect these written descriptions of various peoples through the technique of participant observation. They could hardly have gone to a previously unknown group with a series of questionnaire items to be filled out and returned by mail. Questionnaires assume that the researcher knows what to ask. They also assume that the individuals responding interpret the questions to mean the same thing the researcher intended. Researcher and respondent must speak the same language. While there are methods for testing these assumptions within such a research design, clearly even the pretesting of items by anthropologists studying an unknown aboriginal tribe was not feasible. The picture of an anthropologist running around with a stack of computer-coded questionnaires in the midst of a primitive tribe, encouraging them to use only No. 2 lead pencils in responding to items on attitudes toward industrialization, smacks of a Monty Python or Marx Brothers skit. Detailed descriptions through participant observation of the life lived by such people were a first necessary step in discovering the nature of their social world. As previously indicated, modern social science has not kept faith with this method. Instead there is a tendency to assume, particularly when examining a modern-day institution, that exploratory detailed description is not needed. We charge in with our sophisticated technology and ask questions that take for granted the context of the life lived by our subjects. The end result of such an approach might well be a display of our technical knowledge and statistical sophistication, rather than a description of the social world we are trying to study.

This book takes the position that the criminal justice system is really virgin territory. Again, the reader should try to put aside his or her preconceived ideas about how the system functions, and take the position of an anthropologist about to embark on an exploratory investigation of a previously unknown group. Ethnography, too, counsels us to become naïve observers, suspending our belief in the existence of crime and criminals. We are about to study groups that say such things exist, and they use sophisticated sorting, categorizing, and counting mechanisms to convince us that this is so. These statistics then become a part of the data to be critically examined, a part of our ethnographies. As noted, however, such statistics should not be seen as the real world, only as an image projected by particular groups. Why they project such images, the effects of seeing the world in this particular way, and the function of such symbolic meanings overall are what we will try to discover.

Outline of the Book

Chapter 2 will examine the process of becoming a police officer. It will describe the beliefs, values, and strategies that new police recruits are exposed to as they become socialized into the police role. This examination will help us understand the social world construction of police officers and gain insight into the symbolic manipulations law enforcement people engage in to make sense out of their activity and the activity of others. The chapter will ask you to put yourself in the place of a police recruit and learn the view of the world necessary if you are to function as an officer in this society. Chapter 3 will continue this theme, examining the decision-making process of police officers. In Chapter 3 you will learn how police officers "practice" law. You will see how recruits are taught to apply the law, and you will be right alongside them as they graduate from the academy and are put in the position to make decisions about the applications of law on the street.

The ethnographic data contained in Chapters 2 and 3, describing the round of life experienced by police recruits, were gathered by me during three years of field work with a middle-sized police department west of the Mississippi River. The department had approximately 1,500 sworn personnel. I spent considerable time riding with various patrol officers and attended, as a participant observer, a twelve-week recruit training academy. In presenting this information certain liberties have been taken. While the conversations, stories, and lectures are for the most part verbatim, they have been condensed and presented through a limited number of fictional characters. Hence, while the information given to the recruits was presented over a long period of time by a large number of people, for purposes of illustration the information of three or four individuals is presented through the conversation and stories of only a single character. Further, some bridging material has been added, so that the character portraying the ideas of many appears to present a grammatically consistent message. Nevertheless, the information presented is itself an accurate account of what was said during the course of police training, and of the activity and themes that occurred, both within the academy and on the street during patrol.

Chapter 4 will once again ask you to assume the position of critical observer. In light of your exposure to law in practice, it is now necessary to once more ask the question, "What is law?" This chapter will not only ask what is law, but will also ask "What is law violation?" Theories that attempt to explain law violation will be briefly reviewed to determine if they pay sufficient attention to the dynamics of law application by functionaries of the criminal justice system. Do they really explain law-violating behavior, or do they merely provide a rationale for officials to categorize certain behaviors as deviant?

Chapter 5 will provide exercises that allow you to make the law and propose sanctions for its violation. After critically examining the police, this chapter will invite you to make your own decisions regarding violations and what should be done about them. Chapter 6 will then critically review the factors that may have entered into your decision-making process. Are you any different from police officers, or do you make your decisions about crime and punishment in response to the same factors that affect them?

Chapter 7 will attempt to tie together the previous chapters by discussing in detail the tenets of ethnomethodology and exploring how this theoretical perspective can help us understand law as a process of order construction. This chapter will provide a method for examining and analyzing the social world-building we all engage in and pose questions about the categorizations used by police officers and other criminal justice personnel in their attempts to make sense out of their activity.

Chapters 8 and 9 will describe other actors in the criminal justice system, including attorneys and judges. What conflicts do they face, what pressures are exerted upon them, what values do they utilize in making their decisions?

Chapter 10 will review the correctional process, and will invite you to observe the working day of a correctional officer. Again, the question will be what strategies are used to construct a "sensical" social world. Does the construction process interfere with the aims and values of all the other functionaries in the system or do they mesh with what the police, the courts, the legislatures, and the public have in mind for criminal justice? Do these four groups agree among themselves about how the system should function? If they do not, which group's aims do corrections come most close to meeting? Do they meet any or do they have their own unique aims?

The ethnographic data in Chapters 8 through 10 were gathered from a number of sources using a variety of techniques. Some of the information on attorneys and judges was gathered as part of a research project directed by me. A number of observers recorded courtroom activity and conducted interviews with attorneys. Information was also gleaned from "how to" manuals written by and for lawyers to help them carry out the day-to-day activities of their practice. Data gathered by other researchers concerning judges, attorneys, probation officers, defendants, and so on were used to further fill out the descriptions of the social worlds of these actors. The story of the correctional officer is based on reports of prison guards and their activity that have appeared in both academic and nonacademic sources. Fictional characters are used to present the information thus gathered. What is said and thought by these characters, and the round of life portrayed, is not therefore a description of any particular real-life incident. However, what is presented is an accurate picture of the daily work problems and work strategies that are a part of the routine doing of justice.

Chapter 11 will describe the plight of the victim. How do people become victims? What happens to an individual who enters the justice system in the role of the victim? Is he or she satisfied with the treatment received? Is the person's confidence in justice and the basic worth of societal institutions restored or increased? Are resources available to help the victim cope with the variety of problems he or she may now face?

Of all the roles in the criminal justice system, the role of victim may be one of the most crucial and yet least understood. In a sense, it is the focal point around which the other roles revolve. Police officers respond to victims, attorneys interview them, judges hand down sentences presumably in proportion to the harm done them, correctional personnel correct with the hope of preventing future victims, and some people want more attention given to their rights and less to the rights of their nemesis, the criminal. Despite all the apparent concern with victims, however, very little is actually known about their perceptions of the criminal justice system, the world they live in as a result of being victims, and what they would do if they had an opportunity to change the criminal justice system. Looking at criminal justice through their eyes, then, can perhaps provide the beginnings of answers to the questions posed about victims and victimization.

Finally, in Chapter 12 we will describe policy implications suggested by examining law in process and application. Although the first eleven chapters focus primarily on the social worlds of lower-level criminal justice functionaries, the policy implementers rather than the policy makers, how these individuals use and apply laws and policy reforms has obvious importance to policy makers and others who desire to bring about change. While legislators, police chiefs, prison directors, and so on propose reforms, policies, and laws, the chances of their having the kind of impact desired are directly related to how criminal justice workers choose to interpret them and fit them into their own ongoing activities. Given this, what alternatives are available to change our present system? Are such alternatives necessary or is the current system the best we can hope for? Are the correctives suggested by examining actual law applications different than those flowing from examining the criminal? Are their chances for success any different, or are we caught in a process that requires identification of, and treatment for, deviants that will ensure a ready supply? Can we escape the specter of Salem, or are witches and witch hunters an integral part of the warp and woof of society?

We begin to explore these questions by observing the making of a police officer.

References

1. KAI T. ERIKSON. *Wayward Puritans* (New York: John Wiley and Sons, Inc., 1966).
2. Ibid., p. 149.
3. RUSSELL H. ROBBINS. *The Encyclopedia of Witchcraft and Demonology* (New York: Crown Publishers, Inc., 1959), pp. 492–94.
4. THOMAS S. SZASZ. *The Manufacture of Madness* (New York: Dell Publishers Co., Inc., 1970), p. 34. Szasz in this work goes on to compare the ordeal by water with certain of the practices of modern institutional psychiatry.
5. BOYCE RENSBERGER. "Drugs," *New York Times*, January 26, 1976. © 1976 by the New York Times Company. Reprinted by permission.
6. Ibid.
7. Ibid., third article in the series, January 28, 1976.
8. HARTJEN. *Crime and Criminalization*, p. 165.
9. ALFRED BLUMSTEIN, JACQUELINE COHEN, and DANIEL NAGIN, eds., *Deterrence and Incapacitation: Estimating the Effects of Criminal Sanctions on Crime Rates* (Washington, D.C.: National Academy of Sciences, 1978), pp. 6–7.
10. WILLIAM G. NAGEL. "ACA Convention Speakers Assert That Increased Imprisonment Will Not Reduce Crime Rates," *Criminal Justice Newsletter*, Vol. 7, No. 17, August 30, 1976.
11. NICKOLAS N. KITTRIE. *The Right to Be Different* (Baltimore: Penguin Books, 1973).
12. ERVING GOFFMAN. *Asylums* (Garden City, N.Y.: Anchor Books, 1961).
13. For an excellent overview of the various definitions of law see

Stephen D. Ford, *The American Legal System, Its Dynamics and Limits* (St. Paul, Minn.: West Publishing Co., 1974), pp. 1–28.

14. Ibid., p. 4.
15. STUART L. HILLS. *Crime, Power, and Morality, the Criminal-Law Process in the United States* (Scranton, Pa.: Chandler Publishing Co., 1971), p. 9.
16. HARTJEN. *Crime and Criminalization*, p. 23.
17. ROBERT MERTON in *New Perspectives for Research on Juvenile Delinquency*, eds. H. Witmer and R. Kotinsky (O.A.S. Government Printing Office, 1956).

chapter two

Becoming a Police Officer

Building Patterns

All of us face dilemmas and disturbances in our social environment, in our view of things. People constantly challenge our definitions of ourselves and of the situation. Each challenge invites us to account for our behavior as an example of a logical, coherent act that fits into some pattern.[1] By accounting for behavior, by explaining why we do things, we create the pattern and order of our lives. In a sense we are like an oyster who gets a grain of sand lodged in its tissue. To deal with that disturbance in its environment, the oyster reacts by covering the offending grain with secretions and tissue. Hopefully, the end result is a pearl. People, too, react to challenges and disturbances in their environment and in the process create a pattern for their lives. Whether the end result is a pearl will depend upon each new outcome of our action. Each outcome helps develop the past definition of the situation, so that the pattern is constantly being developed depending on how we meet the continuing challenges we face. Disturbances in a social world, then, lead to a building process, an accounting for action that causes people to relate to, and with, others.

The term "relate" needs explanation. We relate or interact with others by telling them (relating to them) what went on or what is going on in our heads. To relate means to bring into logical or natural association. A relationship is a telling to others the natural or logical associations we perceive among the elements of our social world, trying to convince them that what we do is meaningful or logical. As the last chapter noted, we develop rules for putting together the elements of our environment so that our behavior and that of others appears sensical. When we relate or give an account of our activity, we assume that the people we are talking to are using the same rules for putting together meaning. Of course, they may not be and thus negotiation must occur so that some kind of agreement can be reached, at least temporarily, about the rules for building meaning. Without this agreement, a mutually accepted social pattern or account cannot be built, and a relationship cannot continue. Two examples help illustrate the point.

Try acting toward your parents or spouse as you would act toward a landlady in a boardinghouse. Be very polite. Say "please" and "thank you," but do not show any affection or emotional involvement. Most probably, your behavior will be challenged. Your spouse or your parents will attempt to negotiate the pattern of behavior you and they are engaging in. A number of categories might be offered that will allow them to fit the behavior into a pattern consistent with your previous relationship. "Are you sick?" "Are you angry about something?" "Are you looking for a fight?" These categories are in a sense rules for structuring meaning. "You would only act this way if you were sick" (or angry or whatever). If there can be agreement that a particular rule is appropriate to the situation, your behavior can be made sense of, that is, accounted for. If you answer a polite "no" to all these possibilities, things may get a little tense. When this stage is reached it may be necessary to explain that you were merely engaging in an experiment. If this account is accepted, the behavior can be fitted into a logical, consistent pattern: "my daughter, the scholar," or "my husband, the smart aleck student." Hopefully, the rule for building meaning, "This is what scholars or smart aleck students do," while not articulated, has been implicitly accepted and so the relationship can continue.

Chapter 1 described how the Puritans faced disturbances in

their social world. The rapid changes occurring in their society had to be explained. The accounts took the form of categories called "witches" or "satanic manifestations." The acceptance of the implicit rule that the devil made people do it, allowed the colonists of the era to structure mutually agreed-upon accounts to explain what was occurring in their society.

In the same way, police recruits must create new categories and patterns so they can make sense out of the many contradictions, dilemmas, and problems they will face as police officers. Police academy instructors help in this process by providing new rules for structuring meaning and specific examples in the form of accounts to illustrate how the rules should be applied. Recruits' civilian definitions of situations (their civilian rules for creating meaning) are challenged. New accounting procedures emerge that will allow recruits to make sense out of their behavior, and the behavior of others, as they act out their new social role.

Becoming a Police Officer: The Process Begins

The time is eight o'clock A.M. on a bright, rather warm Monday morning. You enter a classroom that has seating for about thirty people. There are approximately twenty individuals standing around in groups of two or three, talking in modulated tones. The low hum of conversation is only occasionally punctuated by loud, nervous laughter. The group, as a whole, looks eager, but somewhat apprehensive. Everybody is in civilian clothes. Suddenly, an older man in uniform enters and states in a loud voice:

> Everybody be seated. My name is Officer Handlebars. It will be my job to teach you how to defend yourselves in confrontations with the public. This is probably one of the most important courses of instruction you'll be exposed to. If you don't learn the techniques of self-defense, your old lady will collect on your insurance. You've got to start thinking like a policeman; go out there, think defensively. You know, you've got to get a little paranoid. When you're standing in line at a food store checkout counter, start looking over your shoulder. When you come in contact with the public, you've got to be pleasant and polite, but keep in mind each contact has the potential for violence. Don't start thinking that these contacts you will have are just

routine. You may pull over a guy for a burned-out license plate light and this guy knows he's Jack the Ripper and he's just ripped. He thinks you know he's Jack the Ripper and you walk up to the car figuring no one's going to blow my head off for a burned-out license plate light, and he blows your head off. There is no such thing as a routine arrest.

The necessity for being suspicious is a theme that will continually be stressed during the course of training. As the comments made by the officer above indicate, using this rule to pattern relationships can help keep you alive on the street. During the weeks that follow you will learn the specific groups that should be approached with suspicion.

I've seen too many officers hurt by juveniles. They went in with the attitude, "We're dealing with just little kids," and they've gotten hurt. Now we don't mean to make you guys paranoid so that you'll end up thinking everyone's going to do you in, but they might. A couple of you are going to get yourselves killed if you don't get over the idea that girls won't hurt you. Women can be very dangerous. If you arrest one, and she has spiked heels, take them away from her or you'll get your head bloodied. Also, old senile people get nasty when they fight. They can give you as much trouble as anyone else. Now some of you big tough guys may figure that homosexuals are prissy and can be easily taken care of. Well, don't forget, a lot of them are closet queers. If you arrest one who is a respectable member of the community, you're going to be in for a tough time. I had a partner who was almost run over by a clergyman.

Being a police officer means being suspicious of everybody. It also means being suspicious of everything. The former patterning will help keep you alive. The latter will help you meet certain bureaucratic demands, namely, the preventing of crime and the apprehending of violators. Thus, to be a successful police officer, a recruit will have to begin to restructure formerly taken-for-granted situations as possible indicators of potential trouble or crimes in the making. This restructuring process is guided by instructors who relate to the class the situations a police officer should define as suspicious. Situations and people that civilians would define as innocuous, if they noted them at all, must now come to be seen in a different light.

To be effective, a patrolman must be suspicious. What is suspicious? Something that is suspicious is anything that is out of the ordinary. To know what is suspicious you must know what is ordinary. Police work revolves around what is suspicious.

You have to know what to look for when checking a building: open doors and windows; cars parked outside. Know what cars are usually parked there and if there are any new ones, that may be suspicious; when you check windows, you're looking at the ground to check for broken glass. Some burglars if they're going to do their profession right will check a building out and even go so far as to measure the window pane and then have a piece of glass cut to that size; then he'll knock out the window and when he goes in he'll put up that glass, so you look at the ground.

An aggressive patrolman will take every opportunity to approach the suspicious-acting people he observes during his course of duty. What things make a person suspicious: wearing a big coat in hot weather; personal appearance together with the area he's in—he's just not dressed for the area he's in; time of day he's operating may make him look suspicious; know the pedestrian traffic in your area—some parts of town you have pedestrians day and night, other parts you don't have any; know the thugs in your neighborhood; people who turn away from you—the old ostrich trick, if I can't see him he can't see me; or the guy who stares at you too much; or a guy who's running and when he sees you he slows down and tries to breathe normally and tries not to look suspicious; or by the same token a guy who was walking starts running when he sees you.

Besides the need to be suspicious, another rule guides the accounting procedures of police officers. The instructor in charge of firearms makes the following point:

When you're involved in a situation, make sure you're the one that's in charge. That's what the public expects. Most requests for police service come from citizens who telephone headquarters. The types of calls you'll have to respond to are unlimited. It'll go all the way up to a homicide or a kidnapping or one of the biggies, down to helping some old invalid go to the bathroom. You can draw the line at wiping their butt. Why do we get all these "off the wall" calls? Because people don't know who else to call. But when you get there take charge. If you need more manpower, never hesitate to call for help. You must control the situation, you can't leave any doubt in this person's mind about who's in charge. Most of the time, your uniform and the law you represent will be enough to take command of a situation. Like on traffic enforcement, there are so many laws that if you think a guy should be pulled over, follow him a block and he's bound to violate some traffic law or another. But if the law isn't enough, if some guy thinks he's running the show, we've got both the manpower and the weapons to let him know different. This rifle carries a slug that if you hit a human being with it, it will make a hole the size of your little finger and when it comes out it'll make a hole of the size you can stick your head in to see what the hell you missed inside. You got to face it; if they get nasty, we got to get nastier. That's the job.

As the above comments make clear, a police officer is required to normalize abnormal situations by taking charge. Authoritarianism appears to be a structural requirement of the position rather than simply a psychological characteristic. Regardless of one's previous psychological disposition, there is a clear expectation, on the part of the public and police supervisors, that officers will use the authority given them. You must define the situation, you must take charge of the scene. This will be easier if someone calls you and asks for your help. Both you and the individual will probably accept the same rule for building an account, that is, the police officer is in charge because he or she represents the law. The situation becomes more complex if the officer decides to intervene on his own. In this event, different rules for structuring meaning are likely to clash, and as the instructor noted, authority may have to give way to a reliance on power to control the situation.[2]

In their attempts to structure a logical, meaningful social world, recruits face challenges from a variety of sources. The academy commander emphasizes that supervisors will demand an account.

There are two types of discipline, positive and negative. With positive discipline you're appealing to their intellect and education; that's what we do in the academy. But when you hit the field the big bad-ass captain or lieutenant or sergeant will use negative discipline. If you create or do misconduct out there, you'll hang for it, and we could care less.

When you're just out of the academy, you don't know nothing. All you know is the utopian ideal view you learn in the academy. If the senior man says go like hell, and you smash up, that guy's going to go up before the accident review board and say, "I told that squirrel to slow down." He's going to cover himself. You're the one who's out on the limb.

Our biggest stumbling block to becoming a profession is our failure to police our own ranks. We don't meet this requirement of professionalism because you guys haven't got the goddamn guts and intestinal fortitude to let us meet it. You want to be loved. You work with some beady-eyed, slop-headed, bushy-haired clown and let him off for a drink, will you report him? No, because you want to be loved.

Unfortunately, providing an account that exactly meets the formal demands of the police bureaucracy can cause fellow officers to challenge your view of reality.

Of course, you've got to use common sense in reporting departmental rule violations. Don't come on too pure. You may find people shy away from you. Don't tattle on small stuff. What would you do, for instance, if you caught a fellow officer committing a traffic offense?

At this point the recruit next to you raises her hand and says, "Well, for a flagrant violation, I'd write him."

The instructor says, "You would? You know what he's going to do? He's going to sit on your driveway and as soon as your wife, or I should say, your husband backs out the car, he's going to give him a ticket for improper backing!"

The recruit on the other side of you mutters, "Damned if you do, and damned if you don't."

You will also learn that the ever-present public will challenge the accounts of individual police officers, with consequences for the whole department.

Remember, patrolmen are the public symbols of their organization. You represent the organization. If Officer X makes a mistake or looks like a slob, they don't say Officer X is a jerk, they say that the Police Department is a bunch of jerks.

So you've got to be an actor. Look like you know everything and people will think that you do. All of this is good public relations. Give the people what they want, or make them think you're giving them what they want. For instance, never hesitate to call the identification bureau to dust for prints. Now most times, even if you found a fingerprint, it just takes too long to process it for some of these nickel and dime burglaries. But for public relations, it may be necessary to go through the motions. I don't know how big the I.D. bureau is on P.R. anymore, they're pretty busy, but sometimes that's the only way you can get people off your back.

These remarks can be viewed as so many grains of sand. Some of them will obviously disturb the recruit's view of him- or herself and the surrounding world. It is this disturbance, however, that will help recruits begin the process of building a new social world around the contradictions that were presented. During the weeks that follow, your class will have ample opportunity to restructure their social world, amplifying the themes and strategies initially contained in the remarks above. The mapping offered by the Academy Commander appears to contain a number of guideposts for making one's way through the maze of contradictory demands facing the recruit. There is the need to use common sense when building an account. Quite obviously, the term "common sense" may be a misnomer, since what is common knowledge in my individual everyday life may be very uncommon knowledge in the next person's life. Thus, the admonition to use common sense is in effect telling you to learn the knowledge and folk wisdom of the police subculture you are about to enter (that is, the rules the group uses for constructing a meaningful social world). This is essential if you are to adhere to the seemingly impossible dictate of following formal departmental procedures absolutely with discretion. Does the adverb "absolutely" apply to following all the procedures, or does it mean one should always do what one thinks best regardless of the formal norms? The question is answered by pointing out that as a new police officer, you will face a number of problems that cannot be dealt with effectively by either of these solutions. First, recruits must learn to get along with the command personnel. Although there is an implication that obeying all the formal rules will help recruits meet this demand, the Commander notes that recruits will have to get along with fellow officers, a requirement not easily met by reporting officers who violate such rules. The new patrolman who obeys all the regulations and reports those who do not, runs the risk of not being accepted by his colleagues and being labeled with a pejorative term. Further, any attempt to enforce proper behavior on the part of one's colleagues might result in a particular colleague using rules and regulations to harass or embarrass the officer so inclined. Becoming a police officer, then, involves learning to manipulate the bureaucratic structure in order to meet the demands of pleasing both supervisor and colleague. To do this, the recruit must learn the common sense of the department, which includes knowing what violations are serious enough to be reported, as opposed to those that should be overlooked, and knowing which commanders will themselves overlook certain violations and which will enforce all or certain of the rules.

One way of coping with an organization that subjects its members' activity to constant review is for the individual to cover himself and his actions by being aware of bureaucratic consequences and structuring his activity in light of these. The theme "cover yourself" provides a second guidepost to help recruits in their new conceptual mapping. The question now becomes, "What is the best strategy to use to adequately protect yourself from bureaucratic penalties?" (or, in the Captain's phrasing, "from being hanged"). Obeying all the regulations might accomplish this, but as discussed above, there are serious drawbacks to this strategy. Besides, publicizing one's own mistakes or the mistakes of a colleague can have negative consequences for the whole organization. Because people look upon all police officers as the same and use the mistakes of a few to criticize the entire force, it is best to hide rule violations from both the public and the command staff. This strategy forms a social patterning in which patrol officers become a self-protecting group against the contrary social patternings of police administrators and civilians.

The element of danger is a common variable used to explain police brotherhood. Any profession that involves danger develops a strong sense of comradeship among its practitioners, since one may have to rely on one's colleagues to limit the potential for harm. The element of danger, however, seems to combine with certain pragmatic and organizational concerns to bring about the reality of police brotherhood. While it is true that some fellow officers fail to do their job, or drink too much, or are incompetent, all professions contain their share of misfits. Since police officers are perceived to be all alike by outsiders, it is best to trust a fellow officer and protect him or her from outside criticism. This is particularly true since by protecting a fellow officer from outside censure and ridicule one also protects one's own image, both in terms of the public and in terms of police supervisors. Thus, even though you may not be able to depend on a fellow officer in a tight situation (because, for example, he or she has been drinking), pragmatically you had best keep your mouth shut unless the situation becomes so intolerable that you yourself risk negative bureaucratic consequences (as did the senior man who was in the high speed chase). You cover yourself, then, generally by covering for others.

The police academy in a sense demythologizes policing for the recruits. They find that captains, lieutenants, and sergeants may severely discipline their charges. Fellow patrolmen are described as sometimes being unworthy of respect ("beady-eyed, slop-headed, bushy-haired clowns"). Finally, civilians are presented as expecting the impossible from the police but not supporting them in their attempts to give the public what they ask. All three groups must be approached pragmatically. The movement from idealism to pragmatism is further underscored by a third guidepost or strategy, the necessity for becoming a good actor.

The theme "be a good actor" stresses public conformity, and this too seems to encourage the hiding of violations. Thus, appearance rather than actual conforming behavior will allow the recruit to work his way through the maze of conflicting demands that arise from both the bureaucratic system of which he is a part and from the public which he is supposed to serve. The emphasis on military spit and polish in police departments may be due more to this pressure for acting, and to the fact that this is one of the few areas that can be concretely observed by supervisors and therefore controlled, than to any inherent value of neatness.

Challenges to a recruit's civilian view of things come not only from people, but from events. Death, often sudden, violent, and senseless, is a frequent companion in an officer's occupational life. A fatal traffic accident, a shooting, a child-beating, a stabbing, and all of the other numerous ways people come to a violent end, belie society's view of itself as essentially civil and orderly. One reason, however, that society is able to maintain such an image of itself is that certain functionaries perform the task of dealing with sudden, violent death, hiding its reality from a fair number of societal members. One of the major groups assigned this task is the police. Constantly dealing with the abnormal and coping with the contradictions the

abnormal presents to one's self and one's image of the world requires certain strategies. Using police common sense, covering yourself, and being a good actor, introduce you to some of the strategies
seasoned officers use. These are further refined and expanded as
other officers tell you about their specific areas of responsibility.

On a hot, muggy afternoon, Detective Columjack tells you
about homicide and coping.

> Good afternoon, I'm Detective Columjack and I'm here to talk about
> homicide. They always save this lecture until after lunch. Now what
> I'm going to show you may be a little gruesome, but you'd better get
> used to it. Otherwise, when the time comes, and you get a call that
> somebody's been killed, or a dead body's been found, you'll be stand-
> ing around getting sick instead of helping people. The first time I got
> a suicide call, the senior man made me go in and take the report. The
> guy had stuck a shotgun in his mouth and pulled the trigger. Blood
> and mess all over. Naturally, I tossed my cookies. Afterwards, my
> partner made me go with him to breakfast. We were working morn-
> ings. Scrambled eggs and ketchup. Boy, I couldn't eat for a week. But
> I got over it. If you let this stuff bother you, if you don't eat everytime
> you get a dead body, you'll go nuts or you'll starve to death. You'll get
> tired of hearing about all this death shit and all that stuff. How your
> body festers and your eyes bug out, or there's just a neck left. Don't let
> it get to you. These pictures I've got here are of the different types of
> bodies you'll come across. The only thing you miss on these photo-
> graphs is the odor. Just think of it as a piece of meat. Here's one. She
> was a girl who thought there was no bad people in the world. They
> kept warning her not to let strangers in the house, but she wouldn't
> listen. She didn't think anyone would harm her. I think she was
> stabbed sixteen or seventeen times. The guy who killed this woman
> will be out in a little while. He would admit he was in the apartment
> and that he killed her, but the judge wouldn't allow the statement into
> evidence.
>
> Anyway, when you get one of these calls, your main job is to protect
> the crime scene. Get people out of the way, get all their statements,
> and keep everything the same until the detective gets there. Don't
> have people walking all around, destroying physical evidence. Of
> course, if the victim is still alive, your first concern is with him or her. If
> it's an auto accident, take care of the survivors first. Auto accidents can
> be tough to deal with, particularly if there is a little kid involved. Those
> still get to me, but try to remain objective so you can help the survivors.
>
> There are three prerequisites to being a good policeman: common
> sense, bravery, and a sense of humor. You'll find policemen have a
> gross, awful sense of humor. A guy laying out there on the highway,

his decapitated body laying right near the policeman and the cop will be laughing, just having a hell of a time. Sometimes that's the only way they can keep their shit together. You'll see all the poverty, inequality, injustice, and you'll have to laugh at it. Otherwise, you'll start drinking and being a jack-off out there to compensate. You'll be a fucker, fighter, and wild-horse rider. It's not easy to laugh, but if you're going to save your own sanity and perform a service for the public, you'll have to learn.

As Detective Columjack continues to talk about homicides and other sudden deaths, how they are investigated, the various reports that need to be filled out, and the proper activities for patrol officers at such scenes, we might take a moment to contemplate his remarks to this point. His discussion indicates that what is abnormal for the citizen becomes an everyday occurrence for the police. However, initial contact with abnormal occurrences, and the contradictions they may imply, can have a rather disconcerting effect on an individual. Detective Columjack suggests humor as a method for dealing with the problems caused by being enmeshed in the abnormal and contradictory. But to use humor in this way, recruits must also learn to depersonalize the civilian population. At first glance, some of Columjack's comments seem to imply an extremely jaundiced view. It must be remembered, though, that depersonalization is not a one-way process. Civilians, too, depersonalize police officers and tend to overlook their humanness with, it would seem, somewhat less justification. As was pointed out, the law enforcement official must, after all, be able to function in situations that would leave the ordinary civilian helpless. Thus, humor and the development of an impersonal attitude toward tragedy is functional for the officer, because without it, he may not be able to render any kind of service when it is expected of him.

Detective Columjack's remarks seem also to imply that the police officer must in a sense depersonalize himself, at least to the point of becoming a functionary with little or no emotional involvement in the situation he is called upon to handle. This self-depersonalization, while not always successful, is necessary if the officer is to survive his or her exposure to the injustice, poverty, and other contradictions of society. Columjack's closing remarks underscore the point that self-depersonalization helps one cope with the contradictions inherent in modern policing.

Society seems to have developed a double standard. Everyone gets upset when someone gets killed by a gun, but we kill 50,000 a year with cars and no one gives a shit. Of course, we have traffic enforcement to try and cut down on this carnage, but people get upset with you if you enforce traffic laws. I pulled a guy over once for speeding and the first thing he said to me was, "Why don't you arrest all those burglars—they're the real menace."

Funny thing was, just the night before, I caught a guy in someone's house, and as I put the cuffs on him, he said, "I don't know why you're hassling me. Why don't you arrest all those speeders who are killing little kids?"

Most people haven't seen the tragedy that traffic violations can bring about. So people are likely to call you names when you issue a traffic summons. Getting called names is part of the job, like a mechanic gets dirt under his fingernails as a part of his job. You get called names as a part of your job. That's the best way to look at it.

People are also likely to think you're dishonest—you know, they will try and slip you money or something when you are going to give them a ticket. Because of this tendency for the public to think we're dishonest, or all "on the take" or something, I'm telling you, don't get caught alone with a dead body because if anything turns up missing who's the guy who's going to be blamed? If the manager found the body, O.K., the manager. But the next guy to get it is the uniformed officer. Say the person had a ring and it turns up missing. And I may sound a little cynical, but I've never run across a cheap ring. They're all $500 or $1,000. So what we do is we try to be witnesses for each other; if you find a body, leave the door open and then when we get there we'll witness for you and you for us.

These closing remarks present the class with three ideas. First, recruits are exposed to the double standard the community holds regarding law enforcement, particularly when it comes to such things as traffic laws. Exposure to this double standard may reemphasize for the individual recruit the fact that civilians do not play by the rules of the game.

Second, it is evident that police officers can become subject to a great deal of criticism for enforcing laws that the public feels ambivalent toward, even though the violation of certain of these laws, in this case, traffic ordinances, can lead to death and destruction. The officer uses guidelines other than those offered by an individual he catches in a violation for determining the limit and type of his discretionary authority. This, of course, creates hostility and name-calling, something the officer will have to learn to live with by not getting emotionally involved and accepting name-calling as part of the job. The depersonalizing of such an event, by depersonalizing oneself and the other, can help recruits cope with the contradictory expectations of the society.

Finally, recruits learn that civilians can make trouble for an officer and that such trouble often results because of dishonesty on the part of some people. Thus, you are asked to be a hero in a society that will seldom reward or even recognize your heroism, in a society that is itself not very heroic, or honest, or virtuous. Any profession that performs an important social function would ordinarily be reimbursed, either through status or money, for its efforts. As a recruit, however, you learn that such is not the case with police officers and that even though the demands are great, the status rewards are few.

Seeing and Reporting Events as a Police Officer: Making a Record

Recruit training provides fledgling officers with a new repertoire of accounts about the world. By learning "police rules" for structuring meaning, recruits come to see their actions as logical and coherent. At the same time, they are able to account for the actions of others in a way that preserves a police view of the world. Putting together a police report of an event illustrates the process. Since a variety of publics will call for a defense of the police officer's view of things, report writing is one of the most important skills a recruit can learn. Indeed the greatest amount of academy time is spent in teaching report writing.

Recruits discover that superiors will question an officer's action in a particular case and that reports can help meet this challenge.

> The reports and letters you write are the key to success on this job. If you want promotion, report writing will be an indication of how you care. Every report you make reflects on you and you'll make your reputation through your reports. You make a bad one and that's the one someone will see and say, "Look at that jack-off."

Good reports can lead to promotion in an impersonal bureaucracy.

> The Police Department runs on its reports. A lot of our work involves matching known offenders with an incident. We can do that if the reports an officer writes are accurate. The reports help establish a pattern. Each crook has his pattern, and when an incident happens, the detective will try and match it with known M.O.'s on file. M.O. is police talk for Method of Operation. Now detectives won't know you from a load of beans, but they'll get to know you by your offense reports and the letters you write. The more they can establish a pattern from what you tell them on a report, the easier you'll make their job, and the more likely they are to remember your name when an opening comes in the detective bureau.

While accuracy is important, recruits must also remember to anticipate challenges from a variety of sources, and be ready to cover themselves in light of these. An officer may have to justify an action to protect himself from civil suit or criminal indictment, ever-present possibilities in a profession which causes trouble to others. A person questioned, arrested, or trying to hide his own misdeeds may attempt to get back at the officer involved by challenging that officer's legitimacy. Detective Columjack's closing remarks concerning dead bodies and expensive rings illustrate the point. Thus, the officer needs to document his action in a way that covers himself.

> Remember, too, these reports can protect you. When you think you're going to hurt a guy, make a resistance report. That way, if the individual claims police brutality, later on, you can always say he resisted arrest, and you'll have the report to back you up.

In the case of accountability to the body politic, department heads need documentation that the police are doing the best they can do to combat crime, alleviate citizens' fears, and help the city in its efforts to maintain financial solvency. Such records help police administrators make a case for continued or maybe even increased monetary support. Thus, the need to look productive influences the making of a report.

> The selective enforcement program means that if you're out eight hours a day, you're bound to see at least one violation. Tickets are known as "at-a-boys." You can turn in your log sheet and have a

couple of felony arrests on it and the sergeant won't say anything. You turn in a log with a ticket on it, the sergeant will look at you and say "at-a-boy." That's why tickets are called at-a-boys. Let's face it, they make money for the city. Don't go being a "Mr. Goodfellow" out there. Did I ever tell you about Mr. Goodfellow? Well, one day I was feeling pretty good and I was letting all these violators go. All I had on my log was bullshit. So I resolved, the next violator I stopped I would cite no matter what. If it was the Governor or the Mayor, it would make no difference. So this white Studebaker goes whizzing by and I get behind it with my light on and honk the horn, and a little head pops up—don't make no difference to me. I honk again, another little head pops up—old hard-hearted me is going to write it anyway, I don't care if there is a million kids. Anyway, the lady isn't pulling over so I hit the siren and two more heads pop up. Finally, she pulls over and I walk up with my ticket book out, and a pretty little face sticks out the window and says, "Oh, hi Willie." It was my sister-in-law. So I didn't get any at-a-boys that day. So, if you see a good violation you better write it then, and don't just say there'll be another one. But when you write it, be sure you write it correctly.

Most often, a police account will be challenged by court personnel who, as they reconstruct an event, will want to know why the officer acted as he did.

If you don't have the right information on these forms, by the time you get off the stand you'll be agreeing with the defense attorney that you weren't even there. Now remember, 90 percent of the report writing on the P.D. is fill in the blank. The detectives fill in the important lines, as on this report the final charges filed in a sobriety case summary. But the lines you do fill in must be correct. For example, you must have the proper day and month on a traffic citation. Let me tell you what happened to me. On these citations they have on _____ day of _____ month of this year, and I put 4 and 6 in the spaces. The attorney spent the entire time on the cross-examination on the missing "th." "What is the 4 day?" It should have been 4th and it's ridiculous, but they threw it out because of that. I don't know, maybe the judge did it just to get the guy off his back.

Summary

This chapter has attempted to introduce you to the world of a police officer. It has done this by asking you to vicariously take on the role of a police recruit, a civilian who for the first time must now also begin to see the world as a policeperson sees it. As a recruit, you were introduced to the patternings officers create in order to make sense out of their activity and meet demands they perceive as being required of them if they are to successfully act out their roles. To help a recruit restructure his or her social world, certain rules or themes emerge during the course of training that provide strategies for the construction process. The rules discussed included being suspicious, being authoritarian, being a good actor, living with contradiction through humor and depersonalization, covering oneself bureaucratically, and using common police sense. How to apply some of these rules when actually putting together an account are summarized in the remarks on report writing. Thus, report writing can be seen as conveying to a recruit a seventh major theme and strategy for being a successful police officer, namely, the importance of protecting the scene. Protecting the scene can be accomplished through recording events and actions on a document. As already discussed, such documents can then be used to defend an officer's view of the world (and, of course, the actions engaged in by virtue of that view) when he is challenged. The creation of such documents can help a patrolperson successfully negotiate the various milieu of which he or she is a part. Bureaucratically, for instance, the recruit can make himself known. Thus, reports can be a means of mobility within the impersonal bureaucracy of the department. A recruit can also cover himself by producing a report in a particular way, thus protecting his actions from the challenges of both supervisors and civilians. Concerning the former group, recruits can document for them their efforts to meet the production demands of the bureaucracy. This in turn allows them to document for others the efficiency of the department. One's status can be gauged by noting his position in relation to reports (for example, what lines does he fill out, is he the maker or the receiver of the report, etc.), and whole units within the department can claim status on the basis of the records they keep. It could be argued that a police department's major function is the recording of events. Patrolpersons record crime and, indeed, a person with a record is a criminal. The accumulation of such records and files forms a major tool in the apprehension of criminals, since for the most part crime detection involves the matching of a particular event with a known group of offenders. The recording of such events is not, however, a value-free enterprise. What does or does not get recorded depends in part upon the pressures to produce a variety of documents. Hence, whether a person is recorded as resisting arrest will in part depend upon the officer's perception of the likelihood of his actions being challenged by civilians and the necessity of negotiating the interpretation of one's actions within a civilian milieu.

Crime reporting, and therefore crime itself, is clearly an action that needs to be interpreted in light of a particular set of circumstances. Such circumstances may include the immediate situation, but it is clear that the officer takes account of challenges likely to emerge from contexts and groups removed from the actual event. Crime reporting is thus a function of a variety of bureaucratic, civilian, and legal pressures. Reports are extremely valuable in confronting the various publics that can demand an accounting from the police. Crime, then, or more specifically the recording of an event as a crime, is conditional. In our system of justice, cognizance is generally taken of this fact, since the system contains within it built-in challenges to the officer's judgment. How the police officers deal with the other functionaries of the legal system who may question their interpretation of the world, and the consequences of officers' building their social world in the ways described, will be the subject of the following chapter.

References

1. HAROLD GARFINKEL. *Studies in Ethnomethodology* (Englewood Cliffs, N.J.: Prentice-Hall, 1967), p. 59.
2. Reiss documents the increased use of force when officers intervened in a situation on their own accord. See Albert J. Reiss, *The Police and the Public* (New Haven, Conn: Yale University Press, 1971), p. 59.

chapter three

Police Decision Making

Perry Mason, an Unworthy Opponent?

A number of authors have noted the problems and uncertainties created for police officers by our system of criminal justice. McNamara, for example, comments upon the ambiguities created for officers by the growth of procedural law, with its perceived limiting effects on the enforcement of substantive laws. He states that the uncertainties of our legal system are likely to be described by law enforcement officials as "incomprehensible, unpredictable, and inconsistent restrictions placed on police by legislatures and courts that are seen at best as lacking in understanding and at worst as financially, politically, or ideologically corrupt."[1] McNamara finds another source of potential conflict in the fact that police officers are generally drawn from a different population segment than are jurists, and hence each has a different definition of what constitutes serious crime.[2] Clearly, then, judges, attorneys, and even juries represent potential threats to the social world construction of police officers. As a recruit, it is necessary to learn how to deal with such threats and to minimize their impact. Thus, during a part of your academy training you will learn strategies both for applying the law

41

in a manner consistent with your own organizational goals and for defending such applications against the challenges of other criminal justice personnel. Before such strategies can be used, however, recruits have to be given a realistic assessment of the court and its personnel, that is, realistic from the police standpoint.

Even as a naïve civilian you probably possess some understanding of the antagonism that exists between defense attorneys and the police. James W. Sterling accounts for the negative attitudes of police officers toward attorneys by applying a dramaturgical model of social interaction. The courtroom is conceptualized as a stage, with the police officer and the defense lawyer playing the roles of major antagonists.[3] Fans of mystery novels probably have the same view. The relationship between Perry Mason and Lt. Tragg might well represent the civilian's innate understanding of the adversary framework that encompasses these social roles. Yet some of the sociological research conducted within the field of criminal law seems to indicate that defense attorneys often act less as antagonists and more as cooperative participants in the criminal justice arena. The defense attorney is, for example, the one most likely to suggest to the suspect that he or she plead guilty.[4] The relationship between police officers and lawyers and the attitudes they seem to hold regarding one another, therefore, appear to be more complex than either Sterling or Earl Stanley Gardner indicate. Defense attorneys and police officers are at times on opposite sides of an issue. At other times, a conviction can only be assured with the help of defense counsel. A plea of guilty brings, as will be discussed later, a certainty and efficiency to case processing that is absent in trial proceedings. Hence, police officers and defense lawyers do not always face each other as champions of opposing goals. Further, an adversarial relationship does not constitute a sufficient condition for explaining the development of negative or hostile perceptions toward the adversary. Individuals can strive mightily for their point of view without devaluing the opposition. As a recruit you will learn to perceive attorneys not only as adversaries, but as adversaries who at times do not compete fairly. In a class on how to testify in court your instructor makes this clear.

> These defense attorneys are sharp. They make a lot more money than city attorneys and so you get some pretty crafty guys who will try and

trick you. For example, never say the suspect smelled of alcohol. People smell of an alcoholic beverage, not alcohol. Alcohol has no smell. The defense attorney will have a heyday if you say the guy smelled of alcohol. And don't lie up there on the stand. Like I say, these guys are sharp and if they catch you lying you'll embarrass the whole department.

These comments present a methodology for dealing with defense attorneys and at the same time demythologize the justice system. The recruits learn that the system can be easily subverted by an opposing counsel's concern with minor technicalities (smelled of an alcoholic beverage, not alcohol), and that perjury is wrong because, pragmatically, if you are caught it will cause embarrassment, not because it is illegal or unjust. Being exact in the reporting of a situation is viewed primarily as a means of covering yourself. The theme of "cover yourself" quite obviously underscores the adversary relationship the recruit will be involved in when confronting an attorney. Nevertheless, more is involved here than simply the creation of an adversary framework. The latent message contained in this theme seems to suggest that the adversary is not, in some respects, a worthy one. Defense counsel does not play fairly, and he attempts to discredit police officers by trickery or adherence to minute, unimportant detail. This message appears even more clearly in certain of the other themes you will be exposed to that relate to defense attorneys.

As your instructor continues, you begin to realize that he is suggesting that you also need to be suspicious of the questions an attorney is likely to ask you.

> The time is becoming increasingly important in court. You can sometimes pin it down, because they'll pull the plug in the clock. It's nice if you can pin down the time, and say it happened at such and such a time because the guy pulled the plug. That gives the attorney less to bounce around in front of a jury. You say sometime within the twenty-four hour period and they'll harrass you a little bit. And be sure to always jot down the weather conditions. For some reason defense attorneys always ask that question. Also note how you got the call, the time you arrived, the lighting conditions, who was driving. They'll ask you all this stuff to confuse you.

It appears, then, that recruits are taught to be suspicious of the questions directed to them by defense attorneys because such questions are aimed more at confusing the officer-witness than at getting at the truth. Being suspicious is also a methodology for keeping the recruit or the officer on his toes. If the recruit is suspicious, he or she will be alert to any trick questions and will be better able to deal with them.

Sterling's metaphor of the stage, if expanded slightly, is helpful in understanding the dynamic of disenchantment that infects many who deal with law in practice. The courthouse is an arena for a variety of battles, not just for the confrontation between defense and prosecution. Police officers are challenged to defend their construc-tion of events and actions that led to the courthouse arena's being utilized in the first place. More is at stake here than just the guilt or innocence of a particular defendant. What is also at stake is the competence of the police officer in both reconstructing events and justifying his actions as examples of logical, coherent, rational be-havior. If the defendant is found innocent or if he is somehow let off with a lighter sentence, the police officer's sense of justice and his image of himself as a competent interpreter of events is threatened. Of course, everybody in the system has the same things at stake. Attorneys, both prosecutors and defenders, want to see themselves as competent. Judges, juries, psychologists, probation officers, social workers, defendants, and victims also have a stake in the outcome, and all hope that their own view of the world will be validated. Since the battle, however, takes place on what for most of the participants is alien ground (that is, in a legal setting), there is a natural suspicion toward those on whose turf such validation is sought. Attorneys, it is thought, have an unfair advantage in the determination of whose world view will predominate and who will get to see themselves as competent, rational, and so forth. Plea bargaining adds to the suspi-cion that attorneys have an unfair advantage in reconstructing an event for their own ends. The process is carried on largely between the two opposing counsel, with generally little input from police, victim, or suspect. The less severe sentence that ordinarily results from a plea negotiation may then be seen as too lenient from the police perspective and too harsh from the perspective of the defen-dant. Both attorneys, however, can claim victory; the prosecutor can record a conviction and the defense can record a softening of legal penalties for the client.

Being suspicious can keep you alert to the tricks attorneys might use to confuse you on the witness stand. Tricks! What of justice? Is it all just a game? A game in which the motivation and tactics of the major players are somewhat less than altruistic or just? A demythologizing of the criminal justice system continues as you learn the importance of acting as a method for influencing case outcome.

> O.K., we've been talking about how to act up there on the witness stand and how you have to be alert for attorneys trying to trap you into saying something you don't want to say. Now remember, sometimes these guys will really try to play to a jury. And a lot of these juries are made up of people like you. They don't know from nothing when it comes to a court of law. Sometimes the jury thinks that you as a police officer have a bias toward conviction. And that's understandable, but don't let it show. And if you get one of those defense attorneys that tries to make you out a liar, a boob, as someone who is brutal or stupid—keep your cool and you'll get a sympathy vote from them. You might be saying that there will be no problem for me, but wait until it happens to you. Also, to get the jury on your side, you should look like a professional.

> At a hearing, I like to wear a suit. I feel a uniform comes on too strong. Look like a professional, look like a businessman. Besides if you wear a suit you can surprise them; they won't know who you are. Now you may think that's a little thing but juries are funny. There was a stick-up detective who caught a guy coming out of a store with a gun in one hand and the money in the other. Anyway, they go to trial on it, and the guy is found not guilty. So later on the officer went to the foreman of the jury and asked him how come the jury found the guy not guilty, and what could he have done to give better testimony to help the prosecution? The foreman kind of laughed, and he said the reason he lost the case was because he was wearing white socks. You know, this officer wore a business suit and with that he wore white socks and the jury felt that this was not a professional attitude. And the reason the officer wore white socks was that he had athlete's foot and he could not wear colored socks. So juries are pretty unpredictable so you need to act like you are professional. Don't let the attorney get you rattled and for goodness' sake dress the part of a professional.

The above comment underscores two things. Again, the defense attorney is portrayed as the officer's adversary, and by keeping cool and being properly attired (that is, by being a good actor) his job can be made all the more difficult. It is also interesting to note that recruits learn that the outcome of a trial may depend on factors other than the guilt or innocence of the defendant. During your classes on report writing, as the last chapter indicated, you learn that protecting the scene by producing accurate reports (accurate from the officer's definition of the situation) forms an important methodology for confronting a defense attorney and making sure he does not confuse the officer or get his client off on a technicality. The emphasis put on spelling correctly, on watching your grammar, and so forth, also indirectly serves to further demythologize the system of justice. From the recruit's new perspective, the system begins to look as if it is more concerned with minor technicalities than with the question of guilt or innocence. The latter seems to be at best a secondary consideration.

From the above discussion it is obvious that the themes cover yourself, be suspicious, be a good actor, and protect the scene communicate to the recruit a number of things concerning defense attorneys. First, the attorney is placed into a "them–we" framework. The "them" are defense attorneys and the "we" are police officers. Second, these themes constitute a series of methodologies which enable the recruit to both deal with the defense counsel and at the same time begin structuring his new social world in relation to that role. The recruit, therefore, learns how to deal with the ambiguities that arise because of our system of justice. However, neither the adversary relationship nor the presence of ambiguities is sufficient to explain any negative views that may develop regarding attorneys. A third element is present in the themes that are communicated to enable recruits to begin their new social patterning. This element consists of a moral devaluation of the opposing counsel. Thus, he is not only portrayed as an adversary, but as an unworthy opponent interested in things other than justice. Further, the whole criminal justice system is subject to a demythologizing process that begins by pointing out the necessity for viewing the system as a game rather than as a sacred method for obtaining truth and justice. This moral devaluation of opposing criminal court roles and the gamelike nature of justice is further emphasized as your instructor begins to talk about judges.

Some laws have changed; some for the better, some not for the better. You know there is a lot of confusing changes going on—some ridiculous. Some of these judges will throw a case out, and say he'll give the guy the benefit of the doubt. But your job is just to bring the guy to court. You could care less what the court does with them. If you can develop that attitude you'll save yourself a lot of ulcers. It's a frustrating time. But don't take this job home with you. If the court finds some guy not guilty, that's not your problem. I've seen judges dismiss tickets because of the way I approached the car. Also, on a family disturbance, you can't or shouldn't sign the complaint. Your peace can't be disturbed according to some judges and juries, so there's where you might have problems. Whose peace is disturbed in a family disturbance? If you sign the complaint you might be on thin ice in court. Remember, too, that sometimes these judges are not the sterling characters you might think. Hell! Juvenile court is seven months behind in their caseloads. The reason is they don't hear cases. One guy died, and the other is too interested in marrying people and getting gassed. You can't let this stuff get to you though. Your job is to just arrest them. What the courts do with them after that is not your worry; like I say, that's the best attitude to have, you'll save yourself a lot of grief that way.

With the specter of the morally unworthy adversary looming even larger, recruits may well begin to feel that the police officer who bends the law to meet his own needs is doing the only logical, rational thing given the circumstances of justice. The demythologizing of the justice system allows recruits to stretch their own range of permissible behavior. An instructor specifies exactly how the law can be stretched to meet a variety of organizational and personal ends.

We had this girl and the D.A. said to kick her loose. So they were going to kick her loose and I said, "Wait a minute, let's get her to give us something for nothing. Question her and make her think if she cooperates we'll give her something, let her go." So she told us where this guy was dealing out of this house and we went there with a warrant. Anyway we couldn't find anything, and while we were there a guy comes to the door and we search him and find a couple of joints. Here, we've got another illegal search right at the door. The guy turns out to be on probation, and he says, "Hey man, give me a break." So we say, "Sure, you give us six arrests for one." So he tells us about two guys that we never even heard of who are bringing in five hundred kilos every two weeks. One guy was a psychologist at State University and his buddy was an assistant professor of math. He had the stuff in the back yard. The yard was enclosed. So we get a helicopter and went flying over. We put a tap on him and had him under surveillance. Some guy came to him and said he heard down at the district station that the cops were watching him. After that he was real careful. Kind of sickening to think that some cop either accidentally or on purpose let this guy find out we were on to him.

We finally caught him with ten kilos. They were going to give him probation, but we put on such heat they sent him to the state reformatory. Then some psychologist there said the guy didn't belong there, he should be back out on the street. That's kind of sad. I remember ten years ago, a guy could get five years in the pen for having a half of a kilo. Here we catch a guy with ten kilos and they want to give him probation. I think the two guys got seven months in the reformatory.

I think that's a good story that can illustrate what can happen from some of these arrests that may get kicked loose because of an illegal search. Sure you start up the system, and so what if the D.A. kicks him loose. You have a drug arrest and the vice bureau has a card on this guy. Suppose two months from now you hear this guy is selling at such and such a place and you look in the vice bureau and find this guy's card. Hell, he got a drug arrest, and that's one half of an affidavit.

This story describes a methodology for living with the contradictions of the legal system and at the same time meeting a number of other occupational demands. If the recruit adopts the specific method noted, he or she will often be able to obtain information that will lead to bigger arrests. Further, even if an individual is "kicked loose," the officer can still record a drug arrest, thereby meeting a production ethic of the police bureaucracy. Finally, information is on file that can at a later time be used to meet other legal requirements, in this instance an affidavit for a search warrant. Nevertheless, this case still points out that it is necessary to live with some contradiction, namely, the sentencing procedure of judges.

As discussed above, the use of such methods by the police becomes more palatable for the recruit since it appears that the ambiguities and contradictions of the legal system are the result of a moral lacuna in other legal actors. This stretching of norms to allow a greater degree of latitude in the legal behavior of the police is further increased by the knowledge that the courts use informal methods such as plea bargaining for getting around their occupational roadblocks. Hence, a defendant charged with rape might be allowed to plead guilty to a lesser sexual offense. As previously discussed, by pleading guilty to a lesser charge, the defendant gains a less severe penalty than the one he would have been given if he or she were convicted of a more serious offense. Further, the court has saved considerable time and expense by avoiding a trial. From the recruit's point of view, everyone seems to benefit from this mechanism except the police officer. The disillusionment of defendants in this situation is soon forgotten, and the new recruit becomes convinced that in the event of a disagreement over the proper application of a law, the dispute will likely be settled in a way least supportive of the police. Adversaries who will be encountered within the courthouse appear at the outset to have an unfair advantage. This of course adds to the contradictions faced by officers as they confront our justice system. It should be noted, however, that police officers have apparently learned to live with plea bargaining and have in fact used it to their advantage.[5] Offering the suspect a deal whereby admitting to a series of crimes he will only be charged with a few or with one involving a lesser degree of seriousness, allows enforcement officials to show a good clearance record. Nevertheless, this procedure produces greater benefits for detectives, leaving the patrol officer's decision at the mercy of higher-ups within both his own organization and the court system. The scenario offered by the instructor above, however, provides a strategy and a moral justification for decreasing the patrol officer's vulnerability to the social world constructions of other criminal justice role players. Throughout the twelve weeks of training, other instructors, both police and civilian, have also contributed to this fund of knowledge. As you near graduation, you have learned to see the world as a police officer sees it and to play the game of law so that your application of statutes and ordinances legitimates your new social constructs. You are now anxious to "hit the street" and begin playing police officer.

Hitting the Street

The move from recruit to police officer is perhaps not as drastic as the move from civilian to recruit. Nevertheless, the new police officer is still a novice, that is a person who requires socialization into how things "are really done." The new officer will, in a sense, try to become like the veteran, and this becoming a veteran will involve a number of subtle and not-so-subtle alterations in the continuing social world-building process.

Becoming a veteran appears to take place in stages. The first stage, probation, occurs immediately after graduation from the police academy. This career stage is officially recognized by most departments and is of varying lengths of time, depending upon departmental police. Probationary officers are scrutinized by veterans to see if they can "make it" on the street. Learning to make it continues the process begun in the police academy. Strategies for making sense out of one's activity and "doing" police work are expanded or modified in light of actual experience. At this point, the new officer is perhaps the most insecure about his or her new role. This phase of being unsure of one's ability and of one's place in the work group is not alleviated by a departmental policy that allows easy termination of the new officers. Regardless of whether the policy is enforced, new officers are very conscious of the fact that they do not enjoy the job protection afforded older officers through civil service provisions. Terms such as "prob" or "boot," used in some departments to describe those who have just graduated from the academy, further emphasize for the novice the low status and the tenuousness of his or her current position. Therefore, commitment to the formal rules and regulations of the department is likely to be at its peak. Probs are expected to be (and forgiven for being) enthusiastic, hard working, and somewhat idealistic at the outset of their careers. But they are also expected to eventually settle down. The "hard charger" can disturb the routine of the older role incumbents, and force them to redefine and rebuild their social world, a task veterans in most organizations try to avoid. Part of on-the-street training, then, involves learning to "settle in" by adopting the informal work routines of the group.

Veterans are settled in. Between the stages of probation and the settled-in veteran, there appears to be for some officers an intermediate career-development period. This might be termed the "Wyatt Earp" stage. During this stage, the young officer, who has been with the department for between two and ten years, exhibits peak commitment to street patrol and the informal norms of doing police work. The patrolperson during this period is likely to view him or herself as a "crime crusher" or the thin blue line between order and anarchy. Police work becomes a twenty-four-hour-a-day concern, and "street justice" becomes an acceptable response to the pressures of constantly dealing with "dirt balls," arbitrary courts, and unsympathetic brass. Cynicism and resentment toward those who populate the police officer's professional life are at their highest.[6] The officer's personal life may also be in turmoil, since job commitments and street attitudes threaten to invade family life, putting a severe strain on the marriage partner.

Not everyone goes through the Wyatt Earp stage, and for those who do there is great variability in how long it lasts. There are, however, both organizational and extraorganizational pressures to settle down and to lose the starry-eyed notions of the probationary stage and the Wyatt Earp perception that only you can battle the forces of evil. There are constant reminders that you are an organizational employee and not the Lone Ranger.

The process of settling in begins when the district sergeant takes you aside before your first roll call to tell you a little about the district you'll be working in and to give you a little advice.

> We got a pretty good bunch of guys out here. The only big thing I worry about the guys out here is that they're too eager. They're all young guys, and this is the biggest problem I have—slowin' these guys down. Now you take an older officer, and he goes along, you know. You start hurryin' up to get to a family disturbance, and right away he'll tell you, "It's a lot easier to handle two people who's been fightin' for five minutes than to get there when they're fresh." So don't get in no big hurry; you know, take it easy.

Settling in not only means learning to take it easy, it also requires some adjustments to the realities of the actual working life of the police officer. Academy experience prepares the young officer for a world that is dangerous, populated with criminals and those bent on destruction of society as we know it. To cope with such a world, you have learned to shoot a variety of weapons, employ a myriad of sophisticated self-defense techniques, and spot those most likely to give you trouble. Your actual working life, however, is far more mundane. Most of your time is spent responding to noncriminal matters. Eighty to 90 percent of the calls you deal with will not require a crime crusher, but rather a "support agent." Finding lost children, giving information on how to deal with various city agencies (from those that shut off the water to those that help with welfare assistance), transporting the sick and injured, settling neighborhood or family disturbances, and filling out endless reports constitute the majority of your activity during the working day. As you construct your world around these activities, the sentiments expressed by one police officer in a study by Albert Reiss may sum up your own feelings: "I guess 90 percent of all police work is bullshit. All people want is a shoulder to lean on."[7] Reiss's study also gathered empirical data on the police. The empirical data confirm the above officer's comments. The research noted that no tour of duty was typical except that *the model tour of duty did not involve an arrest of any person* (emphasis in the original).[8] This statement is particularly significant since Reiss's research was concentrated in eight high crime rate areas of three major cities (Boston, Chicago, and Washington, D.C.). When he took one city (Chicago) and analyzed 127,861 incidents handled by the patrol division in a twenty-eight-day period, he found that only 17 percent involved criminal matters.[9] Further, an analysis of the dispatches in all of the cities studied showed that in nearly three-quarters of them the patrol officer went to the call in a nonemergency, routine fashion (no flashing lights or sirens).[10]

Clearly, police work is largely a matter of routine. There are times, certainly, when it is dangerous and when the physical and weaponry skills developed in the academy will be necessary. But most often, adeptness at manipulating the environment through words and/or the threat of legal action will be sufficient to allow an officer to take charge of a scene and to create a social pattern most in keeping with perceived organizational goals. You quickly learn how to sharpen these skills as you spend time with older officers. Two incidents take place within your first weeks on the street that illustrate the point.

The time is seven o'clock A.M. The senior officer is driving and you are thinking about soon getting off work. The area you are now in is a lower-class black neighborhood. While you are looking out the window, not really taking note of anything you see, your partner says, "Well, what have we got here?" Your attention is promptly directed to the front, where you observe a blue Volkswagen bus stopped for a light. "What do you mean?" you ask your partner. "Didn't you see that? His brake lights weren't working. We'll have to pull him over. When I get out be sure you approach from the passenger side and look to make sure there is nobody else inside the van. Let the dude see you, so he knows there's two of us."

Your partner honks the horn and the driver of the van, seeing a police car in his rear-view mirror, pulls over. Both you and your partner get out. While he walks up to the driver, you look through the rear window. At the same time you try to watch the driver for any threatening movement of his hands. This takes only a few seconds. There is no one else in the van. In the meantime your partner has approached the driver and asked him to get out of the car. The driver reluctantly agrees. Suddenly, your partner grabs the driver's left arm, pushes up his sleeve, and asks, "What are those marks?" With that the driver is ushered to the back seat of the patrol car. You and your partner get in the front. You are not quite sure what is going on so you just listen. Your partner, who is holding the individual's driver's license, hands it to you. You see that the suspect's name is Arthur and that he is a twenty-four-year-old white male. He has long, rather dirty, light blonde hair.

Arthur: Hey, what's the beef? How come you guys stopped me?

This question is punctuated by a loud sniffle.

Senior Officer: No brake lights.

Arthur: No brake lights? I just had the car in the shop. I can show you the bill of sale for getting it fixed.

Senior Officer: We can make it hard, if you want to go that route. We don't stop you for nothing.

With this last comment your partner starts the car, and you begin to drive toward headquarters.

Arthur: You going to write me a traffic ticket for it? It's a traffic offense.

Senior Officer: We'll write you a traffic ticket for it. Also take you to jail for not having a valid operator's license, you want to get heavy?

Arthur: Not having a valid license?

Senior Officer: You want to play the game that's fine. You want to get heavy, that's fine too. It makes no difference to us.

Arthur: Well, wait a minute, man, you can't take me in. I'm working for Martinson. You know, he's a detective in narcotics. He wants me out on the street.

Senior Officer: Well, maybe you can work for us.

Arthur: Hey, no man, I can't. I already work for Martinson.

Senior Officer: We'll see.

After arriving at headquarters, you, your partner, and Arthur go up to the Narcotics Bureau. Arthur is put in a little room, with you watching him while your partner uses the phone. He hangs up and mutters aloud, "Damn." In a few minutes all three of you are back in the car heading toward the place where Arthur was stopped. Nobody says anything until a few blocks from Arthur's car.

Senior Officer: We'll let you out here. Better you're not seen having us drop you off.

Arthur: Yeah, man. Thanks.

After Arthur is out of the car, your partner says, "Well, that was a waste. Those detectives think they're hot shit, and we're just the dummies. They think they got automatic rights to all the good snitches. Come on, kid, let's hang it up for the day." As you review the above scenario you might, much like a new police officer, be confused as to exactly what was occurring.

At the most general level, Arthur and the senior police officer are negotiating the reality of the situation. Notice the exchange between the senior officer and Arthur. At times, it appears that the two people are really in different conversations, and in a sense they are. Each is using different rules to construct the meaning of the situation. Arthur is telling the officer what he sees to be the natural or logical associations of his current circumstances, and in so doing is trying to convince the officer that he is merely a traffic violator. The officer, however, literally seems to be playing a different game. For the most part, his responses to Arthur are at a much more general level than Arthur's questions and statements. Arthur uses concrete terms like "bill of sale," "traffic ticket," and "traffic offense." The officer, however, uses much less specific terms. "We don't stop you for nothing," and "You want to play the game," are responses at a much higher level of generality than are Arthur's. The only time the officer gets specific, after the initial comment about brake lights, is when he threatens to take Arthur to jail for not having a valid operator's license. It becomes clear that if Arthur insists on defining himself as a traffic violator and will not play the game the officer wants him to play, he will be defined as the most serious traffic violator possible in the circumstances. By the end of the exchange, it is clear that the officer's original definition of the situation will prevail. What is that definition? Arthur is a "hype," that is, an illegitimate user of narcotics. For the police officer, he is much more than a violator of a specific traffic ordinance. In fact, it is not even clear that he violated any specific ordinance. What is clear is that he violated the officer's sense of order. A white male with long hair, driving a Volkswagen van in a lower-class black neighborhood at seven o'clock A.M. was "wrong." This is suspicion actualized to meet organizational goals. If Arthur in fact proved to be a hype, a judgment confirmed by rolling up the sleeve and seeing needle marks, then taking him in could restore order to the beat and at the same time allow the officer to record a narcotics arrest for the shift. Other payoffs might include developing an informant and getting Arthur's name on a file for a more legitimate arrest at some future time.

Arthur, in short, is a cultural caricature. He was pulled over for possessing the typical characteristics of a hype (having long hair, driving a Volkswagen van, being white in a black neighborhood). In the officer's experience, investigating people of this type can result in the positive job outcomes noted above.

The case of Arthur illustrates and expands some of the concepts contained in Jerome Skolnick's book, *Justice Without Trial.* Skolnick notes that police officers develop a shorthand for spotting people likely to give them trouble. Skolnick terms the category used by police to identify such people the symbolic assailant.[11] From their past experience, officers know the traits of those likely to cause them harm. Since such individuals are potentially violent, this use of a perceptual shorthand increases the officer's safety margin. Arthur at first is approached with caution because, based on surface characteristics, he is potentially dangerous. Surface characteristics also make Arthur more than a symbolic assailant, however. He is the officer's symbol of craftsmanship. If handled correctly, Arthur can both demonstrate the officer's competence (at keeping order and getting narcotics arrests) and his initiative and creativity (developing informants that can lead to bigger arrests).

This pressure on the officer to demonstrate his competence can conflict with the rule of law.[12] Procedural law attempts to limit the absolute discretion of law enforcers by prescribing ways in which substantive law should be applied. In our constitutional history, procedural law is meant to guard us from the arbitrary abuse of power by those in authority. Thus, creativity and initiative on the part of law applicators are clearly circumscribed. Who, after all, wants to be the symbol of someone's competence and creativity at law applications, when to be so requires the loss of freedom?

The case of Arthur also underscores another conflict, the one between law and order. The two are sometimes mutually exclusive. For the police officer to maintain his concept of order, it was necessary to violate procedural law. The violation in this case was the rolling up of Arthur's sleeve, which may be the equivalent to an unlawful search. The action of the police officer in this sequence should not be understood as resulting from some kind of psychological predisposition to be overbearing, authoritarian, or to engage in illegal behavior. Rather, the officer is responding to a complex set of organizational and societal demands. Each neighborhood has its own view of what is and is not orderly and expects for the most part that the police will adjust their activities accordingly, even if such order-keeping conflicts with the strict requirements of procedural law. Similarly, as this and the preceding chapter have discussed, the police organization has its goals and its view of what is appropriate production for a police officer. A good officer is one who can meet such a production schedule. But to do so can require using the law and applying it in a way not sanctioned by strict legal interpretation. This is clearly demonstrated by the attempt to turn Arthur into an informant.

"Criminal catching" requires an organized system. As indicated in the previous chapter, police departments run on their reports, and much investigative work involves matching an activity with a known group of offenders. Offenders and offenses become known to the police primarily through the actions of citizens. Citizens call the police to the scene and often tell them who did the misdeed. For certain crimes, however, citizen cooperation is difficult to get. Often, the citizen him- or herself is involved in the illegal activity and derives some benefit from it. Such a person is not very anxious to get the police involved. Most violations of vice laws fall into this category. For the police to operate in this area and to regularize their apprehension of violators, they need informants. Law enforcement depends upon a whole army of Arthurs.

Reliance on informants raises a number of interesting questions about our system of law enforcement. First, it is clear that police officers allow some law violations to go unpunished in order to catch either bigger violators or violators of more interest to the officer's specialty. Skolnick, for example, reports that burglary detectives will allow their informants to use drugs and will not arrest them as long as they continue to provide information on burglars and burglaries. On the other hand, narcotics officers will not question their informants too closely about burglaries they might have been involved in if they provide information on narcotics violations.[13] In light of this, it is rather difficult to argue that various Supreme Court decisions handcuff the police and force them to let violators go. Police agencies regularly overlook violations of one kind to catch those involved in violations of another kind. Given city budgets, this legal barter replaces money as the method of payment for services rendered.

Second, as Skolnick notes, police officers have a vested interest in strict penalties, and the interest is not purely because of a desire to keep criminals off the street.[14] Strict penalties increase officers' bargaining power. Better to work for the "cops" than to be prosecuted for a crime that could result in a long prison term.

Finally, since police agencies are only as good as the information they receive and since, as we have seen, proving one's competency hinges on the information one can gather, there is internal competition among police officers for informants. Unfortunately for the patrol officer, the detectives have the greater stature and hence the greater power in corralling informants. The frustration this causes for the patrol officers is evident. It is also evident that community and organizational demands for order-keeping at times conflict with the officers' desire to make a "big" arrest. As discussed above, sometimes those who violate a community's sense of order (and even their laws) must be allowed to operate if information leading to the occasional "big" arrest is to be developed.

With more street experience, the young officer learns that the gamelike nature of law discussed in the academy was no exaggeration. Putting yourself back in the role of probationary officer, you will learn not only that law is much like a game, but also that you need to sharpen your skills at playing it.

The day after your experience with Arthur you and your partner are again on the street. It is approximately one o'clock A.M. Your partner still won't let you drive. Suddenly a car goes by and your partner says, "I think that's Roger Whitmore. I thought he was wanted." He makes a U-turn and begins to follow the car to pull it over and question the occupant. Apparently, the person in the car does not want to be questioned because suddenly the distance between your car and that of the one you were going to pull over increases. "He's on the run. Get on the radio and tell them we're in pursuit." The chase lasts a little less than five minutes, although going at a high rate of speed down side streets makes it seem a lot longer. Two other officers and a sergeant arrive just as your partner manages to curb the vehicle. The sergeant decides that the two officers not involved in the chase should transport the suspect down to headquarters, while the two of you take a leisurely ride to headquarters alone and get a chance to calm down. On the way there, the following conversation takes place.

> Rookie: We can get him for eluding.
>
> Senior Officer: You can probably write him for that. Maybe that would be best. Otherwise, you know we can write him for about eighty-five different violations.
>
> Rookie: If we write him for eluding, he goes to jail automatically. We can write him for this, and if they reduce it, we can still stick him for the others.
>
> Senior Officer: *(patiently)* See the advantage of writing five separate tickets is that he has to bond out on each one. We got a good eluding case. 'Course we got him on reckless, stop signs, and other stuff. So I think maybe we ought to go with the five separates, that will teach the little . . .

Radio noises make the last word unintelligible. Nevertheless, there are sufficient data in the above conversation to illustrate particular points of police officers' decision-making process and their use of law.

The suspect and his vehicle represented a disturbance in the senior police officer's world. The magnitude of the disturbance was increased by the individual's attempt to escape. That attempt made it more difficult for the officer to get an account from the suspect of his presence and for the officer either to confirm or deny that the individual was wanted. While it is true that the attempted escape confirmed the officer's opinion that the individual was suspicious, having to travel sixty miles per hour to carry out an action reserved for suspicious people (that is, questioning, arrest, etc.) was clearly extra trouble. Therefore, there is an attempt on the parts of both the junior and senior officers to balance the trouble the suspect caused with an appropriate legal charge. The officers are literally "balancing the books." As most citizens probably intuitively know, it is possible to build up credit with a police officer in a traffic situation. If you are polite and show proper respect, the hope is that the officer will go easy on you or perhaps not write the ticket at all. However, the system of credit, that is, the system that says the officer will adjust the charge to fit the trouble caused him by an individual, raises some interesting issues concerning the legal system, the system of justice.

It appears that officers sometimes use law almost in the framework of a tort proceeding or the adjudication of a private wrong. The officer is caused "X" amount of trouble and therefore, to balance the scales, must cause the same amount or more trouble to the defendant. There are various ways the officer can balance the scales. One strategy that has received attention both in the research literature and the popular press is the use of curbstone justice. The officer physically metes out punishment and justifies such abuse on the basis that the courts will not do anything or that the individual had it coming. Obviously, from the point of view of legal philosophy such curbstone justice is abhorrent. It shares problems of primitive tort proceedings (that is, before the introduction of the third party). If wrongs are only settled between the two individuals involved, how can there be agreement on when sufficient justice is achieved? There is a danger of relationships between the police and the public they serve degenerating into a blood war, the good guys against the bad guys, with no clear agreement on which side is which. Is it coppers versus dirt balls, or the people versus the pigs?

Some police departments have attempted to a greater or lesser degree to curb the use of this kind of informal justice. The example illustrates one way of coping with those situations that are potentially ripe for curbstone justice. By having a third party on the scene (in this case, a sergeant) and by giving the officers involved a chance to calm down, the opportunity for physical violence was significantly reduced.

The rookie, however, learns that there are other ways to cause an individual trouble. By taking into account the workings of the legal system, offense categories can be manipulated to cause the individual the maximum amount of difficulty. Such a use of law by police officers underscores an important point about legal categories. The categories, when applied by legal actors, are not simple descriptions of behavior. They contain a large element of evaluation.[15] In this case, behavior is evaluated on the basis of the amount of trouble caused to those who are in the position to apply the law.

The amount of discretion legal actors have varies with the particular circumstances. For certain kinds of activity, the kind represented in the scenario being an example, police have maximum leeway in applying legal categories that, from their vantage point, best describe the social scene, that is, the behavior of the suspect *and* the time and trouble they exerted in the situation to have their view of the world prevail (note that the suspect's legal violation is only one element in the evaluation of the social event). In other circumstances, police officers have less discretion in manipulating legal categories to evaluate behavior. A major crime, such as homicide or bank robbery, may give the street officer less discretion in what categories to apply, but, as will be seen, discretion for other legal actors in the system is still considerable in such circumstances.

The above discussion should raise two cautions for the reader. First, the statistics gathered for and reported in official crime categories need to be looked at with a certain degree of skepticism, as indicated in the first chapter. An official report of an incident is a social construction of the reporting agency and its employees. It is not necessarily a description of the actual behavior of the person who is being reported. As this chapter has demonstrated regarding the police, a variety of factors influence what form a report will take. The legal violation of the individual reported is only one factor in report generation. At times it is not even the most significant factor.

Second, deviance labels (for example, burglar, reckless driver, drug addict) are slippery. To say a person *is* a burglar or *is* a drug addict is to oversimplify human behavior. A person is something only in relation to someone or something else. Labels tell us something about the person to whom they are attached *and* about the person doing the attaching. Thus, social labels need to be looked at in the context of the relationships perceived among the person or persons labeled and the labelers. Deviance labels are parts of accounts used to structure and make sense out of specific relationships within limited time and space parameters. A police officer throughout his or her workday encounters many people. These brief, short-term relationships have only limited goals. The officer wants to cajole, warn, roust, settle, intimidate, instruct, question, and so on with no immediate attempt to bring other legal actors into the relationship. In these instances, the officer concentrates on justifying his presence and the legitimacy of his activity to the individual or individuals he is immediately interacting with. Often, such activity involves order-keeping, letting people know that the "Man" is still on the street, and they had better "clean up their act." Certain labels are part of ready-made accounts that allow such activity to be carried out as efficiently as possible. Terms such as "hype," "dirt ball," and "possible snitch," provide a quick method for indexing a particular situation and for utilizing a strategy that allows the officer to meet certain limited objectives. The scenario of Arthur illustrates the limited and changing nature of labels in this context. Had Arthur been caught with indisputable evidence of a serious narcotics violation, or had it been possible for the officer to develop Arthur into an informant for his own purposes, then more elaborate accounting would have been required.

The accounts and labels used in these more complex interactions must anticipate the likely response of others who may offer future challenges to the officer's construction of an event. The negotiation that took place regarding the appropriate legal category for the individual caught after the high speed chase demonstrates a more complex accounting procedure, wherein an officer must be able to logically link his activity and the activity of an individual interfered with to a broader framework. Often, the officer in such instances is negotiating legal labels to logically account for his activity in light of anticipated challenges. Thus, labels will change, evaluation of events will change, according to the types of relationships indexed and patterned. The new police officer, then, learns both how to relate to specific others to achieve limited goals and also how to weave these specific relationships and activities into mosaics with linkages to the police subculture, the department, and the rest of the legal system. After one learns how to give *police* accounts of events and people, "the becoming a police officer" has been achieved.

References

1. JOHN H. MCNAMARA. "Uncertainties in Police Work: The Relevance of Police Recruits' Backgrounds and Training," in David J. Bordua (ed.), *The Police: Six Sociological Essays* (New York: John Wiley and Sons, Inc., 1967), p. 164.
2. Ibid.
3. JAMES W. STERLING. *Changes in Role Concepts of Police Officers* (International Association of Chiefs of Police, 1972), p. 173.
4. ABRAHAM S. BLUMBERG. "The Practice of Law as a Confidence Game: Organizational Co-optation of a Profession," *Law and Society Review*, 1, June, 1967, 15–39.
5. JEROME H. SKOLNICK. *Justice Without Trial* (New York: John Wiley and Sons, Inc., 1966), pp. 112–15.
6. ARTHUR NIEDERHOFFER. *Behind the Shield* (Garden City, N.J.: Doubleday and Company, Inc., 1967), pp. 231–33.
7. ALBERT J. REISS. *The Police and the Public* (New Haven, Conn.: Yale University Press, 1971), p. 42.
8. Ibid., p. 19.
9. Ibid., p. 96.
10. Ibid., p. 7.
11. SKOLNICK. *Justice Without Trial*, p. 45.

12. Ibid., pp. 231–35.
13. Ibid., p. 129.
14. Ibid., p. 138.
15. DONALD BLACK. "Common Sense in the Sociology of Law," *American Sociological Review,* 44, February, 1979, 20.

chapter four

Law and Theories of Law Violation

Accounts, Sacred and Otherwise

The factors that affect the accounting practices of the police affect the accounting practices of all others involved in creating and maintaining what we perceive as the criminal justice system. In fact, all accounts, in all phases of life, are affected by a variety of social, cultural, historical, and psychological factors. All of us have a tendency, however, to see certain accounts as exempt from such influences. These accounts are raised to the level of the sacred, providing supposedly "true" descriptions of reality unencumbered by any subjective, mundane influences. They literally become part of a sacred text and thereby, in the view of some, unavailable for critical review and analysis. The writings and accounts about religious phenomena are perhaps the most obvious example of the tendency to exempt certain descriptions of reality from the human dynamic.

Three other categories of accounts are, at times, also viewed as exempt from the process of subjective shading. The first of these is our own individual constructions of reality. We often see our view of the world as "right," "objective," "the way things really are," and so on. The first chapter suggested some of the blind spots and consequences that result from a failure to examine our own accounts of reality. The law forms a second category of statements about the world that tends to become enshrined as something removed from ordinary human discourse about events. Chapters two and three illustrated that law itself is subject to the accounting and describing practices of those who use it. Law contributes to such practices and in turn is expanded or contracted in particular situations to meet specific accounting needs. Finally, the theories or accounts of science and the academic community periodically tend to be put on a pedestal and viewed as pristine examples of objective knowledge about the world. Thus, theories about crime, criminals, justice, and law can become the sacred scripture, the bible of those who practice criminal justice. They provide ready-made accounts about the people and events that are a part of the practitioner's life. Unfortunately, as with other sacred writings, there exists the danger of forgetting that academic accounts of the world are shaped and influenced by the same forces that affect common-sense views of reality. When this happens, understanding recedes and blind spots increase.

In order to aid our understanding of law, crime, and criminal justice, this chapter will ask you to focus on a group of individuals not normally included in the catalogue of criminal justice roles. We will term this group "the thinkers." They are the ones who have provided the theoretical statements that have helped many of us categorize and understand law and law violation. You are invited to analyze certain of the influences that have helped shape the postulates of these often hidden, but extremely important, contributors to the accounts available for structuring criminal justice.

Thinkers About Criminal Behavior

Beginning with the nineteenth century, criminological thinkers have thought largely in terms of cause and effect. Prior to the nineteenth century, thinkers about crime were more concerned with the nature and structure of criminal law and how it might be formulated to be both a just and effective deterrent. The former group, those interested in discovering specific, verifiable factors as the causes of crime, is termed the positivistic school of criminology. The latter group form the classical approach to crime and criminals. Positivistic criminology can be divided into four major theory groups: biological, psychological, psychiatric, and sociological. Since positivistic approaches have dominated modern thinking about crime, we turn first to the various individuals who have attempted to account for crime within a framework of nineteenth and twentieth-century science.

Cesare Lombroso (1836–1909) is generally considered the founder of modern criminology. Under the influence of the late eighteenth and early nineteenth century advances in the physical sciences, Lombroso and other Italian criminologists sought the causes of crime in the realm of the biological. Lombroso and his students believed that physical traits set the criminal apart from the normal population. The traits, such as a protruding jaw, asymmetrical skull, retreating forehead, and long arms, were viewed as symptoms of degeneracy or reversion to a more primitive type of human being. This degeneracy was postulated as a cause of crime, and only under exceptionally favorable circumstances could the born criminal type refrain from committing offenses.[1] The influence of Darwin and his theory of evolution is evident in this approach to explaining criminal behavior. Some of Lombroso's students carried the master's ideas even further. They claimed that people guilty of specific criminal offenses could be differentiated on the basis of physical characteristics. Murderers were physically distinct from thieves, and so on. The search for biological determinants of criminal behavior continues. In the 1950s, Sheldon and Eleanor Glueck argued that delinquents were more likely to be of a specific body build,[2] and in the 1970s, certain geneticists attempted to link criminal behavior to chromosomal makeup.

Psychological explanations also have a long tradition in criminological theory, earlier represented by the studies of Goring and, more recently, by the work of Monachesi. Goring, in 1913, challenged the findings of Lombroso, claiming that he could find no difference in the physical characteristics of those incarcerated for criminal offenses and people in the society generally. Based on his study of English convicts, however, he did find that there was a disparity in intelligence between those incarcerated and those in the outside world. Goring thus argued that "weakmindedness" caused crime.[3] In the 1960s, Monachesi, at the University of Minnesota, attempted to predict delinquency with the Minnesota Multiphasic Personality Inventory (MMPI). Using this inventory, he discovered that delinquent boys scored at significantly different levels than did nondelinquent boys on certain scales of the test. He therefore argued that prediction of future delinquency might be possible, since predelinquents should show the same response patterns to test items as those already adjudicated.[4]

The notion of weakmindedness was eventually challenged by psychiatric theories which attributed crime to neuroses or psychoses. Although Sigmund Freud (1856–1939) is considered the originator of psychiatric accounts for explaining criminal behavior, the idea of a sick mind causing crime is quite old. Cavemen, for example, had a method for removing evil-causing demons from the mind. A hole was scraped in the patient's skull for the demons to escape through.[5] Freud was somewhat less drastic in his approach. He and his students viewed criminal behavior as purposive, the purpose being to relieve subconscious tensions or guilt generated in the psyche.[6] In Freud's view, behavior was controlled by the subconscious. Psychoanalysis helps uncover subconscious tensions and guilt so that they can be dealt with in constructive ways. Not all within this approach share such a view, however. Modern-day behaviorists argue that behavior is controlled by stimuli experienced in the environment. They claim that behavior modification techniques, rather than psychoanalysis, are therefore appropriate methods for controlling criminal behavior.[7]

Finally, due largely to the efforts of sociologists from the early "Chicago School" writing in the 1920s and '30s, social factors vied for the crimogenic limelight. These sociologists postulated that crime was the result of social disorganization. Poverty, lack of education, unstable family life, and so on, contributed to a lack of meaningful social bonds that ordinarily helped control behavior and channel it into socially constructive paths.[8]

Besides the social disorganization approach, four other theoretical foci dominate the sociological view of crime and deviance. One focus is a subcultural explanation of illegal behavior. Cohen, one of many researchers concerned with the formation of delinquent subcultures, views lower-class gang behavior as a reaction to middle-class norms and values.[9] The lower-class boy is presented with a cultural ideal that everybody can achieve material success. Yet, from his position it is clear that such success is beyond his reach, particularly if he adheres to the values of middle-class society. Therefore, the boy reasons that such values must be faulty, and the values are then inverted. If middle-class society says hard work is good, the gang boy says it is only for "suckers." If the middle class says deferred gratification is necessary to get ahead, the lower-class gang member, according to Cohen, adopts an ethic of instant gratification. Thus, it is adherence to such subcultural values that results in delinquent activity.

Sutherland's differential association theory represents the second focus, a variation of the subcultural notions of crime causation. In Sutherland's view, associative patterns are seen as causally related to deviant behavior.[10] An individual who associates with a primary group that provides an excess of definitions favorable to the violation of the law over definitions unfavorable to such violations will be more likely to engage in criminal activity. Thus, for Sutherland, crime is learned, like most other behavior, in intimate association with others.

A third focus within sociological explanations of crime centers on the influence of social system factors in the etiology of illegal behavior. Merton, and later Cloward and Ohlin, suggest that the system's failure to provide adequate means for the attainment of culturally accepted goals generates criminal behavior.[11] Criminals are only partially deviant. They accept the goals of society as legitimate. However, they perceive that the traditional means of achieving such goals are not available to them and, therefore, innovative methods of achievement must be employed. Thus, the person who robs a bank is accepting a culturally agreed-upon goal of material wealth but is using innovative means to obtain it.

Last, and most recently, some researchers have begun to explore how the criminal justice system itself contributes to the creation of criminal career patterns. These individuals are known as labeling theorists, and they suggest that to understand crime it is necessary to look at those who label other people as criminals.[12] This last approach comes closest to the account of crime being developed in this book. Nevertheless, as will become evident, there are some subtle but important differences between traditional labeling theory and the approach taken here.

At first glance, the various theories about crime causation may seem entirely dissimilar. Closer examination will reveal that, despite such apparent differences, the theories share, to a remarkable degree, a similar world view. Specifics aside, there are certain common themes that run through the various scientific accounts of criminal behavior.

Just as a reminder, you should approach these accounts within an ethnographic framework. In the two preceding chapters we have examined how police officers account for and make sense of their world. Now we will analyze how scientists of crime do the same thing. From the scientific standpoint, what makes criminal behavior sensical? Does this particular way of making sense out of what is called crime cloud certain aspects of the phenomenon? In short, we want to discover what some of the building blocks of criminology are and what kind of world is built with these materials.

The first common thread is a tendency toward combinations. An example from the advertising annals of the recent past might help to explain this theme. A couple of years ago, a popular mouthwash used to advertise that it killed germs that caused bad breath. You could tell it was effective because it tasted bad. Bad-tasting liquid got rid of bad germs which caused bad breath. At least, that was the association that the advertising attempted to establish. In the public mind, a bad-tasting concoction that attacked germs was like medicine, which also usually tasted bad but got rid of bad things in the body. The Federal Trade Commission put a stop to these advertisements since there was no evidence that the bad-tasting liquid killed germs or even that germs caused bad breath. Despite the lack of evidence, the notion that something that tasted bad was good for you seemed to contain a certain inherent logic. This demonstrates what the Italian sociologist Pareto, writing in the nineteenth century, called the tendency toward combinations.[13] People tend to put together or combine like things. Consequently, an undesirable result (bad breath or crime, for example) is seen as caused by an undesirable or pathological condition. Most of the theories previously discussed exhibit this tendency toward combinations, or the combining of like with like. Crime is accounted for as something caused by bad physique, weak intelligence, psychiatric disability, or those social conditions associated with poverty. Pathological causes for pathological effects.

A second common thread runs through the criminological accounts of crime. This is the thread of determinism. Given a certain preexisting condition, crime will almost inevitably result. Such determinism is most evident in the biological, psychological, and psychiatric approaches to criminal behavior, but it also lurks in the sociological explanations of illegal conduct. There is little attention paid to the operation of free will in the face of adverse social conditions. The criminal is viewed as a victim of circumstance, propelled into law-violating behavior by forces beyond his control. Even the labeling perspective which, according to Howard Becker, takes the position of the underdog or the outsider, contains a heavy dose of determinism. Individuals are labeled, accept the label, and then act accordingly. The people labeled are seen as passive, that is, as uncritical, uncomplaining acceptors of labels.

A third element unites the various scientific explanations of criminal conduct. This is the belief in the essentially orderly, understandable nature of human society. Social life is viewed as rule-governed. Deduce the rules from an appropriate theoretical construct, and it is possible to understand and predict human behavior. This third thread tying together the various theories might be termed the thread of rationalism. The early founders of the modern behavioral and social sciences firmly grounded their new disciplines in the rhetoric and images of the physical sciences. Human behavior, while extremely complex, was ultimately reducible to mathematical-like formulae. Given factor X, Y will result.

As ethnographers, three questions confront us about the accounts of crime proffered by criminological thinkers. First, what kind of social world patterns are woven from the threads of combinations, determinism, and rationalism? Second, what are the consequences for our understanding of crime when accounts are fashioned in these particular ways? Third, from the point of view of the thinkers about crime, why does it make sense to account for criminal behavior in the ways described?

In the world of criminology, crime is largely a lower-class phenomenon or an occurrence more likely to be associated with minorities and those already on the fringe of society. Crime, as an example of behavior that is abnormal or different, will most likely occur among individuals identified as having other social maladies. The influence of associating pathological consequences with pathological causes predisposes criminologists to focus their attention on those previously perceived as different. Most "scientific" accounts of crime are therefore of little use in explaining the deviances of the upper classes. In fact, the peccadilloes of this group are less likely to be accounted for as an example of crime and hence less likely to be seen as something in need of explanation. The world of criminological theory is a world populated by people who are essentially different than the theorist, a "them" rather than an "us." Much like the police officer vis-à-vis his world, the criminologist gains some advantage in perceiving others as essentially different from himself. Depersonalization is made easier. For scientific pursuits, the individual must become "an object of study." Only when the task of objectifying is complete can individuals be categorized as things to be studied. Otherwise, they remain friends, acquaintances, or fellow human beings, and probing questions together with intense scrutiny seem inappropriate. Further, the world of criminology allows for a depoliticizing of crime. If the activities of people (people other than ourselves, that is) are determined by the conditions of society (or biological, psychological, or psychiatric states), the activities do not indict the existing distributions of power within a society. Crime, not the system, is pathological, problematic, and so on. Crime is not a willful statement of protest challenging the status quo. The law is broken, the lawbreaker must be dealt with, but there is no need to look at the decisionmakers or the system itself as contributing to the growth of the problem.

At first glance, the social structural explanations of crime causation (for example, Merton, Cloward and Ohlin) and the labeling perspective may seem exempt from the theoretical blind spot that protects the existing system from criticism. At best, however, such theories imply only a limited criticism of elements of the social system, not the system as a whole. Gouldner, in evaluating some of these theories, notes that any implied criticism stops at the level of the middle-management bureaucrat.[14] Gouldner goes on to note that such limited criticism forms an effective strategy for the social scientist. Social scientists face a world with its own set of contradictions. They should be able, as scientists, to remain impartial in their analyses of a particular social structure or of a whole society, letting the chips fall where they may. At the same time, they need to have their research endeavors funded. The dilemma is, how to remain liberal (that is, not inordinately committed to an existing status quo) and well-financed at the same time. Aiming theoretical salvos at midlevel functionaries accomplishes both goals. The need for change is touted while calls for fundamental systemic reform are avoided. In fact, such pleas often end up being arguments for more efficient handling of criminals, not a meaningful challenge to the whole concept of criminalization. The theoretical blind spots of Salem seem less distant. Witches can be treated more humanely. There is seldom a question of whether "they" should be treated at all.

For people who want to help society or improve the human condition, it is comfortable and profitable to believe that the crime problem can be solved through the application of rational scientific procedures. "Better living through criminology," might be an appropriate slogan for those who account for crime in the various theoretical ways described. The world of the criminologist, then, unlike perhaps the world of the police officer, is an optimistic one. Things can be made better if only the right key can be discovered. The optimism of rationality also contains a dimension of power. The right key or combination of keys will allow prediction and control of human behavior. To date, public policy formulated on the basis of this world view has been both ineffective and, to a degree, dangerous. Programs to control crime have not been an overwhelming success. Decisions about probation and parole continue to be made with the help of predictive instruments that do not accurately forecast future behavior.[15] The lack of sophistication present in predictive instruments, plus the possibility of interfering in a person's life based on what he or she might do, raises a frightening specter. Nevertheless, justification for proceeding along these lines is found in the world view shared by traditional criminological theories.

The world of the criminologist, as articulated through the principal theories of criminal behavior, is one populated by people who are powerless, subject to factors beyond their control, and who have little in common either with the theorist or with people the theorist knows. Since law violators are perceived as essentially powerless, apolitical individuals, there is seldom a question of whether they want or need the ministrations of the scientific community. They are objects to be acted upon, not actors. Thus, as noted in Chapter One, treatment without choice can become an acceptable possibility. Further, scientific faith counsels criminal justice decisionmakers and society generally to believe that a solution to the crime problem is imminent. All that is needed is more money and resources for the pursuit of knowledge.

At this point, it is appropriate to specify and underscore what the preceding analysis of scientific criminological theory does *not* say. It does not argue that such accounts are the result of conscious, conspiratorial collusion among criminologists to keep or obtain power, to control those less fortunate than themselves, to support a particular governmental form, or to con the public into believing their salvation lies within the halls of academia. Like police officers, academics are most comfortable with those accounts that allow them to see their own activity as logical, precedented, and the like. Particular accounts of crime allow particular individuals to meet this goal at particular historical moments. To say this is not to say that such accounts are erroneous, false, or totally lacking in merit. From the ethnomethodological perspective, the way social scientists order the world is not any less accurate than the way a police officer orders the world. It is not, however, assumed to be automatically more accurate. It is just different. Moreover, although no one theory is totally successful either in providing knowledge about, or a program for solving crime, different theories contain elements that have helped illuminate different aspects of criminal behavior. The question is: What dark corners of knowledge are not illuminated by the typical social world constructions of criminological scientists? It seems clear that the theories discussed are not beacons pointing to an understanding of upper-world deviance.[16] Nor do they brightly illuminate the beliefs and values of those doing justice and the consequent impact of their accounts on what we know as crime. Finally, since they focus on the individual violator and not law, thereby assuming a definition of law, they do not light the path to understanding how law is used to construct meaning. As Hartjen remarks, such theories, by attempting to explain criminal behavior without reference to the criminal justice system, were to be as fruitful as attempting to explain slavery by focusing on the slave and not on the economic, political, and social systems which gave rise to that ignoble institution.

In order to further illuminate some of the dark places left untouched by traditional theory, we turn to an analysis of law. The next section will briefly examine the social world constructions of those who have shaped the image of law underlying both criminological and common-sense notions of legal and illegal behavior.

Thinkers About Law

Modern-day theories about law and current legal procedures owe a huge debt to Cesare Beccaria (1738–1794), an eighteenth-century Italian criminologist who convincingly argued for reform of the legal system. Up to that time, the administration of law was viewed as a rather haphazard process, with legal sanctions applied at the whim of the judge or the king. Beccaria, borrowing from the works of Montesquieu, Voltaire, Rousseau, and others, saw law as an expression of the social contract which, if properly administered, could prevent individuals from going beyond the bounds of that contract. When the law was broken, that is, the social contract exceeded, punishment was to be applied according to the harm done society and to the extent necessary to deter others from acting similarly. Presumably, both of these factors were the same for the same type of crime. Therefore, people guilty of the same infraction were all to be given the same punishment. Punishment was to have limits.[17]

Beccaria's account of law and legal process was shaped by a highly rational view of society and human behavior. In fact, even though the behavioral theory was not clearly articulated, Beccaria and his followers had a definite causal explanation of human behavior. Individuals operated on a pleasure–pain principle, seeking to maximize the former and avoid the latter. Before people acted, they calculated the likely amount of pleasure to be gained, weighed against the cost in terms of pain. If the scale tipped in favor of greater pleasure, the act was carried out. If the scale tipped the other way, the act was avoided. Law, then, to deter crime, simply had to ensure that the pleasure of the criminal act was outweighed by the pain that would be inflicted for going beyond the social contract.[18] The rational image of law, legal processes, and human behavior fashioned by Beccaria was the starting point for what became known as the classical school of criminology. Later, positivistic criminology, even though it concerned itself almost exclusively with individual behavior, assumed the image of law fashioned by those in the classical school. Law had definite substance and form, providing clear guidelines and boundaries for agreed-upon community activity.

Compare this notion of law with the idea that law is an emergent, flexible process, applied to situations by a variety of people in a variety of ways. The comparison raises a number of important questions. First, is law a concrete, external, omnipresent phenomenon, or is it not? Second, whose law is it; in whose interest is it exercised? Third, how do the different definitions of law shade our image of the criminal? Fourth, what types of control policies are likely to flow from the differing accounts of law? Put another way, who needs to be controlled, the officials or the people?

The answers to these questions clearly depend on the definition of law with which you are the most comfortable. The comfort index itself, as we have seen, is related to a host of factors external to the law, such as your immediate situation, your past history, the norms and values of your group, and so on. To make matters even more confusing, these external factors are subject to change, which in turn is likely to change your accounts of the world and, specifically, your view of law. For instance, put yourself in the place of Arthur in the last chapter. How does Arthur experience the law? To the outside observer of the scene, law appears to be largely an emergent, flexible process. Yet, it is by no means certain that Arthur experiences the law as quite that malleable. He does attempt to negotiate with it and mold it in a particular way to fit his particular circumstances. However, he also clearly experiences law as something external, with power to coerce and shape behavior. Arthur is in fact a "snitch," whose behavior is controlled in part by fear of this external thing experienced as law. Law is not a totally flexible instrument in the hands of the police officer, either. The law provides parameters for the officers' behavior. They could not, for example, have charged Arthur with homicide. In fact, they probably could not have charged Arthur with the various legal infractions threatened or implied, since the officers' justification for stopping Arthur in the first place was at best legally suspect. Thus, the officers, too, experience law as something external to themselves. It appears that the first question raised by the various definitions of law is best answered by voting a split ticket. Law is experienced as both an emergent, flexible process and an external, concrete, powerful reality with the ability to coerce behavior. The book *The Murder Trial of Wilbur Jackson* illustrates these two seemingly incompatible views of law. Wilbur Jackson murdered his daughter and the three male companions with whom she was living. For the most part, the book consists of the transcript of Wilbur's trial. From the outset there was no doubt that Wilbur had done the deed. He had confessed, his wife was a witness, and there were numerous others who had seen him come out of the apartment with "the smoking gun." Despite the relatively straightforward nature of the event, in his charge to the jury before they retired to consider Wilbur's fate, the judge noted there were nineteen possible findings, each carrying with it various wide-ranging consequences for the remainder of Wilbur's life.[19] Obviously, the law is both flexible and negotiable, and external and coercive. Wilbur spent the next fifteen years of his life in prison.

This discussion helps us confront the second problem raised by the differing views of law. Whose law is it? There are a variety of answers to this question. Aristotle argued a "value-consensus" theory about law—the law is that which we all agree on and/or that which we all know distinguishes right from wrong. Blackstone, an eighteenth-century English jurist, said that law is the prerogative of the supreme power of the state. In this view, the law is what the king says it is or what the legislative body says it is. A third definition suggests that law is whatever the judge who applies it in particular circumstances determines it to be. Other definitions extend the answer to the question of whose law it is by including a variety of political actors, legal actors, and interest groups.

How shall we vote? Again, a split ticket seems in order. Law is any and all of these things, depending upon particular sets of circumstances. The law may belong to a particular person or group, or to the whole society. The law may be what one person or group says it is at a given point in time, but at another point in time a totally different set of actors may exercise the power to determine the law. Clearly, the question "Whose law is it?" is a question of power. Those who articulate the law exercise control in a variety of circumstances. The police had the power to articulate the law in their relationship with Arthur. In the eleventh century, as the first chapter pointed out, the King of England exerted the power to articulate the law over the protests of church officials. In the 1920s, Prohibition represented the success of a relatively small group of citizens to articulate the law. But the power of articulation is not immutable. The police officers lost the power to articulate the law to the narcotics detective in the case of Arthur, and the king's power gave way to the power of parliament and judges. Prohibition, even while still the official law of the land, was articulated by large segments of the community far differently than its framers intended.

Since the ability to articulate the law, what it is and who it belongs to, is also the ability to exercise power, many people attempt to convince others that their legal articulations are removed from the processes that affect other human accounts. Aristotle and Blackstone suggest that law is sacred. Others suggest that it is profane. If you are a monarch, a legislator, or a judge, the former view is probably more appealing. After all, projecting an image of the law as sacred is in your best interests, since it provides a hard-to-challenge justification for your exercise of power. Nevertheless, on this point the evidence is clear. Law is not a sacred account. It is a boundary-setting process, buffeted by those factors affecting all human accounts. Therefore, the boundaries separating the good from the bad, the wilderness of evil from the community of saints, the rational from the irrational, is a flexible one, ebbing and flowing in response to the winds of historical, social, and personal circumstance. In light of this analysis and our previous analyses of police accounting procedures, it seems wise to shade our image of the criminal in tones of gray. As we have seen, the terms of law used to categorize violators often tell us more about the categorizers than about those categorized. They provide a map for understanding how the former view their world and weave patterns to account for their activity as examples of reasonable, logical, and sensical behaviors.

If the law is not a rigid, mechanical, automatic, infallible process for the discovery of truth, the question of who controls the controllers becomes important. Their weaving and processing of law must be available for scrutiny and judgment within the broader community. Procedural law, the law governing legal administration and process, is as important as substantive law, that which provides prohibitions and controls for the behavior of citizens. Beccaria's reforms were partly concerned with limiting the discretion of those who administer the law. Unfortunately, the behavioral theory underlying Beccaria's musings on law and the legal theory underlying traditional criminology then seems to assume that such discretion no longer needs to be considered in accounts of criminal behavior. They take for granted the rightness (sacredness) of the lawgiver or administrator, an assumption certainly appealing to the doers of law. A complex decision leaves the decisionmaker subject to challenge and error; better for people to downplay the discretionary elements of law and the need for control of those charged with its administration.

At this point, what are we to make of law? It is external to the individual and able to coerce behavior. At the same time it is an emergent, flexible instrument used in the construction of personal social worlds. It is used by the powerful to maintain power, but can be used by those out of power to gain ascendancy. It sets boundaries, but once set they ebb and flow in response to circumstances. It has majesty, but is subject to common, profane processes. How then are we to understand law, with its contradictions and dilemmas? An analogy might be helpful. Law is like language. To fully appreciate this analogy, however, we need to momentarily divert our attention and briefly discuss some pertinent facts concerning language.

The Subtleties of Language

Language helps structure the world we see. Different languages mean different world views. The fact that different languages point to different social worlds is underscored by noting that many words cannot be precisely translated from one language to another. This is called linguistic nonequivalence. Obviously, language itself is influenced by physical reality. Thus, there is an interaction between language and physical reality, and that interaction is what shapes our perception of the world. We sometimes underestimate the power of language to shape what we see. Even a physical concept such as color is influenced by language. In English there are six basic colors in the color spectrum: purple, blue, green, yellow, orange, and red. Basa, a language of Liberia, has only two words to describe the color spectrum, one for the blue-green end of the spectrum and another for the red-orange end.[20] Hence, purple would have no exact equivalent translation into Basa, and the world would look somewhat different to a person immersed in the Basa language than it would to a person taught the linguistic categories of the English color spectrum. Some scholars have argued that different languages and the linguistic nonequivalence of languages mean different modes of thought for people of unlike language traditions,[21] that is, reality is construed differently depending upon the linguistic building material available.

It is not necessary to examine fairly esoteric language groups to make the point. Part of police training involves learning a new set of linguistic tags for describing the world, tags that have no exact parallel in the nonpolice world. Words like hype or snitch or dirtball are descriptions of the world as a police officer sees it. A hype is not just somebody who abuses drugs. As the last chapter indicated, a hype is a cultural caricature and includes notions of street drug use (as distinguished from someone who abuses alcohol or prescription drugs), a symbolic assailant, a symbol of police craftsmanship, a potential informant, and so forth. Similarly, a snitch is more than somebody who simply gives information to the police. A snitch generally has a long-term relationship with an officer. The relationship is based on mutual dependence. The officer needs the snitch to keep information flowing, and the snitch needs the officer to gain more leeway in performing his activities, some of which may be illegal. Police training is learning about hypes, dirtballs, and snitches, categories and characters not ordinarily a part of a civilian's milieu.

As indicated above, words interact with physical reality to help structure our worlds. The less physical substance there is to a concept, that is, the more cultural a concept is, the more the influence of language exerts itself in molding that concept. Thus, a concept such as law or justice allows for a far greater play of language than does a concept involving physical quantity. It would be difficult to carry on an extended conversation about the concept "four apples." Alternatively, it would be difficult to have a brief conversation about the concept of justice or about the nature of law.

The discussion of language contributes to our understanding of law in two ways. First, law and language share many common characteristics. Both are external to the individual and are coercive in the shaping of individual realities. At the same time, both are flexible instruments used to construct and maintain particular world views. Both set boundaries on social reality, but boundaries that ebb and flow with some regularity. Finally, each is used to either maintain power or to assault existing power relationships. In the case of language, this last commonality may be less clear. But it underscores the second contribution an understanding of language can make to an understanding of law. The language we use to talk about law influences our concept of law and our concept of those who are enmeshed in its net. Since the ability to articulate the law is also the ability to exercise power, many people have a vested interest in the language used to talk about law. If the "right" linguistic tags are used to describe law, the lawgiver can maintain a world view justifying his or her exercise of power. To illustrate the point, consider for a moment the use of language by government bureaucracies. A false statement, in common-sense language, is termed a lie. What a different aura attaches to the statement when it is termed "inoperative." The moral opprobrium is lifted, and the false statement becomes morally neutral or even legitimate.

Generally, our language tends to overemphasize the rational, concrete, sacred nature of law. We talk about "breaking the law." That phrase conjures up something solid, with mass and substance. It ignores, or at least underemphasizes, the flexibility and fluidity of law. It would be inappropriate to talk about breaking a liquid. You can break chalk or a dish, but you cannot break milk. Terms such as "lawbreaker," "law violator," and "legal transgressor" present over-rationalized, overconcretized images of people caught in the legal system. Therefore, the law itself appears as a readily visible, agreed-upon set of norms, standing vulnerable to intended acts of desecration. The good guys and the bad guys are clearly delineated, with the lawgiver and the law administrator firmly in the ranks of the former.

To better capture the fluid nature of law, new linguistic terms are needed. It would perhaps, for example, be more descriptive of law and legal processes to talk about individuals "being caught in the law," rather than to talk about people caught breaking the law. To avoid linguistic traps that overemphasize the static, rigid nature of law, legal procedures, and law violations, we will use a term that can help illuminate an understanding of law as an interactive process. That term is "quasi-law."[22]

Quasi-Law

Laws are used as potential items in a person's repertoire of accounts. The accounts themselves are the possible descriptions of actions, places, people, and events that allow social life to be seen as logical, coherent, and the like. Laws are quasi- in the sense that their full meaning cannot be understood unless the circumstances surrounding their use are also understood. Therefore, to understand law it is necessary to understand the social occasions of its use—the circumstances surrounding its creation, its application, and something about both the person applying it and the one to whom it is being applied. Two examples illustrate the point.

The first took place in England in 1473 and is known as the Carrier's Case. According to Jerome Hall, changing economic and political circumstances led to the need for a reinterpretation of the law of theft. Until this time, theft necessarily included a trespass. For a theft to occur, property had to be taken from the premises of another. Thus, a problem arose when an individual who was hired to carry goods from one place to another took the goods for his own use instead of delivering them to their intended destination. Technically, the carrier was not guilty of theft since he had not committed a trespass, in the typical meaning of that term, to obtain the property. He originally had legitimate possession of the goods. The jurists who decided the Carrier's Case were in a difficult situation. Clearly, economic circumstances were changing. With the rise of commercialism and the consequent economic interests of both the crown and the wealthy class in the development of various commercial enterprises, the jurists could not simply rule that no crime had occurred. Obviously, the safe transport of goods from one place to another was necessary for the new economy to take shape. The justices eventually decided that the carrier had in fact committed a trespass, since he had to break into the containers to remove their contents.[23] This ruling was a significant departure from the common-sense and legal understandings of what constituted theft. But times were changing. The changes meant that law had to be reinterpreted so that new activities brought about by new commercial interests could be accounted for in a way that protected the interests of those groups that had a stake in encouraging the new economic order. Thus, the law helped make the new world logical and coherent, at least for the merchants.

The accounting function of law can also be illustrated by a modern example. Sutherland, in examining the development of sexual psychopathic laws, found that states usually passed such laws in response to a specific, heinous sex crime.[24] After the occurence of such an event, citizens' groups would often lobby state legislatures to pass sexual psychopathic laws requiring mandatory commitment to a state mental facility. Interestingly enough, however, such citizens' committees were most often directly or indirectly influenced by psychiatrists. Thus, psychiatrists were the most important interest group behind such laws. Within a psychoanalytic framework, it makes sense to treat such offenders in mental hospitals, a world view legitimated by the way sexual psychopathic laws now accounted for such behavior.

As the examples above illustrate, in their inception and interpretation laws will often be formulated to provide particular groups with the accounts necessary to describe and see the world in a way most beneficial, comfortable, and logical to them. However, the term quasi-law cautions against the tendency to chisel even the accounts of powerful groups into immutable stone. Once written down, laws become available to be used in the accounting and describing practices of everyone. Unfortunately, many of the behavioral theorists discussed in this chapter seem to believe that the only legal actors in the system are the lawyers, the police officers, and the judges. As noted, those to whom the law is applied are viewed as passive. But again, the term quasi-law cautions against such an interpretation. Research by Matza indicates that delinquents apply law in particular ways to meet their particular circumstances.[25]

Matza notes that delinquents often see their activities as matters of tort, and therefore feel that criminal procedures and sanctions are inappropriately applied to their actions. If a person's reputation has been challenged, for example, it is perfectly appropriate to defend that reputation by fighting or engaging in a daring activity. Such a response is between the individual and his challenger and is therefore a private matter or a matter of tort. Delinquents, then, apply laws to their activities in a way at variance with courts, police, and attorneys. Moreover, they are not simply passive acceptors of the judgments of these other actors. In fact, it may well be that the conflict that arises over the interpretations of behavior and the applications of statutes to that behavior increases the sense of injustice experienced by delinquents when processed by the legal system. When police officers vary the harshness of the laws applied to a situation in accord with the trouble caused them, they violate what appear to be the formal norms of the system. This provides further rationalizations for the delinquents to continue their own adaptations of law to suit their own purposes. After all, if the system is unfair and everybody is "on the make," why should I be different? This link between the operations of the juvenile justice system and further deviant behavior is certainly made evident by Matza's research and that of his colleague, Sykes.[26]

The notion of quasi-law can be useful, then, in a number of ways. First, it can provide a clearer understanding of legal dynamics by helping avoid an overrigid view of law and its processes. The linguistic rigidity common to definitions of the law has led to numerous misunderstandings about how law operates and, thus, has also led to calls for reform that are doomed to fail.

The term quasi-law also directs us to consider the linkages that exist between the systems set up to correct deviance and the further deviant behavior of those who come before it. Understanding law as quasi- allows investigators to consider the behavior of the labeler as well as that of the labeled. Deviance is then seen as an interactive process. While this notion is contained in traditional labeling theory, quasi-law broadens the conceptualization of who is the legal actor and who applies law. The so-called deviant can be viewed as an active participant in his social world. His or her behavior is not depoliticized. By avoiding depoliticization, we also avoid the trap of considering the system a sacred instrument for imparting an empirically correct, immutable label. Instead, the process of law itself becomes an entity in need of critical scrutiny and control.

Finally, the term quasi-law raises questions about the purpose of punishment. If law is an accounting applied to a situation more or less successfully by individuals, then in essence we are punishing those who fail to convince us of the legitimacy of their use of law. Seen in this way, the typical justifications for punishment must be expanded. Punishment is to a large degree ritualistic. Society selectively punishes deviance in order to symbolize a particular view of the world. In essence, punishment is a way to concretize quasi-law. It is an attempt to convince people that the decisions made about others are not only rational, logical, and coherent, but are in fact the only decisions that can be made given the "reality" of the situation. Thus, if you punish witches there are such things as witches, and the accounts, legal and otherwise, that identify this group are given not only linguistic reality but reality through action. Punishment is the ultimate means of confirming the accounts of particular groups in society. Punishment is a central factor in law, since it attempts to move law from the realm of the quasi- and interactive to the realm of the concrete. There is, after all, nothing quasi- about punishment.

Punishment, then, symbolically gives law its meaning and majesty. In fact, however, people applying law in day-to-day situations give law its form and substance, a form and substance that changes according to who does the applying and in what circumstances. The next chapter will explore your ability to give law meaning and substance in particular circumstances.

References

1. ROBERT G. CALDWELL. *Criminology* (New York: The Ronald Press, 1965), pp. 175–76.
2. SHELDON and ELEANOR GLUECK. *Unraveling Juvenile Delinquency* (New York: Commonwealth Fund, 1950).
3. CHARLES GORING. *The English Convict* (London: His Majesty's Stationery Office, 1913).
4. STARKE R. HATHAWAY and ELIO D. MONACHESI. *Analyzing and*

Predicting Juvenile Delinquency with the M.M.P.I. (Minneapolis: University of Minnesota Press, 1953).
5. PAUL E. DOW, ed. *Criminology in Literature* (New York: Longman Inc., 1980), p. 137.
6. Ibid., pp. 137–38.
7. Ibid., p. 139.
8. See for example Frederic Thrasher, *The Gang* (Chicago: The University of Chicago Press, 1927), and Shaw and McKay, *Juvenile Delinquency in Urban Areas* (Chicago: The University of Chicago Press, 1942).
9. ALBERT COHEN. *Delinquent Boys* (Glencoe, Ill.: The Free Press, 1955).
10. EDWIN H. SUTHERLAND. *Principles of Criminology* (Philadelphia, Pa.: Lippincott, 1947).
11. ROBERT K. MERTON. *Social Theory and Social Structure* (Glencoe, Ill.: The Free Press, 1957), pp. 131–94, and Richard A. Cloward and Lloyd E. Ohlin, *Delinquency and Opportunity* (New York: The Free Press, 1960).
12. See for example Howard S. Becker, *The Outsiders* (New York: The Free Press, 1963).
13. VILFREDO PARETO. *The Mind and Society* (New York: Harcourt, Brace and Company, 1935).
14. ALVIN W. GOULDNER. "The Sociologist as Partisan: Sociology and the Welfare State," *The American Sociologist*, 2 (May 1963), 110.
15. See for example Stephen E. Schlesinger, "The Prediction of Dangerousness in Juveniles: A Replication," and Beverly Koerin, "Violent Crime: Prediction and Control," *Crime and Delinquency*, 24, no. 4 (January 1978), 40–58.
16. One of the few exceptions is Edwin H. Sutherland. See his *White Collar Crime* (New York: Holt, Rinehart and Winston, 1949).
17. CALDWELL. *Criminology*, p. 172.
18. Ibid., p. 173.
19. PHILIP B. HEYMANN and WILLIAM H. KENETY. *The Murder Trial of Wilbur Jackson: A Homicide in the Family* (St. Paul, Minn.: West Publishing Co., 1975), p. 276.
20. Ibid., pp. 315–16.
21. Ibid., p. 317.
22. The term quasi-law is taken from ethnomethodology. See Don

H. Zimmerman and D. Lawrence Wieder, "Ethnomethodology and the Problem of Order: Comment on Denzin," in *Understanding Everyday Life,* ed. Jack Douglas (Chicago, Ill.: Aldine, 1970), pp. 285–94.

23. JEROME HALL. *Theft, Law and Society,* rev. ed. (Indianapolis, Ind.: The Bobbs-Merrill Company, Inc., 1952).

24. EDWIN H. SUTHERLAND. "The Diffusion of Sexual Psychopath Laws," *American Journal of Sociology* (September 1950), 142–48.

25. DAVID MATZA. *Delinquency and Drift* (New York: John Wiley and Sons, Inc., 1964).

26. Ibid. See also Gresham Sykes and David Matza, "Techniques of Neutralization: A Theory of Delinquency," *American Sociological Review,* 22 (December 1957), 664–70.

chapter five

Making Legal Decisions: You Try It

Accounts of Accounts of Accounts

The preceding chapters have underscored the idea that deviance is a slippery concept. Its slipperiness can be attributed to the interactional nature of the deviance-defining process. Somebody (an actor) must do something, that something must be seen by somebody else (a perceiver), the perceiver must then judge the action of the actor to be something negative, and finally, if the behavior is to be identified as legally deviant, the perceiver has to have the power, resources, and knowledge to bring official legal actors into the picture. With the entry of legal officials, new interactional networks are formed and new decision points established. Reflect on this sequence for a moment. It immediately becomes evident that deviance construction is an after-the-fact process, an account of something that has already occurred. Seen in this light, deviance is a fiction. That is, it is a construct put together by a variety of people in order to identify, clarify, and understand the behavior of certain others. It is not reality, but a construct of reality. Different interpretations and constructs are possible. Indeed, we have already seen that people both within and without the criminal justice system disagree among themselves on how to account for particular behaviors. Police officers' accounts of behavior can differ from the accounts of lawyers

87

(both prosecutors and defenders). Attorneys' accounts can differ from those of psychologists, which in turn may differ from those of judges. Judges may account for the activities of defendants differently than defendants themselves may account for them, and defendants at times offer accounts of their activity that are not accepted by juries. Juries construct their own accounts. Whew! After all of that, whose account is the correct one? The legal process offers one method of answering this question. It provides linguistic building blocks for erecting legal accounts of behavior. Such legal accounts can then be compared with one another according to the rules of legal procedure to determine which seems most reasonable. This comparing of accounts takes place formally in a trial situation and informally in plea bargaining sessions, pretrial hearings, and other legal or quasilegal settings. The result is "law" applied to a particular situation, at a particular time, with particular participants, for all practical purposes. Put another way, the result is an account of an account.

In this chapter, you will begin an examination of the process of account comparisons within the legal setting. You will also examine how such comparisons lead to the construction of a new "legal account" of an event. You now have certain tools at your disposal for doing this. You know the purpose of ethnography. You have studied police accounting practices. You have been sensitized to the influence of language on the ways people go about describing their reality. You have observed the tendencies of police officers, scientists, philosophers, and everybody else to try to convince others that their descriptions of reality are "true," that is, sacred, unchallengeable accounts. At this point, one other tool needs to be added to your collection.

Certain psychiatrists claim that individuals cannot be practitioners of psychoanalysis unless they themselves have been through the process. While it is fun to analyze the foibles of others, it is often more revealing to examine one's own. Further, self-examination can lead to an empathetic understanding of others. This chapter will give you an opportunity to analyze your own accounting practices. First, you will be presented with legal accounts of various events. For our purposes, these will be treated as the first descriptions of the events being considered. Next, you will be asked to make decisions about the "facts" presented, that is, to construct an account of an account. You will act as a kind of judge or jury. You will be the final arbitrator of the "facts." Your accounting processes will then be compared to the accounting processes of the legal enterprise. Such comparison will allow us to begin the process of theory building, that is, the construction of disciplined statements about the patterns observed in legal processing and law application. Theory in this instance will literally be an account of an account of an account. The last account in the series is the original description of the "facts." The next account is how you yourself mold the "facts" and come to some decision about what occurred and what has to be done. The first account in the string (the last in order of when it actually takes place) will be the beginning of theoretical statements about the patterns of law. The exercises and discussion in this chapter will do a number of things. First, they will further your understanding of how the criminal justice enterprise arrives at particular reconstructions of events. Second, you will gain some insight into your own accounting process, hopefully discovering some of those factors that help you mold your reality. Third, a foundation will be laid for theory construction, specifically disciplined statements about the operation of law (further expanded in Chapter Six) and disciplined statements about accounting procedures (the topic of Chapter Seven).

To this point we have examined the social world constructions of police officers and thinkers about criminal justice. We now turn to self-ethnography and ask how citizens (you) make sense of crime. What kind of world do you build to account for the perceived misdeeds of others?

The First Accounts

To achieve the goals of this chapter, you should follow a few simple suggestions. Read the illustrations and decide the cases in groups of three or four persons. Ideally, these would be randomly selected groups, not people who are your closest friends. You should make your decisions about the cases and record those decisions before you go on to the discussion sections of this chapter. Finally, limit your decision-making process to thirty minutes for each case. If at the end of twenty-five minutes your group has not made a decision, make a special effort to get something on paper. In no case go beyond forty-five minutes. If you do, consider yourself a hung jury, unable to reach a decision (that is, an account you can all agree on).

The two cases that follow are summaries of actual trials and legal proceedings. Longer versions of the illustrations appear in *The American Legal System: Its Dynamics and Limits,* by Stephen D. Ford.

Case No. 1:

This case had its beginnings on July 5, 1884, when three English seamen (Dudley, Stephens, and Brooks) and a cabin boy were forced to abandon ship during a fierce storm on the high seas. The lifeboat they were in had no fresh water supply. The only food, two one-pound tins of turnips, lasted three days. On the fourth day they caught a small turtle, but it was soon eaten. By July 23, they had gone for seven days without any food whatever, and for five days without any water. Because of such hardships, the cabin boy was near death. On the 24th of July, Dudley proposed to Stephens and Brooks that lots be drawn to determine who should be put to death, in order that the rest might subsist upon his flesh and be saved. Brooks protested. Nobody asked the cabin boy what he thought. No lots were in fact drawn. Dudley and Stephens noted that they had families, while the cabin boy did not. Dudley then suggested that if no vessel were sighted by the morning of the 25th, the cabin boy would be killed. The next day, when no vessel was sighted, Dudley told Brooks to go below. While Brooks was below, Dudley, with the help of Stephens, killed the helpless cabin boy. All three men then fed on his body and blood for four days. On July 29th, the men were rescued, still alive but very, very weak.

After a short recovery, Dudley and Stephens were brought to trial. You are judges assigned to this case. Determine if the accused are guilty of murder and what punishment, if any, should be imposed.

Case No. 2

You are part of a military tribunal assigned to hear the case of Officer Fleming. The events described take place in 1951. Fleming is accused of "willfully, unlawfully, and knowingly collaborating with the enemy by joining with, participating in, and leading discussions that charged the United States with being illegal aggressors in the Korean conflict." He is also accused of making communist propaganda recordings used to promote disaffection among United States troops.

Fleming and a number of his troops had been taken prisoner by the North Koreans. They were told that unless they cooperated all would be killed. Reluctant prisoners were beaten; Fleming finally agreed to cooperate, later testifying that he did what he did only to save his men. None, in fact, perished during their imprisonment. Evidence indicates that Fleming managed to obtain better conditions for his men. However, it should be noted that other groups of prisoners did resist efforts to make them cooperate. Those who did so were sent to "caves," small tin huts which would not permit standing up or lying stretched out. The bodies of those who had not survived remained in the caves with those still living. Nevertheless, some of these individuals continued to resist, survived the caves, and eventually survived the war.

Fleming's defense is that the acts were committed: (1) to protect the lives and well-being of his men; (2) under coercion and duress, and (3) while incapable of adhering to the right.

How do you find?

Accounts[2]

If you carried out the assignment in the way suggested, you are, by this time, probably feeling somewhat frustrated. You might even be feeling a little hostile, either toward your colleagues in the decision process or toward the arbitrary time constraints of the exercise. If you are feeling neither frustration nor hostility, keep reading. The following discussion will underscore the complexities and dilemmas presented by the cases and the attempts to construct logical, consistent legal accounts of the events portrayed.

The first case, known as the *Queen vs. Dudley and Stephens*, raises a very complex issue. How can society symbolize its abhorrence of the act committed while at the same time recognizing the unique circumstances involved? The typical justifications for punishment all seem somewhat inappropriate when applied in this instance.

Clearly, punishment for deterrence's sake makes no sense. There is little danger that Dudley and Stephens would commit the same act again. In fact, after their experience on the seas, it is likely that Dudley and Stephens would look for a new line of work. To argue that there is a need to generally deter people from the killing and eating of cabin boys suggests that many people would be in the circumstances that Dudley and Stephens were in (a highly untenable assumption), or, that given those extreme circumstances, the punishment of two individuals for the killing of a cabin boy would be enough to deter another individual facing starvation from similar conduct. Nor is it really clear that Dudley and Stephens need rehabilitation. The rehabilitation argument suggests that, given the chance, they would engage in like behavior unless treated. In this view, cannibalism is a personal quirk of the defendants, rather than a situational adjustment. Nor does it seem that the general level of safety in society would be increased significantly by isolating this pair. Since the cabin boy is dead, the need for restitution does not seem an appropriate reason for punishing Dudley and Stephens. Unless, of course, the cabin boy had dependents. Then, Dudley and Stephens might be required to pay the family of the boy the equivalent of what he would have earned over a lifetime. This does not restore the cabin boy to his family, but it does, perhaps, lessen the economic impact of his death. Such restitution could not be accomplished, however, if the two were put in prison or they themselves executed. Thus, restitution requires minimum physical restraint, and, consequently, may be viewed by society as no punishment at all. The only other justification for punishment that seems somewhat reasonable in this circumstance is the need for society to express its dismay at this type of behavior. This might best fit in under the revenge motive for punishment. By punishing Dudley and Stephens, society expresses its moral sense that such behavior is wrong. The question then becomes, "What amount of revenge is sufficient to express or articulate moral revulsion?" Keep in mind that the circumstances are indeed unusual.

The way the case was actually handled illustrates a rather innovative use of law that achieves the need to show dismay at such behavior, but at the same time takes account of the circumstances and the fact that most of the usual justifications for punishment do not apply in this circumstance. The court found Dudley and

Stephens guilty of homicide and passed the sentence of death upon the prisoners. The sentence was afterwards commuted by the Crown to six months' imprisonment. Thus, the court served a ritualistic function, its sentence symbolizing society's disgust and moral condemnation of the act, while the Crown served a pragmatic function, the commutation taking into account the unique circumstances of the event.

In the second case, *Fleming vs. the United States,* Fleming was, in fact, found guilty of collaboration with the enemy. He was dismissed from the service and forfeited all pay and benefits. The decision of the *Fleming* case rendered during the 1950s is interesting when compared to the circumstances and handling of the Lloyd Bucher affair. Bucher, his men, and his ship, the *U.S.S. Pueblo,* were taken captive by the North Koreans in January of 1968. The *Pueblo* was an intelligence-gathering ship with records and computers containing highly sensitive, classified information. When the ship was approached by the North Koreans for allegedly straying into their national waters, Bucher apparently made very little attempt to protect the ship or its contents. The ship and crew were surrendered to the North Koreans with little, if any, resistance. During their eleven months of imprisonment, incidents occurred which could have been construed as collaboration with the enemy. A court of general inquiry recommended that Commander Bucher be brought to trial by a general courtmartial for five offenses: (1) permitting the ship to be searched while they had the power to resist; (2) failing to take immediate and aggressive protective measures when his ship was attacked by North Korean forces; (3) complying with the orders of the North Korean forces to follow them into port; (4) negligently failing to complete destruction of classified material on board the *U.S.S. Pueblo* and permitting such materials to fall into the hands of the North Koreans; and (5) negligently failing to insure, before departure for sea, that his officers and crew were properly organized, stationed, and trained in preparation for emergency destruction of classified material. After reviewing the recommendations of the general court of inquiry, the Secretary of the Navy dismissed all the charges against both Bucher and his various officers. He noted in his statement that Commander Bucher had upheld the morale of those under him in a "superior manner," and, further, that he (the Secretary) believed that the Commander and his crew had suffered enough.[1] The differences between the Fleming incident and the Bucher incident seem minimal. The different outcomes can perhaps be explained by the differing times. During the late 1960s, the military, its procedures, and its values were under extremely close scrutiny. The attitude of the 1950s, best summarized by the statement "My country right or wrong, but always my country," had altered considerably by the end of the '60s. Thus, legal accounts of behavior changed in light of the new circumstances. Bucher and the people who served with him were viewed as having suffered enough at the hands of the North Koreans, and punishment for disloyalty to the military hardly seemed appropriate in light of the generally hostile view being expressed toward things military by a large number of civilians. The question still remains as to whether punishment was an appropriate method for dealing with Major Fleming. At the time, however, society felt it appropriate to symbolize the importance of military values, which is what the punishment of Fleming accomplished.

At this point, you should compare your group's discussion and decisions with the points raised above and with other groups who decided the case. This comparing of accounts will show that different people weighed varying elements of the cases differently (that is, they used different rules for putting together reality). As a result, there are probably no two groups that reached exactly the same decision in every case, nor two that see the situations in precisely the ways presented by the preceding discussion. In other words, everybody took the "facts" of the case and reconstructed events in unique ways. Perhaps you are thinking to yourself that, yes, there was disagreement about the way cases should be decided, but that was because there were not enough facts given and we needed to assume certain things. Also, thirty minutes was hardly enough time. Exactly! If you followed the directions for the assignment, including keeping the time limits, you were simulating some of the elements of an actual legal proceeding. In a court, time is of the essence. As we will see, judges need to be concerned about keeping cases moving. Further, as we have already seen, the criminal justice system is largely a reactive system, responding to a scene after an event has occurred. Therefore, the system constantly engages in reconstruction. Police officers take statements from witnesses, who themselves are engaging in a reconstruction process, and in writing their reports try to reconstruct what happened. Again, however, report writing is not a value-free enterprise. A host of factors operate on police officers that lead to the emphasizing of certain factors and the disregarding of others in reconstructing and interpreting an event. As a case moves through the legal system, different pressures operate on different people at different times to further alter original reconstructions and interpretations. From the various reconstructions and interpretations of events, a final reconstruction (an account of an account) is decided upon and then used to justify a decision on how best to handle the case. The important point in all of this is that the decision is based upon a reconstruction of events, not cold, hard, fast, concrete, indisputable *facts*. To assume that the legal account constitutes the only possible reality is to have an overly rationalistic view of the law and how it operates. The whole process can be compared to a wonderful description of how Dashiell Hammett's famous detective, the Continental Op, went about solving a case. The description is from Steven Marcus's Introduction to Dashiell Hammett's *The Continental Op*:

> The Op is called in or sent on a case. Something has been stolen, someone is missing, some dire circumstance is impending, someone has been murdered—it doesn't matter. The Op interviews the person or persons most immediately accessible. They may be innocent or guilty—it doesn't matter; it is an indifferent circumstance. Guilty or innocent, they provide the Op with an account of what they know, of what they assert really happened. The Op begins to investigate; he compares these accounts with others that he gathers; he snoops about; he does research; he shadows people, arranges confrontations between those who want to avoid one another, and so on. What he soon discovers is that the "reality" that anyone involved will swear to is in fact itself a construction, a fabrication, a fiction, a faked and alternative reality—and that it has been gotten together before he ever arrived on the scene. And the Op's work therefore is to deconstruct, decompose, deplot, and defictionalize that "reality" and to construct or reconstruct out of it a true fiction, that is, an account of what "really happened."[2] (From THE CONTINENTAL OP, by Dashiell Hammett, Introduction by Steven Marcus. Copyright © 1974 by Steven Marcus. Reprinted by permission of Harold Matson Company, Inc.)

Of course, what the Op ends up with is simply another account, one constructed by himself, but no more "real" than the other accounts he has encountered. In many ways, the process is the same in the criminal justice system. Events are reconstructed by a variety of actors, the accounts are compared and negotiated, and a compromise account that seems most reasonable and which presents the most coherent view of the world is accepted as "reality." Yet, to a greater or lesser extent, it is always a fictionalized reality, a reconstructed view of the past.

Accounts[3]

The legal processes of comparing accounts, negotiating accounts, and structuring new accounts leaves some with a feeling of injustice. Those whose accounts were not accepted are likely to have a heightened perception of the fictions in the accounts of those that were and feel the system did not work fairly in their case. Thus, police officers at times express hostility toward the judicial system, as do defense lawyers, prosecutors, victims, and defendants. Not everybody's account can be accepted as "reality." Those who lose, those who have their definition of the situation challenged, are likely to feel that the system is defective. Certainly, the delinquents in the study by Matza cited previously felt that way about the juvenile court. Matza notes that delinquents tend to define rules of evidence in a strict legal sense, and, therefore, they see the juvenile court as operating in an unfair manner toward them.[3] Defective cognizance, lack of consistency in sentencing, ineffectiveness, and lack of piety (or professionalism) on the part of the people sitting in judgment are some of the accusations leveled by delinquents at the judicial process. The terms, of course, are Matza's, but the sentiments belong to those juveniles subject to what they feel are the faulty accounting practices of the court.

The term "defective cognizance" means that the court goes about discovering "facts" (that is, arriving at an account of events) in ways not strictly "legal." In other words, delinquents perceive the courts as not playing by their own rules. Indeed, in the juvenile court the presumption of innocence—the accepting at face value the account of the accused and putting the burden of defending alternative accounts on the accusers—seems to be lacking. The juvenile is viewed as needing the help of the court, and, therefore, accounts that tend to deny the need for court intervention are suspect. Research evidence seems to indicate that the charge of defective cognizance might also be leveled at adult proceedings. Blumberg, for instance, shows that the bureaucratic organization of the court undermines commitment to strict legal procedures.[4] Pragmatic values and bureaucratic priorities take precedence over total dedication on the part of the defense attorney to his client. Hence, rules of evidence play a minor role in most courtroom cases. The adversary system is a myth since most defendants plead guilty and, as we have seen, it is usually the defense counsel who first suggests to the client a plea of guilty. This seems a far cry from the image of the court that has the accused's account protected and defended by a champion against the accounts of others who must bear the burden of proof. Further evidence of defective cognizance is offered by Sudnow. In his study of public defenders, Sudnow found that these attorneys assumed the guilt of their clients.[5] During the course of public defender work, the practitioner gains knowledge of the elements involved in "typical" occurrences of criminal behavior. Crimes are carried out in a regular manner, so that most child molestation cases involve loitering around a schoolyard, assaults with a deadly weapon usually start with fights over a woman, petty thefts are generally unplanned and do not involve the use of a weapon, and so on. Hence, clients are approached not with the intention of determining guilt or innocence but to find out whether the crime charged to the defendant was carried out in a "normal" manner. Unlike the Continental Op, then, the court system and its functionaries already possess a set of preconstructed accounts, accounts that both the accused and the accusers may disagree with but that help structure the doing of law to save time, resources, and bureaucratic strain. Thus, for example, if an individual will plead guilty to loitering, the charge of child molesting will usually be reduced to this infraction, and the necessity of going through a trial will be avoided. Public defenders know what accounts prosecutors are likely to accept, and prosecutors know what accounts public defenders are likely to offer in describing a client's behavior. There is still some maneuvering, some negotiation, and the occasional incident where one or another party will not accept the preconstructed accounts. But often, the structuring, comparing, and negotiation of accounts is completed before defendants arrive on the scene. Once they do arrive, it is merely a matter of determining which of the stock accounts come closest to the "facts." Again, what emerges is not reality, but an approximation of reality.

At this point some of you may be thinking, "How terrible. Imagine, child molesting being reduced to loitering!" If your thoughts are running along this line, you are in danger of being trapped in language. You are providing your own preconceived account of what the activity involved. At least court personnel tend to preconstruct their accounts on the basis of some experience. Even though the term "child molesting" connotes images of extreme depravity and the worst type of crime, the "fact" of most such cases is considerably different. Often the cases involve individuals related to the children. The degree of touching is ordinarily considerably less than the term molesting would suggest.[6] Nevertheless, the point is that most of us have preconceived accounts of the activities encompassed by certain linguistic labels used in criminal justice. Thus, terms like robbery, burglary, rape, auto theft, homicide, and so forth all provide a trigger (no pun intended) that releases at least a partially preconceived account of what must have happened. With very little to go on, we can build a plausible story. This same dynamic operates in the doing of justice by the professionals of the justice process. There are two key differences between their accounts and those of the lay person, however. First, criminal justice personnel have some experiential knowledge of "typical" crime, and, therefore, their accounts are often closer to reality. Second, such professionals have available in their world symbols that can be manipulated to present a public image of a process that is much more formal, much more open to the accounts of the accused, and in its result, much more factual, sacred, empirical, and so on, than it might actually be. Thus, legal rules of procedure seemingly provide an objective, rational way of arriving at truth. While it may be true that the formal rules of legal procedure can provide a version of truth, they are used relatively infrequently. This leaves the system vulnerable to charges of defective cognizance and the rest, further alienating those, both the victims and the perpetrators, who are subject to its proceedings.

The gap that exists between the image of the formal procedure for arriving at a case determination and the more informal methods most often used is highlighted by an examination of sentencing procedures. Both Matza and Foote note the lack of consistency in sentencing procedures. Matza, dealing exclusively with the juvenile court, points out that type or degree of offense is not necessarily the telling factor in determining what punishment will be given out.[7] Space in juvenile detention facilities, previous records, home conditions, and a number of other criteria not directly related to the offense appear of paramount importance in whether a child will be given probation. Such factors do not remain constant across time. Two individuals accused and found guilty of the same offense, or a single individual caught and sentenced for the same crime at different times, can and do receive widely varying sentences.

Political considerations (for example, pressure to "clean up" the town), demeanor of the defendant, and his city of residence seem to be crucial factors in the adjudication of a given vagrancy case, according to a study conducted by Foote.[8] Moreover, Foote discovered that the same faces appeared regularly before the magistrate, who would either lecture the defendant or commit him to the county jail for a period of thirty days. But neither lectures nor commitment to jail solved the problems of alcoholism or poverty, two factors common to those picked up for vagrancy violations. Hence, the court appeared both inconsistent and ineffective in dealing with those who came before it.

Given the above factors, the question of piety or professionalism on the part of the officials who administer the criminal justice system is open to serious doubt. Defense lawyers who do not defend, judges who do not adhere to strict legal rules of evidence, plea bargaining, and sentences that are inconsistent, all combine to undermine the veracity of the criminal justice system. As Smith and Blumberg have indicated, judicial decision making is not carried out in a purely objective, legalistic manner, since the social biographies of justices, filtered through an organizational ethos of efficiency and maximum production, tend to override concerns for the ideals of objectivity and uniformity.[9] This sacrifice of objectivity is particularly apparent in Foote's vagrancy study. The author found that magistrates tended to refer to the vagrants that came before them as "bums" and "drunkards" in their presence.

When cases are actually heard before a jury, further questions of objectivity and strict legal interpretation of evidence are raised. As will be discussed in the next chapter, jurors are in fact chosen for their biases rather than for their objectivity or their ability to grasp legal principles.

The review of literature dealing with the operations of the court system seems to support the charges leveled at that system by juvenile offenders. Defective cognizance, lack of consistency in sentencing, ineffectiveness, and lack of piety appear to be part and parcel of the daily operations of the criminal justice system and the doing of law. The question is, why this is so.

As we have observed with the police, the doing of justice is a social world-building process. Actors attempt to make sense out of their activity by fitting or shaping it into a pattern. The pattern we construct is influenced by a need to be able to see our activities as part of a logical, consistent whole. Crime obviously disrupts the pattern. But the urge to pattern is very strong. Just how strong can be illustrated by once again returning to the stories of Dashiell Hammett.

In the *Maltese Falcon* Sam Spade recounts the story of Flitcraft, a one-time successful, happily married, stable, and very respectable real estate dealer who one day disappeared, without apparent cause. Spade, through a series of events, finds Flitcraft five years after his disappearance living in Spokane. He had remarried, had a baby son, a suburban home, a successful automobile dealership, and a standing golf date at four o'clock every afternoon. He had, in short, reconstructed the life he had suddenly abandoned.

Spade asked him why he left behind his "old life." It turns out that Flitcraft had gone to lunch, and as he was walking along a beam suddenly fell eight or ten stories from an office building under construction and nearly killed him. After he got over the shock, he realized that life, instead of being sane, orderly, and rational was fundamentally none of these things. He became a drifter, vacating the rational structure of the life he had built. "He felt like somebody had taken the lid off and let him look at the works . . . What disturbed him was the discovery that in sensibly ordering his affairs he had gotten out of step, and not into step with life."

Spade concluded his story by saying, . . . "I don't think he even knew he had settled back into the same groove that he had jumped out of . . . but that's the part of it I always liked. He adjusted himself to beams falling, and then no more of them fell, and he adjusted himself to them not falling."[10]

Crime, for most of us, is like a beam falling. We construct orderly lives only to have the assumptions underlying such order challenged by random crime. The crime does not even have to happen to us. Being confronted with it in newspaper stories, in T.V. documentaries, and in the accounts of friends and acquaintances raises the suspicion and fear that if we "take the lid off" we will find that our orderly, rational, coherent constructs can all too easily be demolished. Further, when we look at the criminal justice system we find that, instead of treating crime with the drama it would seem to deserve, the functionaries of that system treat it routinely. It's almost as if there were a system established for the routine handling of falling beams that at times randomly kill people! It seems an affront to deal so routinely with something so apparently out of the ordinary. And yet, this is precisely what the criminal justice system does. It attempts to deal with what, for most of us, is the unusual in a usual, patterned manner. In so doing, it shocks and offends those of us whose niche in life, whose pattern, does not include the likelihood of criminal events. But again, the need to build patterns is ubiquitous. The people, events, and situations we deal with day in and day out must form a logical, consistent whole.

Thus, unlike some of the authors cited (notably Blumberg), this book does not subscribe to the view that the doing of justice in America is a disgraceful, deceitful "con game," and that the players, whether police officers, prosecutors, judges, or defense lawyers, are motivated by less than noble sentiments. Undoubtedly some are, but most are simply engaged in what they perceive to be a routine process. The process involves using law (quasi-law) to fashion reasonable, acceptable accounts of events that allow official legal actors to construct a meaningful, logical, orderly, coherent pattern for their activities. Examine the elements that went into your own decision-making process as it applied to the cases at the beginning of this chapter. Your use of law, and the assumptions about the people, places, and events portrayed are probably not all that different than those that affect the decisions of professionals.

Accounts about events are obviously influenced by the values of the person giving a particular account. In the case of Fleming, his activities could be described so that he appears as either a hero or a traitor, or as someone in between, perhaps simply as a pragmatist. In part, the description of Fleming and his activities will depend upon how highly you regard the military, whether you are politically liberal or conservative, and so on. In the next chapter, a more detailed description will be given as to how the value commitment of judges influences their decision making. But, as already noted, knowing the social biographies of judges can help in understanding variations in legal decision making, and it is in living such biographies that values are formed. What you value is symbolized in the accounts of activity which you give. Such accounts, in turn, help structure your decisions about what to do about a particular situation.

Besides the values you bring to a decision situation, the stereotypes you hold regarding people and events influence your accounting practices. What you decided to do about Dudley and Stephens or Fleming, in part, depended upon the preconceived notions you held regarding seamen, military personnel, and the historical time period of the event. The disagreements you may have had with your colleagues about a case are probably due, in part, to the different stereotypes each of you holds regarding actors and situations. The literature discussed in this chapter demonstrates the role stereotypes play in the decision making of legal functionaries. Sudnow's public defenders had stereotypes of typical crimes and criminals, as did Foote's magistrates of drunks. In the preceding chapters on the police, we saw that part of the training involved developing particular stereotypes so that officers could more quickly assess the situations they were likely to encounter, thus, the importance of the symbolic assailant.

In reaching decisions on the cases, you also had to utilize some preconceived notions about the value of punishment. Your faith, or lack of it, in the efficacy of punishment helped structure the plans for dealing with the particular problem before you. In the case of Dudley and Stephens, for example, some people probably thought that a penal approach was inappropriate, and that instead a treatment approach should be used. The differences between the two are, however, more apparent than real. The treatment approach and the penal approach stem from the belief that without official intervention, such behavior is likely to continue. But beliefs, values, and stereotypes might well have hidden that similarity, and, thus, a person arguing punishment for deterrence's sake may have encountered stiff resistance from a treatment-oriented colleague. If, on the other hand, you argued the need for severe punishment to express societal dismay at the crime of Dudley and Stephens, you end up in a quagmire that would have delighted Sam Spade. A crime as horrible as the one committed by Dudley and Stephens "takes the lid off" and presents to us a picture of humanity reduced to its most basic, primitive level. This is certainly a threat to our belief in an orderly, clean, rational existence. Some would argue that the penalty for taking the lid off, for showing the essential irrationality of life, should be maximum. If it isn't, others might act in a similar manner. Such an argument, of course, simply gives credence to the notion that life's orderly, rational, coherent constructs are tenuous at best and need to be reinforced and shorn up at every opportunity. Thus, a belief in the need for drastic punishment for heinous crimes (and even those not so heinous) is sometimes unconscious testimony to the belief that, given the least chance, the orderly structure of society will tumble down around us. The sentencing behavior of the magistrate when confronted with vagrants becomes more understandable in this light. Even though demonstrably the sentences had little effect (since the same faces appeared again and again before the bench), they expressed the belief in the importance of a rational, orderly society and, ironically, at the same time, the tenuousness of such a society.

If you had occasion to argue about solutions to the cases presented, undoubtedly some statements concerning the propriety of particular solutions were met with rebuttals similar to "Sure we can do it; we can do anything we want. We are the ones with the power." When we say certain individuals have legal authority or power, what we are saying in part is that they have the wherewithal to define and give meaning to certain situations. The pattern they want to impose on those situations becomes the publicly accepted one. This again demonstrates the elasticity of law. It expands and contracts according to the beliefs and values of its users and in response to particular societal arrangements. As we have seen, however, the growth of legal patterns for defining situations gives distinct advantage to particular segments of society. The Carrier Case and other legal episodes involving the rise of the mercantile class meant a growth in law and legal relationships that concentrated the power to define particular situations in the hands of relatively few. Legal decisions, then, are influenced partly by a desire to keep or expand such power of definition.

Nevertheless, the power of legal functionaries to define particular situations is to an extent limited by the very legal pattern they create. As already pointed out, law is used by a variety of actors. In the modern criminal justice establishment, the needs of at least some of these others must be taken into account if a pattern is to evolve which will allow a majority of participants to see their activity as logical, meaningful, and coherent. This pattern might be termed the "courthouse subculture." Police officers, prosecuting attorneys, defense lawyers, judges, and probation officers have to work with each other on a daily basis. What emerges from these day-to-day interactions is an agreed-upon method of operation which allows most of the participants to feel that they are doing justice most of the time. Prosecutors learn what cases the police will particularly want them to pursue and what cases the police consider less important. In the less important ones, the prosecutor may feel he has more room for compromise and leniency. As Sudnow's study noted, defense attorneys learn what prosecutors will accept in plea bargaining, and prosecutors, in turn, learn how far they must be willing to reduce charges to avoid going to trial. Judges, too, although apparently the most powerful actors in the system, must also learn to play by the rules of the game. If too many plea bargains arrived at between prosecution and defense are rejected by the bench, a judge can suddenly find that his or her cases are backing up and the docket is overloaded. Judicial efficiency is lowered, a situation both professionally and politically undesirable. Probation officers even get caught up in the emergent pattern of the courthouse subculture, writing their reports to fit with decisions already made about a particular case.[11] Chapters 8 and 9 will describe the day-to-day doing of justice within the context of a courthouse subculture. At this point, suffice it to say that if you were working for a long period of time with the same four or five people you worked with on the cases at the start of this chapter, your group would establish a decision-making pattern that would allow you to deal with even complex cases in a relatively quick fashion. You would each begin to get a feel for the values, stereotypes, and other nonrational factors influencing your colleagues. You would know what each would be likely to accept in the way of compromise. The pattern that would emerge would mean slightly less power for everyone, but slightly more logical, coherent meaning in your day-to-day decisions about cases.

This emergence of a pattern that would contribute to the efficiency of decision making would be important. This is so because one of the realities of modern-day justice is the constraint of time. We are a production-oriented society, and the course of justice is influenced by the concern with processing as much as possible as soon as possible. You probably feel that you could have come up with a better decision, if only you had had more time. But, if there were twenty or thirty or forty other cases waiting to be dealt with, and you took an inordinate amount of time with just one, many different people would be upset with your procedures. Your fellow judges, who are already overworked, would feel put upon if they had to take some of your cases. Defendants, some of whom must spend the time in jail until their case is heard, would feel that justice delayed is justice denied. The attorneys, both the prosecutor and the defender, and particularly the former, would have a difficult time presenting their cases, since witnesses die, move away, or simply lose interest as the time between the actual event and the trial increases. So, while wisdom may need time to come to fruition, justice, for both pragmatic and philosophical reasons, cannot wait. Thus, time is an ever-present factor in legal decision making.

Finally, the decisions you reached no doubt exhibited an underlying faith in the essentially rational nature of humankind. Your decisions in each case were probably premised on the assumption that the participants acted rationally, that is, they weighed the pros and cons of their activity, foresaw possible consequences, and acted accordingly. A modern legal approach to social problems assumes a rational world. It is only within this context that punishment makes sense. If a person's act was irrational, it makes no sense to punish. Again, a penal solution to a problem assumes that actors take into account the consequences of their behavior and that if one of those consequences is punishment, that will cause the rational individual to avoid such activity. Within a criminal justice framework, even a recommendation of treatment assumes rationality is at least attainable.

This belief in rationality has a number of consequences. As

discussed previously, it leads to an emphasis on individualized justice. One rational actor, making a decision about one particular situation, to be treated as a case. Thus, I would be surprised if any of the recommendations concerning the cases of Fleming or Dudley and Stephens suggest the need for systemic rehabilitation. Did anyone recommend that lifeboats be equipped with better provisions and safety gear? Did anyone suggest that perhaps military training was inadequate and that Fleming was merely a victim, together with his men, of inadequate preparation? The answer to these queries is "Probably not." The emphasis was on dealing with individuals as rational actors, not as persons presented limited alternatives by broader, unwieldy, sometimes irrational events and systems.

Belief in rationality also means that decisions must be justified as examples of well-thought-out, practically scientific enterprises. In the process of doing this, the irrational elements of the decision are hidden or glossed over. Values, stereotypes, concerns with time, and the like are left out of public defenses of decisions arrived at. We do not even talk about a decision process, but instead use language that emphasizes our belief in rationality. Persons "break the law" and must "pay" the penalty so that others will be "deterred." Such language allows us to see ourselves as "giving answers to problems." Once again, we have slipped into viewing law as concrete, scientific, anything but quasi-.

This approach means that, in our practice of law, we really do not give much attention to questions that cannot be dealt with in a framework of rationality. Thus, for example, a question is seldom asked about what values we are trying to symbolize in our doing of law. Instead, a more rational question is framed, to the effect of what problem can this or that law solve. The end result is a system that deals very inadequately with both social problem solving and the need for public ritual to symbolize agreed-upon values.

It is easy to criticize, however. The cases at the beginning of this chapter presented situations to be dealt with in a legal manner. Quasi-law means that the cases and the applicable statutes provide a blueprint with plenty of spaces left blank. The blanks are to be filled in by us. In filling in the blanks, you were in all likelihood affected by the same factors that affect police officers, lawyers, judges, and others as they apply the law in day-to-day life. Values, stereotypes, a belief in your power to define situations and a desire to keep such power, a quest to appear rational, preconceived attitudes about punishment, all of these provided the building blocks from which you created legal patterns to deal with the cases. And you probably did no better or no worse than the police officers discussed earlier or the other legal functionaries discussed in this chapter. Most of us construct and use law in pretty much the same way. We may arrive at different conclusions about appropriate legal applications, but the process of using law is similar. Thus, law forms recognizable patterns in response to value constructs, societal pressures, and so on. These patterns of law and the factors that shape them will be further discussed in the next chapter.

References

1. STEPHEN D. FORD. *The American Legal System, Its Dynamics and Limits* (St. Paul, Minn.: West Publishing Co., 1974), p. 85.
2. STEVEN MARCUS. Introduction to *The Continental Op*, Dashiell Hammett (New York: Random House, 1974).
3. DAVID MATZA. *Delinquency and Drift* (New York: John Wiley and Sons, Inc., 1964), pp. 101–51.
4. ABRAHAM S. BLUMBERG. "The Practice of Law as a Confidence Game: Organizational Co-optation of a Profession," 1 *Law and Society Review* 15 (June 1967).
5. DAVID SUDNOW. "Normal Crimes: Sociological Features of the Penal Code in a Public Defender's Office," *Social Problems*, 12 (Winter 1965), 255–76.
6. Ibid. See also Nicholas A. Groth and others, "A Study of the Child Molester: Myths and Realities," 41 *LAE Journal of the American Criminal Justice Association* 17 (1978).
7. Matza, pp. 101–51.
8. CALAB FOOTE. "Vagrancy-type Law and Its Administration," 104 *University of Pennsylvania Law Review* 603 (1956).
9. BLUMBERG. "The Practice of Law as a Confidence Game."
10. MARCUS. Introduction to *The Continental Op*.
11. ARTHUR ROSETT and DONALD R. CRESSEY. *Justice by Consent: Plea Bargains in the American Court House* (New York: J. B. Lippincott Company, 1976), pp. 77–78.

chapter six

The Factors of Justice

This Thing Called Law

As we have already seen, law, like language, is both external and internal to the individual. For the most part, the book to this point has stressed the use of law by individuals to account for certain of their actions. This perspective focuses on law's internal dimensions. The emphasis has not been accidental. Law's externality has, it seems to me, been overstressed in theories about both law itself and law-violating behavior. To use a somewhat Beccarian-type analogy, the scales needed to be balanced. However, to better understand the quasi- nature of law, it is helpful to consider law's externality and to momentarily ignore the fact that law acts through individuals. Again, the perspective can be carried too far, but as you read this section, emphasize law's body and substance, giving it the ability to respond to its environment. Like a kind of energized Silly Putty, law pulls and pushes, stretches and molds, grows and recedes in response to changes in society. In short, law behaves. If you think of law as behaving, you will be able to better grasp law's external dimension and, at the same time, avoid falling into the trap of thinking about law as a rigid, static, never-changing embodiment of "truth." The following, then, is simply an ethnographic description of law's behavior.

Donald Black describes certain dimensions of law's behavior and the sociological circumstances to which law responds. His book is entitled, appropriately enough, *The Behavior of Law*.[1] Black notes that the amount of law can vary from situation to situation. In particular instances, there is either more law or less law. To illustrate the point, consider the case of a bus rider who lights up a cigar beneath a large "No Smoking" sign. Nonlegal attempts to control such behavior can be employed. The bus driver can remind the individual that there is no smoking allowed on the bus, and fellow passengers can give dirty looks.

Historically, social control has moved away from such informal methods and towards written statutes, specially designated control agents, and bureaucratic processing. Modern society has increased its dependency on law and in so doing has increased its absolute numbers of laws. Thus, were a police officer to get on the bus, he would, in most cities, have the legal authority to intervene with the behavior of the smoking passenger. The amount of law present in the situation would have increased.

Law's style can also vary. It can be penal, where the solution to the problem is punishment, or it can be compensatory, where the problem requires some type of monetary payment in order to be set aright. Law can be therapeutic, requiring the individual be given help for his problem. Finally, according to Black, law can be conciliatory, requiring that a problem be solved through some type of negotiation.[2]

Law not only varies in terms of amount and style, it also varies in its movement. It can move up or down or sideways. The direction it goes will influence both its style and amount. To plot law's behavior, its movement, style, and amount, it is first necessary to briefly review the dimensions of the terrain law traverses. The terrain is society, and it is a multifaceted landscape. Societies, for example, vary both among and within themselves according to the degree of stratification they possess.

The term "stratification" in the social sciences has been borrowed from the geological sciences. In geology, a stratum is a discrete layer of rock or earth, relatively uniform within itself and distinct from the strata above and below it. Thus (and this is simply by way of illustration and makes no claim to be an actual geological description of a location), a top layer of earth may be mostly dirt, the next layer sand, the next layer a particular kind of rock, and so on. Each layer forms a separate, distinct band. Societies, too, can be organized in terms of distinct layers, each layer differentiated from the others by the amount of power, prestige, and wealth the individuals within it possess. People possessing the greatest amount of societal resources form the top layer of a society, those with the least resources, the bottom layer. There may be a number of layers between the top and the bottom or none at all. To do some violence to the geological analogy, but to accurately portray the variability of society, there may only be one layer, everybody sharing equally in the resources available.

There is a question as to whether modern American society forms itself into the distinct levels suggested by the geological term strata.[3] In the United States, the dimensions of status (power, wealth, and prestige) often do not occur together. A person can possess prestige, for example, without necessarily having power or wealth. College professors as a group illustrate the point. Politicians have power, but assuming their honesty, they often do not have wealth. Many would also argue that the occupation of politician is not a particularly prestigious one. Police officers also play a role that contains a great deal of power, but has very little wealth or prestige associated with it. Finally, a gangster might be a good illustration of someone who has wealth and power, but little prestige or social acclaim. At any rate, it is clear that our society has a highly complex set of stratified relationships, and, depending on the particular status dimension present in a social encounter, individuals will adjust their behavior in response to perceived social differences.

The complex set of stratified relationships which exist in our society can be contrasted with the relative absence of such relationships in primitive, simple societies. There people are generally equal with one another, with little variation in terms of wealth, power, or prestige. In such societies, there are no groups who can claim societal honor on the basis of a greater share of resources. There is no "other side of the tracks."

Situations, as well as societies, can differ according to the degree of stratification. While the classroom is a stratified setting, a party of friends is not. The absence of stratification will alter the way people relate to one another. Formal titles will not be used, and people will feel free to "let their hair down." Just as the presence or absence of stratification and its degree affect the behavior of individuals, so, too, does stratification affect the behavior of law. Black proposes five propositions which capture stratification's effect on law: (1) "Law varies directly with stratification;" (2) "Law varies directly with rank;" (3) "Downward law is greater than upward law;" (4) "Downward law varies directly with vertical distance;" and (5) "Upward law varies inversely with vertical distance."[4]

According to Black's first principle, modern American society would have far more law than a simple Eskimo or Plains Indian society, because the more stratification a society has, the more law it has. Further, since stratification can vary with particular situations, Black's first proposition would lead us to expect more law in the stratified situations, less in the unstratified ones. Thus, there is likely to be less recourse to legal solutions with problems among neighbors, colleagues, friends, and relatives than there would be among people of different strata. Black notes, for instance, that in an accident between people of different ranks, a lawsuit is more likely. The more equal people or societies are within and between themselves, the less law; the less equal, the more law.

Black's second proposition, "Law varies directly with rank," means that higher ranks have more law, lower ranks less law. Thus, in disputes between poor people there is less likelihood of recourse to the legal system than in disputes between wealthy individuals. Consider for a minute the kinds of problems most lawyers deal with most of the time, that is, wills, trusts, property disputes, and so on. To have these problems, it is first necessary to have a certain amount of resources. If you are poor, you do not have to worry about who will inherit your estate. In general, then, the legal system is more oriented toward dealing with the problems of the wealthier members of society. This variation in the amount of law between ranks also holds, Black argues, in criminal matters. A crime committed by a poor person against another poor person is less likely to be reported, and if reported and processed, the perpetrator is less likely to receive a severe sentence than if the participants had been wealthy. Thus, criminal events in lower-class neighborhoods among members of the neighborhood are often considered "routine for the area," and not worth a great deal of police effort. Many economically disadvantaged citizens, in fact, complain about the relative lack of police responsiveness, as measured by the time it takes an officer to respond to a scene in their area.

Propositions (1) and (2) deal with how the amount of law is affected by both the degree of stratification within a society and the stratum in which a dispute takes place. Highly stratified locations and higher ranks have more law than less stratified locations and lower ranks. But law also varies by direction. Law can move from the higher stratum to the lower, and vice versa. Black's last three propositions regarding the effects of stratification on law deal with this directional dimension. To say that downward law is greater than upward law simply means that, in most instances, a crime committed by a lower-class person against an upper-class person will result in far more serious consequences for the perpetrator than if the reverse occurred. The higher-class person, when calling upon the law to deal with the transgression of the lower-class person, can expect the law to respond swiftly and harshly. The lower-class person, though, when asking the law to deal with the transgression of the upper-class individual, can expect mostly frustration. The political turmoil in the United States during the 1960s and '70s provided numerous illustrations of the point. For example, Vietnam war protestors were dealt with harshly by the government, but a nearly impeached president forced to resign his office was pardoned. In the first instance, law was moving from the top down, in the second, from the bottom up.

Not only is downward law greater than upward law, the amount and seriousness of the law in a downward direction will increase as the distance increases between the upper-class individual applying the law and the lower-class person receiving it. Proposition (4) means, therefore, that the seriousness of an offense by a lower-class person against a higher-class person is greater as the differences between the two in power, prestige, and wealth increase. Alternatively, proposition (5) means that the seriousness of an offense by a higher-ranking person against a lower-ranking individual decreases as the rank difference increases. Simply put, the higher the individual's stratum, the more legally untouchable he or she becomes by those of progressively lower strata.

Black's discussion of law's directionality by stratification clearly indicates that law favors the higher strata against the lower strata. This not only refers to the amount of law but also to its style. Thus, law in a downward direction is more likely to be penal in style, while in an upward direction it is likely to be conciliatory, compensatory, or therapeutic. Hence, police officers are, for the most part, the legal agents who deal with the poor, while regulatory agencies and special commissions deal with the problems of the more favorably situated members of society. If a higher-status person does become enmeshed in the criminal justice process, we can expect that, generally, he or she will fare better than a lower-status individual. Recall from your police academy experience the lecture of the narcotics officer bemoaning the fact that a professor caught with a large amount of marijuana received a comparatively light sentence (Chapter 3). Black's proposition about the behavior of law would lead us to expect this type of outcome. The same outcome would not be expected if Arthur (also in Chapter 3) had been caught with a large cache of a controlled substance.

The behavior of law in response to stratification helps explain the behavior of criminological theory in attempting to explain crime. As we have seen, for much of criminological theory upper-class crime does not exist, only lower-class crime exists. This is because criminology accepts the definition of the legal system as to what constitutes crime. But, since law is more likely to define the transgressions of the lower class as criminal to begin with, criminological theory, as discussed in Chapter 4, ends up explaining very little. In fact, it seems mainly to provide a rationale for conceiving of a social world made up of good guys and bad guys. The social scientist, of course, is a member of the former group.

Society's terrain is not unidimensional. People do not only relate to each other vertically, they also relate to each other horizontally. Society, therefore, has both an up-down dimension and a dimension of intimacy. Some relationships are emotionally charged, others are emotionally neutral. Most of our daily encounters in modern society are of the latter type. We have a preponderance of secondary relationships as opposed to primary relationships. The secondary relationships are impersonal, in which we show only a limited facet of our personalities. We are teachers or students or police officers or drugstore clerks, and we relate to each other on the basis of these limited, functional roles. Before students sign up for a class, they do not ask whether Professor Jones is a good spouse, parent, or community participant. Instead, questions are likely to be asked about his or her grading habits, teaching procedures, lecturing ability, and work expectations. The relationship with Professor Jones is expected to be limited to certain very pragmatic concerns. As noted, most of our relationships in modern society are of this variety. There are few relationships in which our whole personality is exposed and in which we can expect support or nurturance for who we are rather than for what we do. The impersonality of modern society can be highlighted by recognizing that people wait for buses, they do not wait for bus drivers. In our day-to-day lives we are, for the most part, considered extensions of machines or organizations, to be used briefly and pragmatically.

The way people relate to each other, the degree of impersonality in a society, has an impact upon the behavior of law. The growth of impersonal, secondary relationships in turn depends upon increases in the complexities and differentiations of societal roles. In simple societies, people relate to one another on the basis of shared values, beliefs, and functions. Everybody believes in the same things, holds the same world views, and generally performs the same tasks. There is little, if any, social differentiation. But if a society begins to grow, and the growth combines with certain other social conditions, differentiation of function occurs. Some people cultivate, others administer, protect, pray, and so on. People become unlike but are tied together because now, instead of sharing values, beliefs, and work, they share a need for each other's skills. The cultivator needs the protection of the soldier, the skill of the administrator, and the luck brought by the incantations of the religious leader to bring in a good crop. And, of course, they all need the cultivator in order to eat. As society becomes more complex, we relate to more people with increasingly less involvement of our whole selves. Black, in describing the effects of the horizontal aspect of social life on the behavior of law, notes that for law to operate there must be some relationship between people, but not so close and personal a relationship that the connection would be considered a primary one.[5] Thus, a society that has a preponderance of secondary relationships, that is, a preponderance of relationships where there is limited functional involvement of people with one another, will have a greater amount of law than a society where primary relationships predominate and there is little differentiation among roles and tasks. Moreover, a society with a preponderance of secondary relationships will have more law than a society in which separate tribes or families have nothing to do with one another and, in effect, live in different social worlds, even though they may share the same territory. In brief, a society of secondary, functional relationships provides a hothouse for the growth of law. From this framework flow two of Black's propositions concerning the effects of differentiation and the effects of relational distance on law: (1) "The relationship between law and differentiation is curvilinear;" and (2) "The relationship between law and relational distance is curvilinear."[6] In the first proposition, Black asserts that where there is no differentiation by function, and thus little necessity for exchange among people, there will be little law. Further, since the relationship between law and differentiation is curvilinear (that is, law is minimal at either extreme of the differentiation continuum and maximal at the midpoint), complete differentiation of function results in a dearth of law. In an exchange relationship, total differentiation would mean that there is only one supplier for a commodity. An example will illustrate why the absence of choice in an exchange relationship constrains the use of law. If I am a shopkeeper who makes chairs, I need a supply of wood screws. But, in order to have the option of pursuing legal action against my ordinary supplier of wood screws, there must exist the possibility of being able to take my business elsewhere. If there is only one supplier and I sue him, it is unlikely I will, in the future, be able to obtain my wood screws from him. Where there is a choice of suppliers there exists a degree of differentiation between the suppliers I choose to patronize and myself. He makes wood screws, I make furniture. At the same time, we are to a degree dependent on one another and, therefore, less than totally differentiated, since he depends on me for my business and I depend on him for his wood screws. But neither of us is so dependent on the other that we cannot afford a legal confrontation. The relationship provides fertile ground for the blossoming of law.

The second proposition also notes a curvilinear relationship. As already indicated, the ideal situation for law's growth is that in which people relate to one another, but in a secondary manner. If people are either so close that the relationship is primary, as for example, lovers, or so distant (either emotionally or physically) that people have no contact with one another, law will be inactive.

A third factor, in conjunction with emotional involvement and degree of differentiation, molds the horizontal relationships of individuals within a society. People vary according to their degree of integration into a society, that is, the number and kind of societal institutions they belong to, their degree of community participation, and so forth. To grasp this dimension of social life, it is helpful to conceptualize society as a series of concentric rings, like a target with a bull's eye at the center. The most highly integrated individuals are those at the center. Degrees of societal integration decrease as you move from the center outward, so that those on the periphery of the concentric circles are the least integrated individuals. The degree of integration will affect the amount and type of law. Obviously, people who are most integrated into society, that is, those who most use and participate in the institutions of society, will use law more than those on the periphery who are marginal to society. Therefore, the amount of law is greatest at the center of the circle and decreases as one moves outward. Thus, as Black indicates, lawsuits among marginal people are relatively rare.[7] When people differentially integrated come into contact with one another, however, as when a highly integrated individual from the center circle meets a less integrated individual from the periphery, and a legal proceeding ensues, law favors the more highly integrated societal member. When law moves, then, from the center outward (a centrifugal direction), it will be greater than when it moves from the periphery to the inner circles (a centripetal movement). This means that, generally, an integrated person who is the victim of an offense by a marginal person will have an easier time applying law to the offender than if the circumstances were reversed. The amount of law moving from the center outward will be greater and possess more severe style.

Black asserts a number of propositions concerning the impact of social integration on law, of which the following two are illustrative and provide examples of the points made in the above discussion: (1) "Law varies directly with integration;" and (2) "Centrifugal law is greater than centripetal law."[8]

Certain consistencies concerning the behavior of law seem to emerge from Black's analysis. First, more complex societies have more law than less complex societies. Second, higher-status individuals (status measured by wealth, prestige, power, or degree of societal integration) within societies have more law than lower-status individuals. Third, when individuals of different strata or variable levels of integration interact and legal behavior is applicable, law tends to favor the higher-status, more integrated individual over the lower-status and/or less integrated individual. Other social factors, such as culture, organization, and social control, similarly affect the behavior of law. An examination of the influence of these factors provides further evidence that law finds its most fertile soil on a social terrain which is complex and unequal in its distribution of resources.

Culture can be defined as the symbolic aspect of social life. Culture is made up of all the beliefs, values, and physical artifacts of a society, and, thus, when cultures are compared with one another, they can vary in their quantities of these elements. If you live to the ripe old age of one hundred, it is unlikely that you will ever understand every facet of modern Western culture. On the other hand, if you lived in a hunting and gathering society, you might grasp the totality of that culture in a relatively short period of time. There would be fewer tools to learn about, fewer beliefs to master, and probably no competing values. Since, as we have seen previously, law itself is in part a symbolic representation that embodies beliefs and values of a society, it seems likely that a growth in the amount of culture would be accompanied by a growth in the amount of law. This is, of course, consistent with the notion that law increases as society becomes more complex. Individuals can also be described in terms of both their amount of culture and their degree of integration into a culture. Considering these two dimensions and their impact on the direction of law, we would expect that the more cultural individual would have an easier time applying legal sanctions to the less cultural individual than the reverse, and that the more conventional person (conventionality being a measure of cultural assimilation) would be favored in a legal action involving a less conventional person. The three propositions that follow are illustrative of both these points and Black's analysis of the influence of culture on law: (1) "Law varies with culture;" (2) "Law is greater in a direction toward less culture than toward more culture;" (3) "Law is greater in a direction toward less conventionality than toward more conventionality."[9]

The last chapter noted that law (and theories about law violations) contains an individualistic bias. Law tends to focus on individuals rather than on organizations. Black's analysis of the effects of organization on law, which follows, underscores the same point. Organization is defined as the capacity for collective social action. There are a number of indicators that point to the amount of organization in any group, whether a family, a club, or a nation-state. Such indicators include according to Black, "the presence and number of administrative officers, the centralization and continuity of decision making, and the quantity of collective action itself." Law can move in a direction from more organization to less, or in the reverse direction, from less to more. But, since organizations have the capacity for collective action, we would expect that an organization acting against an individual legally would be more successful than the reverse. One of Black's propositions about the effects of organization on the direction of law asserts that this is, in fact, the case: "Law is greater in a direction toward less organization than toward more organization."[10] To exemplify this, Black describes research findings that show that in most circumstances a business is more likely to complain to the police about an individual than vice versa, and when a business pursues such a legal action it is more likely to be successful. Thus, there is a higher likelihood of arrest, confession, prosecution, conviction, and a severe sentence. Flowing from this, it is clear that membership in an organization provides protection from law. Offenses committed by an organization or its representative are likely to be considered less serious than an offense committed by an individual on his own.

Note that most law dealing with organizational infractions tends to be of the regulatory rather than the criminal variety. But even this style of law does not seem particularly effective since, as organization increases, so, too, does immunity from the law. Thus, an examination of the Federal Government's efforts in the area of white-collar crime shows that larger organizations are less likely to feel the burden of law than are smaller ones. During the two-year period from 1977 to 1979, the Internal Revenue Service was responsible for bringing 3,360 indictments for criminal violations of federal tax laws, only nine involving major corporations. The Securities and Exchange Commission referred 420 cases of questionable domestic and foreign corporate payments by major companies to the Department of Justice; of these, ten have resulted in guilty pleas, thirty are under continuing investigation, and the rest have been dropped. In no case has a corporate executive been prosecuted individually. At the midpoint of 1979, the Justice Department had filed twenty-three criminal antitrust cases. Three involved major corporations. Even the rapid growth in environmental law has apparently meant little in terms of the ability to control large corporate violators. Since 1974, the Environmental Protection Agency has referred about 130 criminal cases to the Justice Department for prosecution. Six have involved major corporations, and of those only one actually had a criminal charge filed against it. One top Justice official is quoted as saying, "It's just a lot easier for us to pick on the small guy." Presumably this is so because major companies with complex operations and a multitude of resources can inhibit any legal proceedings against them. The size and complexity of such organizations would require an extensive commitment of both investigative time and expertise. Both of these commodities are, however, in short supply in regulatory agencies.[11]

Concerning the amount of law, it will increase as organization increases. An increase in organization can occur in two ways. There can be an increase in the absolute number of organizations in a society. An increase in the number of organizations in a society signals an increase in the complexity of that society and, hence, the need for more law. Organization also increases when there is an increase in the degree of organization of a particular group. For example, Black discusses the ebb and flow of organization within a certain Indian tribe and how the differing levels of organization affected the amount of law present in the tribal community.[12] During buffalo hunts, when the need for organization was high, a police force came into being to ensure that people worked together and shared hunting resources with one another. After the hunt the force would disband. Black captures this behavior of law in response to organization with the proposition that "Law varies directly with organization."[13]

Finally, Black notes how law varies in response to other forms of social control. First, concerning the impact of the quantity of other forms of social control on law, he states that "Law varies inversely with other social control."[14] Thus, as other forms of social control decrease, law increases. The less the influence of the family and other primary group associations in the controlling of behavior, the greater is the reliance placed on law. As the illustration of the errant bus rider presented at the beginning of this chapter points out, informal means of social control such as embarrassment, public ridicule, and the like seem relatively ineffective, as do, according to Black, the more formal methods generally applied by family, friends, church groups, and other nonlegal associations. It might be hypothesized that the relative ineffectiveness of these nonlegal sanctions in the control of behavior are, in part, due to the sociological circumstances already discussed. While law requires some minimal relationship between people for its application, other means of social control might require a deeper, longer-lasting relationship between individuals than is ordinarily present during many of the daily encounters in modern life. Embarrassment, for instance, will be most acute when we are with those with whom we must associate for longer periods day-in and day-out. Associations on public conveyances and in most other public places are transitory, so that it would be difficult for you to develop a reputation affecting other parts of your life. The transitory nature of many of the daily encounters in the modern city and their lack of consequence for our reputations and long-term self-images might account for the growth of formal legal constraints and the demise of the less formal methods of keeping individuals within certain agreed-upon behavioral bounds.

Reputation is itself a factor affecting the behavior of law. Thus, respectable people, those more concerned with their reputations, will also have a greater concern with keeping their environment and their relationships within the parameters of respectability. Therefore, Black postulates that "Law varies directly with respectability."[15] Respectable people will have more law (and more social controls generally) among themselves than will nonrespectable people. To illustrate the point, Black notes that ex-convicts are less likely to complain to the police about each other than are more respectable people.

As might be expected from the preceding points, when the influence of respectability on the direction of law is examined, more respectable people have an easier time applying law to less respectable people than the reverse. A number of consequences follow from this. First, as discussions in Chapters 1 through 5 underscored, less respectable people are more likely to have their deviance recorded and defined as crime than are the respectables of society. Thus, outcasts are more likely to be identified as witches, drug abusers, and so on. We have already noted the theoretical blind spot this creates for the theories about criminal behavior. Second, both Black and this book suggest that once a person has a criminal record (that is, has his respectability diminished) his chances of having official sanctions leveled against him in the future increase. Third, the seriousness of deviance will, in part, be determined by its direction. If a more respectable person victimizes a less respectable person, that act will be considered less serious than if the reverse had occurred. That is because, in the former case, law will be moving in an upward direction and, therefore, will be less severe in both style and amount than if it were moving in a downward direction (a situation brought about by a less respectable person victimizing a more respectable person). Thus, unrespectables are victims of the law in two ways. They feel the weight of the law for their transgressions much more severely than do respectables. Further, they can expect less protection from the law when they themselves become victimized. An example of the propositions Black formulates regarding this dimension of the behavior of law is "Law is greater in a direction toward less respectability than toward more respectability."[16]

Black's work can easily be considered a seminal piece in the sociology of law. Yet is is not without its critics. Michael Gottfredson and Michael Hindelang attempted to empirically test certain of Black's propositions.[17] Using data collected from several victimization surveys, the authors examined variations in calls to the police to determine if such variations could be predicted by Black's schema. Generally, calls to the police (a measure of quantity of law) did not vary in the ways predicted. Instead, the researchers discovered that "seriousness" of crime was more significant than the factors postulated by Black for determining calls to the police. Thus, for example, variations in income could not predict calls to the police.

Black, in a rejoinder to his critics, describes a theoretical blind spot that pervades both the sociology of law and, at times, sociology in general.[18]

> What people consider to be "crime" varies with its location and direction in social space. Any given person will describe some conduct as "crime"—or "robbery," "theft," "rape," etc.—but this will depend upon such factors as the social status of the people involved as "offender" and "victim," the nature of the relationship between them, and the larger context in which the incident occurs. Thus, what is an "assault" or "theft" in one setting is only "teaching someone a lesson" or "borrowing without asking permission" in another setting.[19]

In brief, then, the data used by the authors cannot provide a test of Black's propositions, since the quantity of law includes the tendency to label behavior as criminal. A true test of Black's theory would have to include information on the differential propensity to label various occurrences as criminal. Presumably, such data would show that higher-ranked people are more likely to label particular occurrences as criminal (and thus expect or utilize legal intervention) than are lower-ranked people, and so on. The basic problem of the study is that the authors accepted the building blocks used by respondents in their social world-building process and, therefore, did not really test how uses of law (as building material) vary among populations. It would be as if somebody took your categorizations of Fleming's behavior, or that of Dudley and Stephens, and accepted them as simple descriptions of fact without asking either why you categorized the behavior in a particular way or whether there were alternative descriptions. The individual proceeding in this manner would discover very little about how you use law. Perhaps the only thing discovered would be how an administrative problem (that is, what to do with these people) was solved.

It is clear that more research needs to be done on how people build social meaning and what factors influence different building strategies. This is particularly true if we are to understand the process of criminal justice. Black's work and the discussion it has generated can give us some insight into the behavior of law on a macro-level. Work has also been done on a micro-level, as researchers have sought to discover those factors associated with variations in legal decision making. We now shift our focus and once more examine the behavior of legal functionaries and their use of law.

Here Comes the Judge (and the Lawyers and Jurors, Too)

We have already seen that a variety of factors, both personal and organizational, influence police decision making. For instance, who recruits learn to identify as symbolic assailants and the organizational pressures for production and efficiency influence the legal applications of police officers. Considerably less research has been done on the influence of these factors on other legal functionaries, such as judges and lawyers. (Perhaps sociolegal research, like law itself, is greater in the direction toward the less prestigious legal occupations. Judges and attorneys, after all, may have greater resources than the police to protect themselves from the prying eyes of the sociologist.) Nevertheless, there have been some attempts to sort out the personal, political, and organizational factors that influence judicial decision making. The research emphasis, in attempting to determine factors affecting judicial decision making, in part has been due to the wide discrepancies found in both judicial case determination and sentencing practices.

As early as 1914, a New York City group was beginning to suspect that logic and legalities were less important than were personality factors in influencing judges' decisions. Comparing how different judges handled similar cases in Magistrates Court, the Committee on Criminal Courts of the Charity Organization Society found wide variation. One judge heard 566 cases of alleged intoxication. He determined that 565 of the allegations were true and declared the individuals guilty of the offense. Only one person was discharged. His colleague, on the other hand, had 673 people come before him charged with the same offense but found only 142 of them guilty, discharging 531. Similarly wide variations were found among judges handling other kinds of cases within the magistrate court. Apparently, the committee was deeply disturbed by these findings, since they discontinued their study.[20]

A more rigorous study of judicial decision making, Frederick J. Gaudet's 1930s analysis of judicial sentencing behavior, also reveals marked inconsistencies. Gaudet examined 7,442 cases of certain select crimes assigned to six judges of a New Jersey County Court over a ten-year period. His conclusion was that personality, in the broad sense of social background, education, religion, experience on the bench, temperament, and social attitudes, was of primary importance in determining a judge's decision of the appropriate sentence to give a person found guilty of a crime.[21]

A 1970s Rand Corporation study of local sentencing practices in California continued to underscore judicial sentencing inconsistencies. One judge imposed felony sentences in 6 percent of dangerous drug possession convictions, while a colleague imposed such sentences in 62 percent of the possession cases he heard. Imposition of felony sentences for burglary ranged from 9 percent of the cases for one judge to 82 percent for another.[22]

In summarizing some of the studies done on judicial decision making, Anne Steick states, "Sentencing . . . depends less upon punishment fitted to crime, upon the contextual circumstances of the case, or even upon the particular criminal's history, than (in Judge Marvin Frankel's words) 'upon the wide spectrums of character, bias, neurosis, and daily vagary encountered among occupants of the trial bench.' "[23] The reader should exercise the normal caution of the social scientist when confronted with such a strong statement. Actually, the research problems confronting an investigator of judicial decision making are significant. Nevertheless, despite the admittedly serious methodological problems that have to be considered when examining such an issue,[24] the weight of the evidence to date is certainly suggestive of the need to analyze judicial decisions in light of unique judicial backgrounds. One of the most widely quoted studies in this regard is Stuart Nagel's study of the influence of certain background characteristics on judges' decisions. He found significant differences between Democratic and Republican judges, non-ABA members and ABA members, non-former prosecutors and former prosecutors, Catholic judges and Protestant judges, and relatively liberal judges and relatively conservative judges, as measured by their off-the-bench attitudes. Democratic judges were more likely to favor the defense than were their Republican counterparts. Not belonging to the ABA, not being a former prosecutor, being Catholic, and being scored as liberal in off-the-bench attitudes were also factors significantly associated with being more favorable to the defense position in criminal cases.[25]

In attempting to understand how various legal functionaries "fill in the blanks" of quasi-law when it comes time to apply such law to an actual situation, remember that individual background factors are only one source of social world construction material. We have already seen in the studies by Matza, Foote, and others that bureaucratic and political considerations affect the decisions of judges. Whether somebody gets sent to the reformatory may depend in part on how much room is left in the facility. Political pressure to "get tough with criminals" can also influence a member of the bench. Finally, we have also noted that the working relationships that judges develop with prosecutors, defense attorneys, and other courthouse personnel affect the decisions judges render in particular cases.

Summarizing the evidence of the influence of extralegal factors on judges' decision making, it seems clear that extralegal factors are at least as significant as statutory law in understanding the dynamics of case processing. Certainly the legal profession operates on this premise. Lawyers, police officers, and defendants familiar with how the criminal justice system actually works try to get the judge who would be most sympathetic to their particular plight. Such "judge shopping" is common practice and, as one judge has said, "Lawyers are always trying to psych the judge out, like people at the race track trying to figure out the horses. . . . That is what you pay a trial lawyer for—assessing the judge's discretion."[26]

Obviously, jurors, in their applications of the law, are affected by the same factors that affect judges and other legal functionaries. In fact, in the case of jurors, such background and personality characteristics are paramount in their selection for hearing certain cases. Lawyers do not attempt to pick impartial juries during the process of *voir dire* (literally, "to say the truth"). During the *voir dire*, lawyers question jurors in an attempt to discover which jurors are likely to be biased. Each lawyer is allowed to remove a certain number of jurors he or she feels would be biased against his or her side. Of course, each lawyer tries to get and to keep those jurors who would be biased for his or her side. The importance lawyers place on the biases of the jurors for winning or losing cases is illustrated by this excerpt from an interview with the attorneys involved in *The Murder Trial of Wilbur Jackson,* cited previously. Recall that Jackson, a white blue-collar worker, was on trial for killing his daughter and three hippie companions.

> Prosecutor: Jury selection in this case was completely different from the way it is in other cases. I wanted to get the most intelligent jury I could find, which is not the way I would normally approach it. Normally, I want followers. I want people who will follow the lead of one strong, middle-aged factory worker type who dislikes crime and whom the other jurors will follow. In this case, I wanted a really bright intelligent jury who would disregard the clothes and beard and all that.

> Defense: Ordinarily, if you defend a homicide case in Pittsburgh, it would be fair to say that you are defending someone between seventeen and twenty-six who is charged with the commission of a felony murder, a murder which was committed in the course of the perpetration of a robbery, burglary, an arson, or a rape. About 90 percent of the time, but perhaps even more often than that, you're defending a black who is between eighteen and twenty-six and you want one particular kind of jury to try that kind of a case, but you want a very different kind of a jury to try Wilbur Jackson. . . . What I was trying to do, to be quite frank with you, was to get as many people on that jury who came from the north-east part of Pittsburgh and who had Polish or Italian surnames.[27] Reproduced by permission from THE MURDER TRIAL OF WILBUR JACKSON by Phillip B. Heymann and William H. Kenety, copyright © 1975 by West Publishing Company. All rights reserved.

Case determination is the result of compromise between the various world views and consequent moldings of quasi-law of the legal actors involved. Police officers, witnesses, victims, judges, lawyers, probation officers, and others all bring their idiosyncratic blueprints of how the world should look to the building materials represented by legal statutes. Each takes the law and shapes it according to his or her own blueprint. The constructs are then compared with one another, parts of the various structures are discarded, and the resulting structure is law in a particular case. As the last chapter noted, this is the procedure of the Continental Op writ large. But keep in mind that certain of the builders are always on the building site. These functionaries, the judges and the lawyers, and in some instances the police, deal with and shape the law day-in and day-out. Therefore, they act as the construction foremen, attempting to guide the uninitiated in the use of the materials. As we have seen, these professionals work out patterns that may require them to slightly alter their view of the world but that, in the long run, allow them to handle most matters routinely and to formulate and play the game of justice so that everyone *on the professional team* (lawyers and judges) can be a winner. The patterns that are hammered out lead from the unique individual world view of a particular legal actor to the routine behavior of law, as discussed by Black and as illustrated by Sudnow's study of the routine handling of cases by defense attorneys, with their attempts to fit individual acts into normal crime categories. Quasi-law, then, as it is shaped and applied by individual actors, ends up forming a mosaic or a kind of puzzle where the outline of the eventual picture is already provided. It then becomes a matter of trying to fit the individual pieces into already existing patterns. Thus, the behavior of law becomes routine and classifiable.

In the course of our discussion in this chapter, we have moved from an examination of behavior of law to the behavior of certain legal actors and back again to a discussion of general patterns. In the course of our travels from the general to the specific and back to the general, we have come across a seeming paradox. Legal actors attempt to shape and apply law to fit unique circumstances, but in the course of doing that they have created patterns that are, upon analysis, not unique but regularized. Just how regularized can be illustrated by an examination of arrest rates over an eight-year period (1969 to 1976). Eugene Doleschal noted that in the period

1969 to 1976 arrests for Index Crimes (murder, rape, robbery, aggravated assault, burglary, larceny, and auto theft) remained essentially stable (between 19 and 22 percent of total arrests). Arrests for victimless crimes (drunkenness, disorderly conduct, vagrancy, etc.) decreased significantly, from 51.5 percent of total arrests to 35.9 percent of the total. Arrests for Part II crimes (simple assaults, embezzlement, vandalism, etc.), however, increased from 29.5 percent of the total to 41.3 percent. Doleschal shows that the end result of the various fluctuations in arrests for different types of crime is an arrest rate per 100,000 population that remained virtually unchanged over the eight-year period. To quote Doleschal; "What this apparently means is that police have been busy arresting serious offenders at roughly the same rate throughout the eight years and that as pressure mounted to leave victimless crime alone, they took up the slack by concentrating on nonindex offenders."[28] Even though Doleschal's data are for a relatively short period of time, his analysis presents strong indications that the criminal justice system tends toward homeostasis (in maintaining a stable level of both defining and processing acts as criminal). A disturbance in one part of the system, such as pressure to decriminalize certain activities, results in an attempt to regain the balance by efforts at increased criminalizing of other activities (bus smokers, look out). Hence, it seems that law not only acts in certain regularized ways (Black), but that the criminal justice system itself maintains a certain regularized volume of those to whom the law will be applied (Doleschal). The end result is predictable patterns in both how and to how many the law will be applied. Such regularity in the face of individual actors molding law to fit unique social world blueprints!

The dynamics of this paradox will form the central issue of the remaining chapters.

References

1. DONALD BLACK. *The Behavior of Law* (New York: Academic Press, Inc., 1976), pp. 3–4.
2. Ibid., pp. 4–5.

3. ROGER BROWN. *Social Psychology* (New York: The Free Press, 1965), p. 103.
4. BLACK. *The Behavior of Law,* pp. 13–25.
5. Ibid., p. 42.
6. Ibid., pp. 39–41.
7. Ibid., p. 49.
8. Ibid., pp. 48–50.
9. Ibid., pp. 63–69.
10. Ibid., p. 92.
11. *St. Louis Post–Dispatch,* July 17, 1979, p. 10A.
12. BLACK. *The Behavior of Law,* p. 89.
13. Ibid., p. 86.
14. Ibid., p. 107.
15. Ibid., p. 112.
16. Ibid., p. 114.
17. MICHAEL GOTTFREDSON and MICHAEL HINDELANG. "A Study of the Behavior of Law," *American Sociological Review,* 44 (February 1979), 3–18.
18. DONALD BLACK. "Common Sense in the Sociology of Law," *American Sociological Review,* 44 (February 1979), 18–27.
19. Ibid., p. 20.
20. ANNE STRICK. *Injustice for All* (New York: G. P. Putnam's Sons, 1977), pp. 145–46.
21. FREDERICK J. GAUDET. "The Sentencing Behavior of the Judge," in *Encyclopedia of Criminology,* eds. V. C. Branham and S. V. Kutash (New York: Philosophical Library, 1949), pp. 449–61.
22. STRICK. *Injustice for All,* p. 147.
23. Ibid., p. 147.
24. For a discussion of some of these problems see Edward Green, *Judicial Attitudes in Sentencing* (London: Macmillan & Co., 1961), pp. 8–20.
25. STUART S. NAGEL. "Judicial Background and Criminal Cases," *Journal of Criminal Law, Criminology and Police Science,* 53, no. 3 (1962), 333–39.
26. JUDGE TIM MURPHY. "His Honor Has Problems, Too," *The Center Magazine,* 3, no. 3 (May /June 1971), 51, quoted in Strick, *Injustice for All,* pp. 153–54.
27. PHILIP B. HEYMANN and WILLIAM H. KENETY. *The Murder Trial of*

Wilbur Jackson (St. Paul, Minn.: West Publishing Co., 1975), pp. 296–97.

28. EUGENE DOLESCHAL. "Viewpoint: Input to the Criminal Justice System Remains Constant," *Criminal Justice Newsletter,* 8 (November 21, 1977), 5.

chapter seven

How People Build Meaning

Old Bags and New Bags

We all carry around with us a bag labeled "Things in Need of Explanation." The items in the bag simultaneously expand and restrict our understanding of the world. For example, if you were a medieval monk, your bag might contain an item such as "How many angels can sit on the head of a pin?" The answer to the question provides a certain understanding of the world, but the question itself delimits the type of world you are able to perceive, thereby also limiting your understanding. Had you lived in Salem during the colonial period, your bag might have had an item such as "Why are there witches?" Again, the answer to the question both advances and limits understanding. Just by assuming the existence of witches, you assume certain things about the world. Often, the assumptions about the world contained in a particular question remain hidden. Emphasis is put on trying to answer the specific query, not on the nature of the query itself. As a result, hidden assumptions are seldom subjected to any kind of rigorous scrutiny. Without such "questioning of the questions," understanding remains limited.

The bag labeled "Things in Need of Explanation" has a shorter name in the philosophy of science. The bag is simply called a paradigm. A paradigm provides scientists with questions or problems about the world and models for answering or solving "those things in need of explanation."[1] In social science there are two such paradigms, one called the normative paradigm and the other called the interpretive paradigm.[2] Each provides a bag of questions about social life, together with a method for answering them. The questions and the procedures of investigation form the theories of the paradigm, that is, specific accounts of specific social events. By examining some of the assumptions underlying the paradigms of particular theories, the nature and limits of a theory and the questions it poses about social phenomena are uncovered. For example, Chapter 4 discussed a number of theories regarding crime, most of which flow out of the normative paradigm. The normative paradigm argues that human behavior is rule-governed.[3] The behavior occurs in response to natural laws. The laws themselves can be biological, psychological, or social. The task of the scientist is to uncover these preexisting laws so as to explain the social order. Recall that the image of society suggested by these theories is a concrete, "out there" one. Society imposes order on individuals and therefore determines their behavior. The limits of this perspective have been noted.

The interpretive paradigm states that social life and social interaction are not, in essence, rule-governed, but instead come about through an interpretive process in which meanings evolve and change over the course of social interaction.[4] In this view, people impose order on society (and, in the process, are continually constructing it), society does not impose order on individuals (and, in the process, create them).

The differing assumptions about social life contained in each of the paradigms and the theories that flow from them mean that each asks an essentially different question about the nature of the social order. The normative paradigm is concerned with the issue of why the world is what it is. The interpretive paradigm focuses on how people do what they do, making very few assumptions about the "natural order" of the world. Therefore, the interpretive paradigm contains within it the seeds of a radically different view of society, social order, and the appropriate methods for investigating human behavior. To fully appreciate the radical view of society contained within an interpretive social science paradigm, we turn to an examination of two theories developed from an interpretive framework, ethnomethodology, which we have already briefly discussed, and symbolic interaction, a theory that undergirds the labeling approach to deviance.

Since we have already done a kind of ethnography of traditional social science thinkers, fair play demands that we do a similar analysis of nontraditional theorists. But be forewarned! Certain of the theories and theorists to be discussed are not very popular with many social scientists. In fact, ethnomethodology is distinctly unpopular. It, perhaps more than any other recent theoretical innovation, has seriously challenged the pretensions of traditional social science and the sacred precepts of the scientific method, particularly its relevance for the study of social life. Consequently, those who had accepted the legitimacy of the "normal" scientific approach to the study of social life reacted with vigor to the tenets of what they considered a bizarre alternative. From the social "scientific" point of view, the collection of individuals calling themselves ethnomethodologists were uninformed radicals at best and incompetent methodologists at worst. There was a sneaking suspicion among many of the more traditional social scientists that ethnomethodologists were those who could not master statistics when in graduate school.[5] Even sociologists sympathetic to the ethnomethodological perspective found it difficult to believe that its adherents were really saying and meaning what, indeed, they were saying and meaning. As a result, some tried to explain ethnomethodology as just another method for observing society. Theoretically, it was seen as a variant of symbolic interaction,[6] which, although it comes out of an interpretive view of social life, at least pays lip service to certain of the taken-for-granted assumptions of "normal" social science.

Ethnomethodology was and is revolutionary (and still fairly unpopular). But, ironically, by being that, it conforms to a rather common process of the scientific enterprise. Contrary to popular belief, science seldom advances the frontiers of knowledge in a step-by-step process of incrementalism. More often, startling advances in human understanding occur through revolution.[7] The investigators, researchers, and discoverers of today do not simply stand on the shoulders of scientists who have gone before. If they did or had, our pace of discovery would be much slower. Science pushes and expands the frontiers of knowledge through the introduction of radically new ideas and principles. These challenge accepted under-standings by providing a bag of new questions to be discussed and researched. "Breakthroughs" come about when new questions allow for new answers to old dilemmas. Ethnomethodology, regardless of whether it is accepted as science, is therefore part of a long scientific tradition. By carrying the assumptions of the interpretive paradigm to their extreme, a new set of "Things in Need of Explanation" can emerge. If this occurs, our understanding of social life will be altered and social inquiry will be prevented from atrophying. It will be as if somebody replaced our old bag, loaded with questions about witches, with a new bag full of questions assuming a different kind of world.

Of Bent Pennies and Other Things

During the late 1960s and 1970s, Washington, D.C. was the scene of many mass protests. Certain law enforcement agencies, particularly those concerned with narcotics control, regularly sent agents to infiltrate these gatherings. The agents were charged with discover-ing, investigating, and apprehending those individuals violating federal drug laws. While many questions can be raised about the propriety of such law enforcement activity, generally these were not being asked in law enforcement circles at that time. Be that as it may, the particular instance we are concerned with takes place at one of the last large-scale peace demonstrations to end the war in Vietnam. A number of federal narcotics agents were assigned to work under-cover, and it was decided that they would not carry any official credentials. Instead, each agent would carry a bent penny. The bent penny would identify agents as members of this particular federal enforcement group. All fellow agents and those of other federal law enforcement bureaus were informed of this identification proce-dure. Unfortunately, however, nobody bothered to inform the Washington, D.C. Police Department. During one of the periodic roundups of demonstrators, a practice later to be found unconstitutional, a federal narcotics agent was apprehended. As the police were moving the demonstrators toward police vans and buses for transport to the areas used for detention, the hapless agent moved toward the edge of the crowd. He motioned to the officer nearest him. The police officer, his helmet unbuttoned and face shield lifted to reveal a weary and frustrated countenance, came over to the hippie character trying to get his attention. The agent opened his fist and pointed to the bent penny resting in his palm. As he did so, he whispered knowingly to the officer, "Bent penny." The officer looked at the penny and then at the long-haired male in front of him. He looked again at the penny. With a resigned shrug, he pushed the individual back into the crowd and said, "Listen, buddy, don't give me any trouble." The agent moved toward him again and again pointed to the defaced coin in his hand and said in a loud, urgent whisper, "Bent penny!" The officer ignored him for a minute and then said impatiently, "Come on, keep moving." The agent, however, was persistent. He said loudly, "Bent penny, bent penny," and held the coin close so that the officer could indeed see that it was bent. The officer motioned the agent out of line. He indicated to him that he wanted to whisper something in his ear. The agent bent close to his brother law enforcer. The officer slid his baton halfway out of the ring on his belt. He got close to the agent's ear. With his right hand he pointed to the wooden shaft protruding above his left fist and whispered, "Nightstick!" He then let the baton slide back into its ring and pushed the funny-looking man with the bent penny back into line. The agent wisely stayed there.

What happened in the above scenario? The various answers to this question can help illuminate the differences between ethnomethodology and symbolic interaction. Further, an analysis of the bent penny incident can clarify some of the assumptions of the interpretive paradigm, underscoring how these provide a world view quite distinct from the view of social life found in the normative paradigm. Finally, an analysis of the above story will highlight the uses of theory, both the kind found in the social sciences and the kind found in every-day life.

The term theory carries a variety of meanings for a variety of people. To some it equates with terms like "impractical," "ivory tower," or "foolishness." Others view it as philosophy, speculation about how things are—an armchair sport. Still others view it as deadly dull and, in their estimation, the bane of the social sciences. And yet, as the incident portrayed shows, all human actors use theory. We all have a story to tell about the world and the relationships and events that occur in it. And that is all that theory is: a story about what we see that explains a particular phenomenon and our relationship to it. Again, theory is simply an account of an event. There are a variety of different accounts that can explain what happened in the story, each a kind of theory about the event.

The police officer in the story might theorize about the occurrence in this way:

> A commie demonstrator tried to get smart. The dirt ball must have been high on something. Tried to convince me that a bent penny meant something. I showed him what my nightstick meant, and that got him shaped up.

The federal agent, in contrast, would probably find the following theory a more accurate explanation of what happened:

> The cop screwed up. The dumb bastard forgot what the hell a bent penny meant. Boy, I wish those guys would get on the ball. I kept my cool, so the cop wouldn't go berserk. He'd have hurt me or blown my cover if I didn't cooperate. He may have even screwed up some legitimate arrests. So I just went along with him.

A symbolic interactionist is likely to structure his or her account in this way:

> The police officer and the agent are capable of taking on each other's roles. The officer, for example, can literally put a part of himself in the place of the other—walk in his shoes (or sandals), as it were. The ability to take on the role of the long-haired male allowed the officer to interpret the behavior of this individual and then act toward him on the basis of the interpretation. Similarly, the agent takes on the role of the police officer, saying to himself that when a police agent acts this way (for example, points to a nightstick) he means business. The ability of the self to take on the roles of others allows individual subjective meanings to be modified so that an objective, mutually agreed-upon definition of the situation emerges. At the end of the interaction, both participants agreed that the police officer's orders

were to be obeyed. Such mutual role-taking and the emergence of common situational definitions are made easier, since participants in social interaction generally come to the exchange with agreement on the meaning of certain societal norms, values, and symbols. In the scenario, both participants accepted the meaning of a nightstick or, more generally, the societal symbols of power differentials, legitimate authority, and so on. While the bent penny could have represented a new symbol of power, authority, and legitimacy, the negotiations favored the more generally agreed-upon symbol.

The last theoretical explanation to be proffered is ethnomethodology. An ethnomethodologist would argue:

The two participants in this sequence did not and will not agree on what took place. This is because each was using a different set of rules to establish meaning. The police officer was invoking a rule to the effect that "a police officer should be obeyed." The agent invoked a different rule, "A bent penny exempts me from obeying your orders." When it became evident to each participant that the other wanted to build or assemble order and meaning differently from himself, new sets of rules were invoked. The police officer, on the one hand, invoked the rule, "I have more power than you do, so you better get back in line." This rule was reinforced with a push. The agent, on the other hand, invoked the rule that if you speak louder and with more urgency people will understand what it is you are saying. Thus, he merely repeated in a louder voice the phrase, "Bent penny." Each outcome forced the individuals to redefine the pattern they were engaging in and to invoke new rules for putting together meaning. For the officer, the situation changed from "this is a demonstrator," to "this is a troublemaker," to "this is somebody who needs to be taught a lesson," to "those people sure are weird." For the agent, the pattern changed from "this is a brother law enforcement officer," to "this is a brother law enforcement officer who did not understand me," to "this is a mistake and I better just cool it, because this fellow obviously doesn't know what he is doing." If new information is received by the parties, the scenario will be redefined once again, with a still different set of rules. If the police officer finds out the official meaning of a bent penny, he will probably report that, "Those feds never communicate with us locals. I am glad I taught the guy a lesson." When the agent finds out that the police were not properly informed, he might be inclined to say, "It's a good thing they didn't know because they probably would have blabbed. At least this way I can keep my cover." The final outcome is that each individual thinks the other is "wrong," "strange," "in error," and so on, because each invoked different rules for assembling the situation. The only point of agreement is that one individual (the police officer) was more successful in convincing the other individual (the agent) of the appropriateness of his, the police officer's, rules, *for the moment.*

Reviewing the above accounts, you once again find yourself in the position of the Continental Op. Something has happened, and you must compare the various stories presented to you in order to assemble and assess your own view of the world and of your place in it. How will you proceed?

If you rummage around in your common-sense bag of "Things in Need of Explanation," you are likely to pull out a rather obvious question about the accounts that confront you. Unfortunately, the obvious question, "Which of the theories is true?" does not take you very far in establishing the validity of the theories for understanding social life. Each theory is true, more or less. How much more or less depends upon an individual's point of view, that is, the meaning each theory provides that individual. To examine this question of meaning or the assumptions each statement makes about the nature of social life, dip into a bag labeled "Philosophy of Science, Things in Need of Explanation." The questions that pop out should take you further along the road to understanding the nature of theory than did the questions from your common-sense bag.[8]

The first question you might ask is, "What are the theories trying to explain?" At one level, the answer to this question is quite simple. The first theory (the police officer's) is trying to explain "weird, hippie demonstrators," the second, "dumb cops," the third, "subjective meanings," and the fourth, "accounting practices." But what are the consequences for one's view of social life in asking questions about those particular items?

The first two theories, examples of what might be called everyday-life theories, raise issues about concrete, situationally specific items. The questions implicit in the statements assume the empirical realities of the things they try to explain (that is, there really are such things as dirt balls and dumb cops). Most such theories are pretty narrow in scope. That is, they do not generally apply beyond the particular circumstances of a small group of people. The conceptual category of dirt ball, for example, has little applicability to my day-to-day world of college teaching; at least, hopefully, this is so. The term class clown, however, forms a conceptual category that has some meaning for me but is probably useless for the police officer. Scientific theory contains more general conceptualizations of "Things in Need of Explanation" than does everyday-life theory, which tends to focus on narrow, situationally specific elements. Thus, one kind of social science theory speaks of deviants rather than dirt balls or class clowns. This more general category allows the scientist to get above the particulars of a specific instance and construct stories of relationships that explain or account for a wide variety of behaviors that share similar traits. The more generalizable theory of the scientist can, therefore, be useful to a wide variety of people. Since it takes the broader view, it can also avoid to some extent the prejudices and blunders likely to influence personal theory and thus lessen its accuracy of prediction. Professors and police officers are not in positions to either find out about or appreciate the economic circumstances, personal histories, and psychological factors that influence the behavior of class clowns or dirt balls. Since they are not, they are likely to base their actions toward individuals so defined on answers to questions that elicit only very limited information. For example, the officer in the scenario probably asks himself the question, "What can I do about this hippie?" while the agent asks, "What is with this dumb cop?" The information each question elicits provides only narrow, highly subjective "facts" upon which to act. Such actions, in turn, may worsen the situation. As we have seen, sometimes the actions we take toward our personal categories of deviants create the very thing we wish to avoid. The action of Salem residents toward witches created more, not fewer, just as the actions of police officers, legal functionaries, and teachers can create more dirt balls, law violators, or class clowns. The conceptual categories that are the focus of the questions implicit in personal, everyday-life theory restrict the ability to gather information, thus restricting the ability to act creatively.

Generalizability, avoidance of narrow biases and prejudices, and a wide informational base distinguish scientific theory from everyday-life theory. Yet, we have seen that the conceptual categories about which much social science theory asks questions are themselves restrictive. While the term deviant may be a more general term than dirt ball, there is still an assumption that something "out there" exists that *is* a deviant. The term takes on an untested, empirical reality, thereby restricting the amount of information a question about deviants can elicit. Theories flowing out of the normative paradigm, while more general than everyday-life theories, tend, as has been noted, to overconcretize social life. Compare the words of the theories discussed in Chapter 4 with the interpretive accounts of the bent penny incident presented in this chapter. In these interpretive accounts actors take, negotiate, reflect, exchange, interact, invoke, account, and so forth. In short, they act. They are not simply acted upon. Both ethnomethodology and symbolic interaction attempt to explain how actors act, thus, each assumes that the individual human actor should be the primary focus of social science inquiry. Questions about social structure, institutions, and other large-scale social entities are considered less important in the interpretive paradigm than they are in the normative paradigm, because such questions are viewed as limiting rather than expanding insight into social life. Normative questions contain a greater number of untested assumptions than do interpretive questions that focus on process (what can be rather than what is).

Compare the ethnomethodological account of the bent penny incident with the symbolic interactionist perspective. Of these, which makes the fewer assumptions about human activity in the questions they pose?

Symbolic interaction is specifically concerned with the subjective meanings social objects have for individuals. The assumption that symbolic interactionists make is that human social behavior results from people's ability to symbolically represent to themselves the world outside. The representations thus made form a basis for deciding how to act in a particular situation. The symbolic interactionists agree with their colleagues from normative science that there is a world "out there," but people perceive it "in their heads" and, in so doing, negotiate and change the world outside, or what they perceive as the real, objective world.[9] There is a rather detailed story that justifies the assumption that human behavior is largely a product of symbolic, subjective manipulations on the part of human actors. George Herbert Mead was one of the first to articulate the story so that it could be used by the social sciences.[10]

Focusing on the subjective meanings of human actors contains fewer assumptions about the nature of the world than focusing on a category such as deviants. Nevertheless, symbolic interactionists do assume some empirical realities that, within the theory, are not tested. An ethnomethodologist would argue, for example, that the subjective meanings possessed by actors have to be assumed, since they cannot be empirically observed or verified. Ethnomethodology, therefore, does not concern itself with subjective meanings. For the ethnomethodologist, the only observable social phenomena are the reporting practices of members of a society. One cannot assume subjective meanings or, for that matter, mutually agreed-upon norms and values. As Harold Garfinkel, the major ethnomethodological theorist in the United States, notes, people use ethnographies in their daily round of life.[11] They literally describe their own behavior just as anthropologists describe the behavior of primitive peoples. The descriptions people give of their daily behavior are the only things available for social scientific scrutiny. By describing behavior, people are able to recognize a pattern and uniformity in their activity. Thus, how individuals use ethnographies is of central importance to understanding the nature of social life.

The question, "How do people use ethnographies?" (that is, how do they account for their own behavior) seems to contain the fewest assumptions about the nature of social life. Therefore, while both symbolic interaction and ethnomethodology view social life as a fluid, flexible, ever-changing entity (a view at variance with the perceptions of both normative science and everyday-life theories), ethnomethodology seems much more radically committed to this notion than does symbolic interaction. The point can be made more clearly if you will once again dip into your bag of philosophy of science questions. The question that you pull out is, "How can people gain knowledge about such a fluid, flexible phenomenon?"

Obviously, how you categorize those "Things in Need of Explanation" affects how you go about gaining understanding and knowledge. If you are interested in how many angels can sit on the head of a pin, your assumptions about how to answer the query will be different than if you were interested in how to split atoms. Simply put, the question you have just extracted from your philosophy of science bag asks if your world is knowable and, if so, how.

Everyday-life theories assume that the world is knowable and that, if pressed, everybody, based on their own experience, knows what is true. This is "common sense." Unfortunately, as we have seen, common sense varies considerably according to an individual's experience. Police officers have a different common sense than civilians, for instance. Moreover, individual experience is sometimes a poor teacher. One incident caused by a communications foul-up does not mean that all police officers or all federal agents are dumb or incompetent. Yet, the first two theorists in our scenario are likely to defend such an assertion based on a limited, incomplete, individually unique experience.

If you believe that social life is rule-governed (the assumption of the normative paradigm), then you approach how you understand that world differently than common-sense understanding dictates. The assumption is that laws governing social life are knowable and that the best method for uncovering them is by using the canons of the scientific method. One tests the formulations of scientific laws through the use of deductive logic. You start with a theory about particular relationships and deduce from the theory a hypothesis. A hypothesis asserts what one would expect to happen under a given set of circumstances, if the theory is correct. Testing hypotheses deduced from theories forms the major activity of the scientific enterprise.

If social life is not governed by immutable laws, then deductive logic (that which moves from a general design or scheme of things to a specific instance) is not an appropriate method for gaining understanding. Ethnomethodology and symbolic interaction, therefore, both reject this approach to knowledge. Instead, they argue that it is necessary to proceed inductively, beginning with specific behaviors and extracting from them those elements that are common across the behaviors. Social scientists should begin their inquiries with human behavior and move to general statements, rather than beginning with general statements or theories and view behavior in light of these.

The rejection of deductive logic by the interpretive paradigm means that the term "concept" takes on a different meaning, both within symbolic interaction and ethnomethodology. Both perspectives attempt to deconcretize the term. Concepts should be sensitizing rather than definitive. That is, the investigator should approach a social phenomenon without preconceived notions of what will be found. The term deviant is a definitive concept, and if one approaches an instance of social behavior looking for deviants, one narrows his or her ability to perceive the nature of what might be encountered. An example from the last chapter can help illustrate the point. Remember that Black's statements about the behavior of law were challenged by investigators who tested them through the application of normal scientific procedures. Black responded to the challenge by claiming that the investigators missed a crucial element in understanding the behavior of law. The investigators found that seriousness of a crime was more predictive of calls to the police than were such factors as social location postulated by Black as important in determining the amount of law. But the researchers, in Black's view, treated the descriptions of seriousness as definitive concepts. They did not ask, for example, what people meant when they reported that they had been victims of assault. Thus, it might appear that, regardless of social location, all people report a serious assault to the police. But, as Black notes, what people consider to be a serious assault may vary by their social location. An upper-middle class person who gets decked by a parking lot attendant may consider that a serious assault. Were the same thing to happen to the parking lot attendant, he might just consider the incident an example of a business negotiation. When the attendant reports a serious assault, the behavior being reported may include guns, knives, and serious bodily injury. The two instances of serious assault are, therefore, not the same, a point missed if the term serious assault is taken at face value, that is, treated as a definitive concept.

Sensitizing concepts, rather than defining for the researcher what he is to see, merely suggest directions along which to look. Deviants become "people who are perceived as acting differently from others," and serious assault becomes "behavior considered by the individual affected to be extraordinarily hurtful." This use of concepts allows for maximum description of the actual group life of individuals as it occurs in an ongoing process.

The rigorous description of group life is the first step in the interpretive method of understanding social phenomena.[12] A study of the police should, therefore, begin with a rigorous, detailed description of what police officers actually do. After this is accomplished, the researcher then attempts to construct general statements applicable to a wide variety of specific behaviors.[13] The concept symbolic assailant (a concept arrived at *after* Skolnick spent time with the police and rigorously described their activity) helps in understanding a wide variety of police behaviors. Once such general statements or categories are formed, the investigator next attempts to describe linkages between the general themes he has discovered. For example, learning about symbolic assailants, learning to de-mythologize the court system, learning to con the public, and so forth, constitute the process of building a particular kind of social world. Discovering the linkages among general patterns of social life allows for prediction within the interpretive paradigm. Howard Becker's study, describing how an individual becomes a regular user of marijuana, provides an example of the type of prediction possible within interpretive social science.[14]

Becker first described the careers of regular marijuana users. He then abstracted from these individual descriptions those elements that were common to them and constructed several general statements that captured the process of becoming a marijuana user (learning to smoke correctly, learning to identify effects and connect them with smoking, and learning to enjoy the effects). These statements were linked among themselves by a general theme of social learning. Hence, a person became a regular user of marijuana by learning how to appropriately pursue this career. An individual who goes through the process described by Becker will meet a point that leads inevitably to habitual drug use. A social scientist observing a person at this stage can thus predict his or her eventual drug-use pattern. The problem, however, with this type of prediction is that whether a person will in fact reach a particular point or become involved in a particular process leading to regular use cannot be determined. Nevertheless, such an approach does allow a continuous redefinition of concepts so that these continually represent the nature of the empirical entity under study.

Interpretive social scientists emphasize that human actors continually act. Logically, then, the paradigm counsels those who follow it to also be continually active in the structuring and restructuring of the data they gather. Interpretive social scientists should approach their data playfully, interacting with it and allowing intuition to guide the researcher in discovering new meanings and understandings. Intuition is also recognized within the normative paradigm. The serendipity pattern in traditional empiricism notes the tendency for data to yield unexpected results through the investigator's intuitive examination of it. In the interpretive paradigm, however, such intuition is legitimized and given a central place, rather than being merely considered an accidental side effect.

To this point, it appears that both symbolic interaction and ethnomethodology share the same understandings about the appropriate ways for gaining knowledge. Both urge the use of sensitizing rather than definitive concepts when approaching data. Symbolic interactionists actually use the term sensitizing concept in their discussions of how to approach a social scene free of preconceived notions. The term quasi-law in ethnomethodology similarly stresses the need to remain open to a wide variety of influences and stimuli in order to understand a particular instance of social behavior. Both theories stress the need for rigorous descriptions of what people actually do and for proceeding inductively from these specific observations to general statements. Yet, ethnomethodology again departs radically from symbolic interaction in what it perceives as knowable.

If you were to meet an ethnomethodologist on the street (Lombroso would probably argue that they are easily recognizable), you might ask him or her, "Is there such a thing as society?" The answer would no doubt take you aback. "Who cares?" would not ordinarily be the response expected by most people. "Who cares," however, sums up the attitude ethnomethodologists have regarding the existence of an objective, external social order. From an ethnomethodological perspective, the answer to whether an external social order exists is ultimately a matter of faith. "Society" or "social order" cannot be observed directly. The only thing that can be directly observed is how people account for social order, that is, the methods they use to describe a particular pattern. Thus, sociological research should center on how people go about convincing each other that a social order exists. Whether it does or not is beside the point, since the existence of society (a thing out there) can only be inferred from such accounts and not empirically demonstrated. What is "really real" are the accounts, not necessarily the things being accounted for. When ethnomethodologists say they are concerned with the methods people use to build order and logic, they are serious. Methods, not content, form the proper focus for social science inquiry. Talk *about* status, society, social control, and power are important, *not* the dimensions (if indeed there are any) of the concepts themselves. In short, not only are subjective meanings not knowable through observation, but also society as it has been typically conceived of by sociologists and others is not knowable through empirical means.

Imagine for a moment that you have invested a good deal of time and effort in the study of society. How would you react to a group of individuals who insinuated that you had wasted your time. The things that you studied were viewed by this group as having little value. In fact, it was implied that the objects of your scholarly attention did not even exist except in the recesses of your mind. Symbolic interaction at least allows for the existence of an external social order. Ethnomethodology makes no such allowance.[15]

Therefore, while symbolic interactionists see symbols and shared meanings as having existence that requires negotiation and interpretation, the ethnomethodologist claims that such symbols and meanings have no existence at all outside of the members' accounting and describing practices.

Your immediate reaction to these notions would no doubt be one of hostility. You certainly would not welcome the ideas of such a group with open arms. It should now be clear why ethnomethodology is considered both radical and unpopular within the traditional social scientific community.

Another question from your philosophy of science bag will further demonstrate the radical nature of ethnomethodology. The question you extract asks, "What explains how human beings construct meaning?"

Since symbolic interaction and ethnomethodology each focus on different aspects of human behavior, each postulates a different explanatory variable for the activity they examine. Subjective meanings which precipitate social activity in symbolic interaction come about through a process of self-interaction, literally a self-conversation about the meaning of a situation. A joint act (two people acting in accord with one another) comes about through a fitting together of the subjective meanings that each interprets from a situation. These mutually agreed-upon interpretations allow shared meanings and a system of symbols to emerge.

Ethnomethodologists, who are concerned with how people account for activity and thereby convince one another that there is a social order or an orderly pattern to what they do, view human actors as accomplishing this through rule-invoking behavior. People convince others by invoking rules. "My behavior fits into this pattern (is logical) because. . . ." What comes after the "because" is a rule that the individual wants others to follow in assembling the meaning of a situation or an activity. The ethnomethodological account of the bent penny incident illustrates the function of rule-invoking behavor. The police officer invokes a rule that he should be obeyed because he is a police officer. He pushes the individual back into line because he has the power to do so (the rule: people with power can push people without power). He can keep the individual in line because he has a nightstick (the rule: people with nightsticks will use them if necessary). As the ethnomethodological account indicates, however, the agent invokes a different set of rules. "A bent penny exempts me from your order because it means I am a federal agent." "I will obey you because you will blow my cover." The ability to invoke rules allows an individual to pattern his or her activity in a way that allows it to be seen as logical, coherent, and the like.

Two points about rule-invoking behavior need to be emphasized. First, to say that individuals invoke rules to convince others of order is not the same thing as saying that the rules themselves are empirically "real" or refer to "real" objects in the social milieu. For example, I have a fifteen-month-old child and I am constantly trying to convince him that there are rules. Some of the rules I invoke are, "All toddlers go to bed at eight o'clock P.M." "Toddlers must stay on the sidewalk when they are out. They cannot go in the street." "People do not rub cereal in their hair." All of these rules that I invoke give the child a sense of order (and me a sense of peace and control). But the rules themselves do not empirically exist. Likewise, to say a police officer must be obeyed because the social order demands it does not offer proof that there really is such a thing as a social order. The social order is invoked merely to convince another of the rightness of the police officer's action.

The radical implication of this view, as we have seen, is that social order does not exist independently of how people account for it. But there is a second radical consequence to using rule-invoking behavior as explanatory of how people build meaning. Since order, shared meanings, and symbols have no existence independent of accounting practices, action is seen as taking place first, and *then* interpretation and negotiation take place to establish the structure and coherence of the action with some relation to ongoing activity. Members act and then account for the act as an example of logical, coherent behavior. In symbolic interactionism, the definition of the situation determines the action. In ethnomethodology, each outcome develops the past definition of the situation.[16]

This distinction can be elucidated by noting the place of reflexivity in each of the approaches. For the symbolic interactionist, the actor's reflecting on an object allows him to act in a given way toward that object. For the ethnomethodologist, reflexivity deals with the actor's reflecting back on an action already taken, thereby giving meaning to that action. The former theory sees order and shared meaning being created by a fitting together of divergent lines of activity, whereas the latter sees order as resulting from the way people analyze and account for action already taken. Ethnomethodology argues that much meaningful social activity involves *looking backwards* in order to make the past fit the present. The outcome of each action provides another piece to fit into the puzzle of meaning we are assembling. But each new piece can cause a radical restructuring of the entire puzzle. When we get a new piece that does not fit into the pattern we are assembling, we must disassemble that pattern and rearrange the pieces to account for the new outcome. This view of social life is similar to that uncovered by Sam Spade in his discussions with Flitcraft. The pattern of Flitcraft's life had to be rearranged to account for the random occurrence of a falling projectile almost killing him. But even his new pattern of life did not remain constant. He rearranged the puzzle again, this time into a design similar to the one he had. Although the account does not say so, we can speculate that this new rearrangement was precipitated by the need to fit a new element into his life, perhaps the meeting of his second wife.

At this point, you might well ask, "What specific tools does an investigator use to observe either rule-invoking behavior or the construction of symbolic meaning?" To observe accounting practices and the rule-invoking behavior they involve, Garfinkel suggests disrupting normal social activities. Such disruption requires a member to account for a particular action and invoke the rules that should be used to assemble the meaning of a situation. In an earlier chapter, you were asked to act impersonally in an environment where such behavior was not expected. The response you elicited was an attempt to negotiate the situation and to invoke rules to explain your behavior or assemble meaning.

Since symbolic interaction requires an understanding of the subjective meanings possessed by actors, the investigator must see the world through the eyes of the individuals he observes. Therefore, symbolic interaction counsels the use of participant observation by researchers, thereby allowing them to become a part of the social life they observe.

There are certain problems inherent in the specific methods or tools of the interpretive paradigm, and these affect the implementation of either a symbolic interactionist or ethnomethodological perspective. For the symbolic interactionist, there is the question of whether one can really put him- or herself in the place of the actor. Further, there might be a tendency for the researcher's presence to change the phenomenon. By participating in the social life of the group, the investigator can significantly alter the behavior of the people he studies. This has been termed the "Hawthorne effect."[17] One way of preventing this is for the investigator to spend a long period of time with his subjects, thus, in a sense, becoming one of them. This too, however, has drawbacks. The researcher himself can be changed and thus lose objectivity.[18] He or she may begin to take for granted the same things the subjects do and thereby miss crucial elements in a particular interaction process. The methodology of ethnomethodology is particularly vulnerable to the possibility of changing the phenomenon being observed. Dreitzel summarizes the difficulties involved:

> Disrupting taken-for-granted activity has problems not only ethically, but also technically, since the planned change in appearance would, according to the theory, also change the underlying patterns. The

point, however, is that the basic rules of everyday life thus made visible are not necessarily a free product of the subjectivity of members in search for meaning. These rules can also be a result of factors outside the intention of the members' activities and interpretations.[19]

Such criticisms are not meant to imply that the interpretive paradigm generally, or symbolic interactionism and ethnomethodology in particular, have no value. To understand social life, it is necessary to understand both the subjective states of human actors and the accounting practices of those actors. At the same time, however, it is also necessary to give attention to those forces outside of the actor's individual perspective. For example, language, a key element in constructing an account of the world, is itself influenced by such forces as technology. Technology, then, can influence how we build meaning, regardless of whether we consciously take its influence into account when we assemble a particular pattern for our activity. However, the blind spots of the interpretive paradigm can be partially cleared up with a micro- (rather than macro-) perspective. Replication and verification of the understandings gained is possible. Remember that the paradigm sees the human being as an active participant in his or her environment. Thus, the subject of the research can talk back to the researcher and tell him wehther his interpretation of an event is correct. The depiction of key elements within a particular phenomenon can be verified when such elements are subject to probing and critical discussion by a group of well-informed participants in a given world.

Looking Backward to Find Meaning

You might well be saying to yourself, "Well, that was interesting, but what does it all mean for criminal justice?" Simply that ethnomethodology seems to be a promising theoretical perspective for generating new questions about and insights into the criminal justice enterprise. The last six chapters, which, for the most part, have adopted an ethnomethodological perspective, have hopefully demonstrated the utility of ethnomethodology for examining criminal justice phenomena. The criminal justice enterprise is largely a reactive one. Events occur, and the system responds in an attempt to understand, clarify, and interpret the occurrence after the fact. Ethnomethodology is a perspective that directs our attention to the importance of after-the-fact strategies for creating social meaning.

Ethnomethodology can also help us with some of the difficulties encountered in trying to bridge the everyday-life theories about crime with scientific ones. As noted, everyday-life theories can be narrow and uninformed. But scientific theories, particularly within the social sciences, also become narrow and uninformed, because they lose touch with their basic subject, that is, the activities and actions of people living out their daily lives. Hence, the scientific theories themselves become means or strategies used by scientists to explain and justify a world that is comfortable for them. Ethnomethodology provides a framework for comparing everyday-life theories and strategies with scientific ones, thus providing to each a constant prod to expand visions and stay immersed in the broadest possible informational base. This theoretical perspective directs us to look for and uncover the theories and strategies people use to make sense out of their everyday lives. Applied to criminal justice, this means that the system itself becomes a thing to be explained rather than an unquestioned given. From this perspective, as noted previously, the term criminal becomes a conditional one, and thus the theories used to explain criminal activity also become available for critical scrutiny. Just how conditional the term criminal is can be illustrated by noting the percentages of crime not reported to the police. Doleschal reports that 82 percent of all larcenies, 60 percent of aggravated assaults, 56 percent of rapes, 54 percent of burglaries, 51 percent of robberies, and 32 percent of auto thefts go unreported.[20] Theories that purport to explain behavior on such a small sample of known criminals are not immersed in the broadest possible informational base. Thus, the traditional theory of criminology can be helped by examining the decision strategies of criminal justice personnel and citizens (a group whose importance in the defining process of criminal justice has been underscored by Black) when they decide to index a pattern as criminal.

Ethnomethodology also notes that patterns indexed and created are fluid. Thus, a pattern defined one way at one time can, through future events and outcomes, be redefined and restructured to fit a new set of circumstances. The meaning of this insight for criminal justice should be obvious. First, it should sensitize researchers to questions of why people fail to pursue legal action against perpetrators of crime who have in some way harmed them. Second, it should direct researchers to ask what events and outcomes make it sensible, logical, coherent, and the like for certain individuals to continue to define their situation as one that makes future criminal behavior expected and likely. This second question raises a whole series of issues about the convincing procedures used by criminal justice personnel. Why do legal actors fail to convince some individuals of the "rightness" of a particular image of social order? Does the image of social order being sold have a broad appeal or is it more palatable for some individuals than for others? Are there alternative images of social order that might have broader appeal? Is the product being sold (that is, the image of reality) faulty, or is the method of selling in need of improvement? All of these issues can be subsumed by approaching the criminal justice enterprise with the query, "Who attempts to convince whom of what, and for what purpose?"

The general failure of reforms in criminal justice, reforms which have been largely based on the findings of normative science, suggests a need to go back and look at how criminal justice personnel actually go about interpreting events and dealing with disturbances in their social world. Such an approach might help expand and redefine traditional theory by continuing to expand and redefine its informational base. Moreover, by understanding the everyday-life theories of criminal justice personnel and by examining their rule-invoking behavior to construct meaning, effective policy decisions for improving the course of justice are possible. But policy must proceed inductively, grounded in the lives of the people who will implement it. Therefore, we move on to examine the assembling processes of other builders who construct for us our images of justice and crime.

References

1. THOMAS S. KUHN. *The Structure of Scientific Revolutions* (Chicago, Ill.: University of Chicago Press, 1970), p. viii.
2. THOMAS P. WILSON. "Normative and Interpretive Paradigms in

Sociology," in *Understanding Everyday Life*, ed. Jack D. Douglas (Chicago, Ill.: Aldine Publishing Company, 1970), p. 59.

3. Ibid.

4. Ibid.

5. NICHOLAS C. MULLINS. *Theories and Theory Groups in Contemporary American Sociology* (New York: Harper & Row, Publishers, Inc., 1973), p. 198.

6. NORMAN K. DENZIN. "Symbolic Interactionism and Ethnomethodology: A Proposed Synthesis," *American Sociological Review*, 34 (December 1969), 922–34.

7. KUHN. *The Structure of Scientific Revolutions*.

8. The following comparison is based on a more detailed article by James F. Gilsinan, "Ethnomethodology and Symbolic Interactionism: A Comparison," *The Rocky Mountain Social Science Journal*, 10 (January 1973), 73–83.

9. See Blumer's most recent statement of Symbolic Interaction in Herbert Blumer, "Mead and Blumer: The Convergent Methodological Perspectives of Social Behaviorism and Symbolic Interactionism," *American Sociological Review*, 45 (June 1980), 410.

10. GEORGE H. MEAD. *Mind, Self, and Society from the Standpoint of a Social Behaviorist*, ed. Charles W. Morris (Chicago, Ill.: University of Chicago Press, 1934).

11. HAROLD GARFINKEL. *Studies in Ethnomethodology* (Englewood Cliffs, N.J.: Prentice-Hall, Inc., 1967), p. 10.

12. See Herbert Blumer, *Symbolic Interactionism: Perspective and Method* (Engelwood Cliffs, N.J.: Prentice-Hall, Inc., 1969), p. 43 and Garfinkel, *Studies in Ethnomethodology*, p. 4.

13. See Blumer, *Symbolic Interactionism*, pp. 43–44 and Herbert Spiegelberg, "The Essentials of the Phenomenological Method," in *The Phenomenological Movement: A Historical Introduction*, 2nd ed. (The Hague: Martinier Nyhoff, 1965), II, 655–70.

14. HOWARD BECKER. "Becoming a Marihuana User," *The American Journal of Sociology*, 59, no. 3 (November 1953), 235–42.

15. DON H. ZIMMERMAN and D. LAWRENCE WIEDER. "Ethnomethodology and the Problem of Order: Comment on Denzin," in *Understanding Everyday Life*, Douglas, pp. 293–94.

16. GARFINKEL. *Studies in Ethnomethodology*, p. 38.

17. The term "Hawthorne effect" is taken from the Western Electric Studies conducted in Chicago. During this research, it was discovered that the researcher's presence significantly altered the behavior of his subjects.

18. GEORGE KIRKHAM. *Signal Zero* (Philadelphia, Pa.: Lippincott, 1976) is an example of what happens when a social scientist becomes too involved in the social life of the group he is observing.

19. HANS PETER DREITZEL. ed., *Recent Sociology* (New York: The Macmillan Company, 1970), II, xvii.

20. EUGENE DOLESCHAL. "Crime—Some Popular Beliefs," *Crime and Delinquency* (January 1979), 1–8.

chapter eight

Attorneys: Worthy Opponents or Cooperating Colleagues

Rules About Rules

The last seven chapters have discussed the making of patterns. The particular patterns evolved by various criminal justice actors are what people experience as law. Therefore, law is a doing. As has been discussed, it is not a mechanical, static set of principles automatically applied. Rather, it is people policing, lawyering, legislating, judging, negotiating, sentencing, administering, and so forth. Law is action and, more specifically, it is action taken at a particular time, by a particular individual, to make sense out of a particular set of circumstances, to meet a variety of ends. To this point, we have focused largely on "the doing of policing" to illustrate law as process. In this chapter, we will look at another group of individuals which patterns what we know as criminal justice, the attorneys, and will examine the doing of law by these actors. Our focus, then, is not on lawyers as such, but, from a more action-oriented perspective, on "lawyering." Consider the "ing" at the end of the word a suffix that means "rule-invoking behavior." The focus on lawyering raises the question, "What are the rules invoked by criminal lawyers to construct a logical, coherent pattern for their activity?" Literally, attorneys invoke rules for how to apply the statutory articulations known as law. In other words, there are rules about the rules. A prosecuting attorney articulates certain of these rules as he explains what factors affect his decisions regarding case dispositions. Some of the rules underscore the importance of other legal actors in helping shape a prosecutor's account of an event.

> —Who the judge is, is a very important factor . . . you even know ahead of time whether it's worth arguing. There are certain judges you know that will never undercut a state's recommendation. Other judges, you know always will.

> —Who the defense attorney is. If you go to trial, how good is he? Then there are a lot of [defense] lawyers who, subconsciously, are considered more reasonable . . . But some other guy comes in who still may be a very good lawyer, and maybe you wouldn't want to go to the mat with him, who is just a complete jerk. Subconsciously you recommend those a little higher. There is almost a sense of challenge—I want to get you in the court.

Of course juries, too, have to be taken into consideration when applying law to a particular set of circumstances.

> My superior tries to evaluate a case in terms of what reasonably could be expected to be gotten from a jury.

> Our county has relatively conservative jurors. Our juries are white, middle-aged, sometimes young, but a prosecutor's dream. That's why if you have a young white kid they're gonna go easier than if you have a young black kid. The former has a lot less jury appeal. It may be racist but it's a fact.

The account of what juries will and will not do, influences the perceived amount of legal proof necessary for a conviction.

> Property crimes to our juries, on the one hand, outrage them. That's our biggest type of crime here. But on the other hand, if you do get a sympathetic defendant, they are reluctant to hit him too badly and they will spend a lot more time arguing over the fine points of the case because they feel at the same time it's no big deal if we let him go on this. With our juries, on a sloppy case you are more likely to get a conviction if it's a rape, or a robbery, or a murder, than if it's a burglary or stealing an automobile. They hold you to much higher

standards then. Or if I'm looking and it's marijuana, say the sale of marijuana as opposed to the sale of heroin or almost any other drug, you really want to make sure it's a lot tighter. On a sale of marijuana case we're much more likely not to issue the warrant because the police have screwed up or left something out of the case. Because that's the kind of case that jurors get so particular about. See that's always in the back of your mind.

A person's past record together with the strength of the current case influences the accounting practices of the prosecutor.

You start with the evidence. How strong is the case. Then you look at the defendant's background. One big thing is whether or not he has priors, not only because that will determine who does the sentencing, the judge or the jury, but it's going to affect whether or not he testifies. If he testifies, his prior convictions are going to come out. If you try a guy for assault and he's got three assault priors, that'll kill him. At the same time, this is one other thing about the kind of juries we get, on the whole it's almost impossible for a defendant to get acquitted if he doesn't take the stand. In certain cases it's almost better for him to get up and admit his priors like when he says, "In those other cases I did those but in this case I didn't and that's why I went to trial." And that can be very effective for a jury to hear. So you look at all that.

Notice that although the prosecutor is talking about the importance of evidence and a person's past record, such things are considered in light of a mythical jury's supposed response to the "fact." The jury is mythical in the sense that it is a construct based on experience and the rules for creating meaning learned from being around the courthouse.

You learn about this by osmosis. Nobody ever comes in and sits down and says you can't win this, you can't do that.

You learn from doing it yourself and listening to other people talking about their experiences.

If you're around the courthouse long enough, you see what juries do, you see what judges do, you see what cases have what appeal and how strong your evidence is and you just pick all that up through experience.

Again, it is clear that the phrase "strong evidence" does not denote a simple empirical reality. The evidence is only as strong as a jury, or more accurately, the constructed image of a jury, says it is. As we have seen, juries make such judgments based on a host of extra-legal factors, the combination of which helps the prosecutor form rules for putting together the meaning of an event. A final set of rules deals with when to go to trial and when to take a plea.

> Next, is the jury gonna sentence him or the judge. If the jury is gonna sentence him, then I'm gonna look more at the defendant. I'm gonna look at the nature of the case which might be solid for conviction but it may not be a serious case. If I got a $5 till tap, the jury is not gonna send the guy away for a long time on a $5 till tap. Even if he's got a bunch of priors. [Then there are cases when] the evidence is weak. Even if he's convicted he's not going to get a lot of time. It's a car theft. His arrest record shows that he is definitely in that criminal involvement but he's never been convicted before. This time, let's take a quick plea. Get a felony conviction. Let him have credit for jail time. He's back on the street, but at least next time, because of his priors, he'll get into judge sentencing and he'll get hammered.

Reviewing these remarks and some of the previous statements by the prosecutor, it appears that there are four rules governing the decision to go to trial or accept a plea. These are:

> —You take a plea when it is a weak case with no jury appeal.
> —You go to trial if it is a weak case but has strong jury appeal.
> —You take a plea when you have a strong case with no jury appeal.
> —You take a plea as a means of establishing priors, so the next time the individual will be sentenced by a judge.

The assistant district attorney makes a final comment that emphasizes the importance of some of these rules for structuring an account of a given criminal event.

> Cases go more smoothly with public defenders than with private lawyers. But there is a handful of private attorneys who do mostly criminal work. They understand the system and know what a case is worth.

This last comment or rule seems to indicate that not everybody accepts these procedures for building meaning. Interestingly enough, however, those attorneys who do a lot of criminal work, whether they are public defenders or private lawyers, understand

and accept the rules, and this allows for a smooth-functioning system or pattern of activity. Of course, private attorneys and public defenders each have their own sets of rules germane to the specific problems they encounter as they go about lawyering.

A number of authors have noted that private defense attorneys, because they are in business, have to be concerned with collecting their fee.[1] There are, therefore, rules relating to this necessity. For example, a lawyers' manual suggests that the private attorney not go to visit a client in jail unless a suitable fee arrangement has been made with the defendant or unless a relative can be contacted who will provide a retainer. Such precautions can, however, be waived if the individual is an old client.[2] Abraham S. Blumberg has argued that the need to collect a fee even affects the swiftness with which a case will be brought to a conclusion.[3] By asking for delays in court proceedings, the defense lawyer wields a powerful tool to insure that his efforts are appropriately compensated, since relatives and the individual being represented are reluctant to have the accused in jail for longer than is necessary. The rule is, "Do not proceed with a case until you have been compensated for the work you have done or will do. Once the guy gets off, there is little you can do to collect."

There are also rules for convincing an individual that the attorney deserves his fee. Lawyers sometimes have difficulty convincing a client that he really benefited from professional legal assistance. After all, the accused may be found guilty or convinced to plead guilty by his attorney. If the client ends up in jail or is currently in jail awaiting trial, it might be difficult to persuade him that he is getting his money's worth. The same lawyers' handbook suggests that attorneys explain to their clients exactly what will take place as their cases sojourn through the ways of justice. If this is done at each stage of the proceedings, the defense lawyer is able to justify his retainer and convince the individual that everything is being done on his behalf.[4]

Public defenders, while not faced with the burden of fee collection, do have the burden of meeting the constitutionally and judicially mandated responsibility of doing their best for their client. As with other criminal justice roles, however, there are a variety of obligations and responsibilities, besides the formal, publicly recognized one, that compete for primacy when structuring a meaningful social world.

The public defender is a government employee, not an independent knight who can give his or her all to one case. There are many cases that must be processed. Further, the public defender finds his or her position a dilemma-filled one. He or she is a middle-class lawyer who deals mostly with lower-class losers who often are guilty. Granted, in some cases it is not all that clear exactly what the clients are guilty of, but in others it is uncomfortably clear what the clients have done. In any event, it is hard for someone with eight or so years of higher education and middle-class dreams and values to either relate to those who are guilty of simply being poor and unlucky or to those who are guilty of being burglars, rapists, and so on. A public defender, then, faces a variety of problems in relationship to his or her clients. He or she may find it hard to identify with their impoverished state. Further, it will be hard for the defender to identify with the actions of certain of the clients, regardless of what circumstances resulted in a particular crime. Somehow, bragging about getting a burglar or a rapist set free does not fit in with the imagery of the knight in shining armor protecting the poor and downtrodden. Finally, a public defender will discover that his clients do not particularly like or trust him. The phrase, "Shit man, I didn't have no attorney, I had a public defender," sums up the feeling of many of the individuals served by that office. Add to these problems the further difficulty of low prestige among fellow attorneys, and the dilemmas of the position become even more apparent. In most jurisdictions, the routine handling of criminal cases is a prosecutor-dominated process, since it is that office that does the initial screening and has the greater investigatory resources to build its cases. As one public defender noted, "Most cases we get are pretty hopeless—really not much chance of an acquittal."[5]

Given this, many public defenders become primarily educators to, rather than advocates for, their clients. They inform the client of the options and attempt to convince him or her that within the unique social world of the courthouse, the individual is getting the best deal possible.

Research by Lynn M. Mather describes some of the methods public defenders use to both assess their client's chances and structure their own decisions on how to handle a case.[6] The public defenders in this study appeared in part to be guided by the following rules:

—You take a plea when there is a serious charge, but the prosecutor is willing to consider a lesser degree of criminal involvement than originally assessed.

—You take a plea when the charge will not result in a heavy sentence, and the prosecutor has a strong legal case.

—You go to trial when the charge will not result in a heavy sentence and there is reasonable doubt that the defendant committed any crime.

—You go to trial when the case is serious and the prosecutor has strong evidence, since the defendant has little to lose and much to gain.

The most difficult decision the public defender faced was in those cases where there was a serious charge but a reasonable doubt that the defendant was in any way involved in the act. Going to trial was a high risk-high gain venture due to the vagaries of juries. Bargaining for a lesser charge appeared to be the preferred strategy, but public defenders would go to trial on such cases if either the prosecutor or the client was unwilling to deal. Fortunately, from the public defender's standpoint, such cases were infrequent. Most cases were judged to be legally strong, but with comparatively light sentences, involving either probation or a short jail term. Thus rule two was the most frequently invoked in the structuring of case accounts by public defenders.

The discussion above, together with evidence cited previously by Sudnow and others, suggests that from a defense attorney's standpoint, directly asking a client whether he is guilty or innocent is of little importance. Accounts presented on police reports and various other case documents provide the more "realistic" assessment of how a case will be perceived by those who will structure the final "legal" account of an event. Moreover, by avoiding a direct inquiry as to a client's guilt or innocence, the defense attorney can also avoid the ethical dilemma of the client who insists on testifying under oath to his innocence after having admitted the deed to his lawyer. By not asking the client, the attorney can put the individual on the stand without suborning perjury.

The process of justice is guided by a series of hidden rules about how the formal, public, legal statutes should be applied. To illustrate the importance of some of the hidden rules for doing justice, we will return to the case of Arthur. The circumstances will be altered slightly so that Art gets a chance to experience other than police accounts of his activity. Arthur has now been arrested for possessing a significant quantity of marijuana. How significant will be determined by the accounts of the various legal practitioners who will process Arthur's case.

I Am Arthur's Case

Arthur's case, as distinct from Arthur himself, is a collection of pieces of paper that proceed from one part of the system to another, triggering various segments of the criminal justice process into action. To fully appreciate the importance of these pieces of paper, you might think of this section in terms of the subtitle, "I Am Arthur's Case," a concept in line with the anthropomorphic treatment given certain parts of the body in popular magazine articles with such titles as "I Am Arthur's Liver," "I Am Arthur's Lungs," and so forth. In this instance, what happens to the pieces of paper called Arthur's Case is as important to him as what transpires in various parts of his body. The remainder of his life may well be shaped by the paper processing about to take place.

Arthur's case, in its infant stage, consists of the police report of the incident and an arrest slip indicating the specifics of Arthur's physical description, the charge he is being held on, and a prisoner number. These pieces of paper must be taken by the arresting officer to the District Attorney's office, where they will be reviewed by an assistant district attorney assigned to that function. In this capacity, the attorney's job is one of initial screening, weeding out those cases which, in his judgment, are either too weak to pursue or too petty to waste time on. If, in the judgment of this individual, the case has some merit, he will take the pieces of paper, add to them, and help move Arthur's case to the next stage. The next stage is the issuance of a warrant for Arthur's arrest. The attorney who applies for a warrant after he or she initially reviews the charges brought by the police is called the warrant officer.

Before we follow Arthur's case further, one note of explanation may be in order. Arthur may be held only a limited time by the police acting on their own authority. The actual time Arthur may be held on police authority varies from jurisdiction to jurisdiction, but is generally between twenty and forty-eight hours. To hold somebody beyond the time set by state legislature (or, if none is set, beyond a "reasonable time"), a judicial officer must issue an arrest warrant, which certifies that there is probable cause that the individual being confined committed a crime. This procedure is mandated by Fourth Amendment guarantees against unreasonable searches and seizures.

Procedurally, this amendment is carried out by the warrant officer's taking Arthur's case to a judge or magistrate, who will be requested to issue a warrant, based on a complaint from the police, to hold Arthur until his first appearance before a judicial officer. This whole process is rather bureaucratic. If the warrant officer agrees with the police that a warrant should be issued, the actual issuance of the warrant by a judicial officer is almost automatic. In fact, in some jurisdictions, a clerk of the court may be assigned the function of judicial review and issuance, a practice that raises some knotty constitutional questions, since a clerk is not a judicial officer. At any rate, despite the almost automatic bureaucratic procedure at the point of the warrant officer's requesting a warrant, the document which allows for the longer detention of Arthur is a piece of paper that is very formal and official-sounding and which helps maintain the legal niceties of an unfolding play that will increasingly have little to do with Arthur's actual circumstances. In the jurisdiction Arthur is in, the arrest warrant now added to his growing case reads as follows:

> To Any Peace Officer of the State:
> You are hereby commanded to arrest the above named defendant on the above named charge, alleged to have been committed within the jurisdiction of this court and in violation of the laws of the state, and to bring him forthwith before this court to be here dealt with in accord-

ance with law, and you, the officer serving this warrant, shall forthwith make return hereof to this court.

From the sound of the official arrest warrant, it seems that Arthur is not yet in custody. In certain cases, of course, the actual sequence of events is first, the issuance of a warrant, and, second, the actual apprehension of the individual. But, in the majority of cases handled day-in and day-out by the criminal justice system, the person is detained first and later "arrested" under authority of a warrant. Arthur's case is typical. The peace officer (the policeperson who arrested Arthur in the first place) receives a copy of the duly authorized warrant back from the assistant district attorney who was the warrant officer for the case. Looking around the police lockup (at least figuratively), he finds that, lo and behold, Arthur is already in custody. It is at this point in the process that Arthur and his case once again converge because, as noted in the warrant, the peace officer must bring Arthur before the court. In many jurisdictions this is known as the "first appearance," and it must take place within a reasonable amount of time. Although "reasonable amount of time" is a relative term, in most jurisdictions it is operationalized to mean that Arthur must be brought before a magistrate within forty-eight to seventy-two hours of his initial detention.

The stage of initial appearance does not generally include the arresting officer, again despite the official wording of the warrant commanding the peace officer to bring the said individual before the court. The jurisdiction that Arthur is in is a large city, so the process is a highly structured group activity. All the people arrested within the forty-eight-hour time period are transported to the court en masse.

Arthur's first day in court, including his initial conference with his lawyer, will take approximately ten minutes. A magistrate, after briefly reviewing the folder containing Arthur's case to this point, will publicly read the charges as the defendant stands before him. Arthur will again be informed of his right to remain silent. Bail will be set. He will be asked if he can afford an attorney. If he cannot, a public defender will approach Arthur and, after the formalities, have a hurried conference with him introducing himself as Arthur's lawyer.

Arthur's fellow detainees will experience a similarly rapid assembly line during the initial appearance. A few will manage to arrange bail. Those who do not will be taken to the county jail to await the further processing of their cases. Arthur is one of these. Arthur and his case once again will go their separate ways.

The Lawyers Get Busy

Arthur's case has now grown and multiplied. Copies are kept at court, at the District Attorney's office, and at the Public Defender's office. There is also a copy with the Department of Welfare, the department in this jurisdiction responsible for maintaining the jail and its inmates.

The file will again be hurriedly reviewed by the public defender Arthur met at his initial appearance. The file will also be reviewed by an attorney in the District Attorney's office, in this jurisdiction an office that uses a zone system. The warrant officer has passed the file on to another individual, who will be responsible for handling the case through the arraignment hearing.

Within a day or two of his initial appearance, Arthur will once again meet with his public defender. The public defender will at this time inform Arthur of the various options open to him. He will also attempt to get Arthur's account of the events leading up to his arrest. These "facts" combined with the "facts" in the police report will enable the public defender to construct his own account of what the case is worth and what he can reasonably be expected to do for Arthur.

> Public Defender: I like for all my clients to know what to expect, so I want to explain to you the various steps your case will proceed through. Then I want to get some idea of what happened from your perspective. All right, you've had your initial appearance. That's where you hear the formal charges against you. You also got bail set this morning. By the way, I don't suppose there is any chance that you'll make bail.

Arthur shakes his head no and asks about personal recognizance.

Public Defender: Well, let me ask you a few questions. Do you own a home?

Arthur: No.

Public Defender: Do you have a steady job, where you've been employed for six or more months?

Arthur: No.

Public Defender: Have you been a resident of this state for at least five years?

Arthur: No.

Public Defender: Have you got any prior arrests for drug-related offenses?

Arthur: Yes.

Public Defender: Well, you see, I don't think they'd consider you such a good candidate for release on your own recognizance. You are not what they'd consider over in the pretrial release center your more conventional citizen. Besides, the police and the District Attorney charged you not only with possession, but with possession with intent to sell.

Arthur: There wasn't hardly enough in there for myself.

Public Defender: Well, let me get your side of it in a minute. First, I want to tell you the procedure. Probably in the next week or two you'll have your preliminary hearing. The judge will review your case and decide whether or not the police had probable cause to arrest you in the first place. A couple of things can happen here. In a misdemeanor case, you can plead guilty, and that would be the end of it. The judge would then set sentence. Or, the judge can decide that the police shouldn't have arrested you in the first place, and kick the case out. If he did that, you'd be free to go. But, at this point, you are charged with a felony. So, if he finds that the police did make a good arrest, and there is probable cause that you did the deeds in question, he'll bind the case over for further proceedings. All that means is, it will move to the court that has jurisdiction in felony matters. The case moves out of magistrate court, and moves into circuit court. The District Attorney will file an Information, which simply means he'll give formal notice to the circuit court of the charges against you. The Information is put together on the basis of the police report and any further investigation done by the police and the District Attorney's office.

Of course, if the D.A. wanted to, he could bring the whole matter before the Grand Jury. He'd present all the facts to the Grand Jury.

They are just twelve citizens who get called to serve in the capacity of Grand Jurors for a year. They meet mostly at night, so it does not interfere too much with their jobs. But the District Attorney uses this infrequently. Only for cases that he sees as "hot potatoes," if you know what I mean. You know, if he suspected a popular politician or somebody like that of doing something untoward, he'd be better off to let the Grand Jury bring in what they call a true bill, which is just a legal term for any indictment that issues from a Grand Jury. By using the Grand Jury in a case like that, he takes some of the heat off himself. Of course, the D.A. really controls the Grand Jury. If he calls somebody before the Grand Jury to testify, they don't get to have their lawyer present in the room. So the Grand Jury is a pretty powerful weapon in the hands of a smart D.A. Pretty open to abuse also. But like I say, they only use the Grand Jury in a politically sensitive case or in a really big case. They won't use it in a case like this. It would be like using a cannon to kill a fly. Well, never mind about the Grand Jury, where was I?

Oh yeah, so after the preliminary hearing, if you're bound over to circuit court, the D.A. will file an Information with the court, literally informing them what you're charged with.

The next step is the arraignment. This will be your first appearance in the circuit court. You can enter your plea at this point. If the plea is "not guilty," you can tell them whether you want a jury trial or a trial by judge. The judge will also once again review probable cause, and see if there is enough evidence to hold you for a full-blown trial. If the case isn't dismissed, and you don't plead guilty, we will make a pretrial motion about what evidence should be admitted for use in the trial and so on, and then the trial. If you get to trial, figure about a day, maybe two of actual trial time.

Now let me just list the steps for you, so you have a clear idea about what's going on.

First, you've had your initial appearance.

Second, in a week or so there will be a preliminary hearing where the charges will be reviewed and the judge will decide whether there is probable cause to proceed.

Third, if the judge decides there is probable cause, the District Attorney will file an Information with the circuit court, and the proceedings will move from the magistrate court to the circuit court.

The fourth step is the arraignment. That would be about four or five weeks from now. At that time, the judge will once again review your case, weigh probable cause, and decide whether to proceed. You enter a plea at this time, and if you plead not guilty, decide whether you want a jury trial or a trial by the judge. Then your court date will be set. Generally, you can get on the docket within three to six months.

Arthur: What about the Grand Jury stuff?

Public Defender: Don't worry about that. I shouldn't have even mentioned that. But just so you'll know, the Grand Jury would be instead of the preliminary hearing. And instead of the D.A. filing an Information with the circuit court, the Grand Jury would issue a true bill. In the case of a Grand Jury that would be the legal instrument used to bind you over for arraignment in the circuit court. The steps would be the same after that.

Arthur: How long before my trial?

Public Defender: Oh, if it got to go to trial, probably eight months to a year from now. They're a little backed up.

Arthur: Shit.

Public Defender: Well, there are a few questions I'd like to ask you. When the cop pulled you over, was it raining or dark or anything like that?

Arthur: No, it was about eleven o'clock in the morning. It was a pretty nice day out as I remember it. 'Course, I was a little high.

Public Defender: When you saw the cop get out of the car, did you make any sudden move?

Arthur: No way. Man, you don't think I'd drive around with the stuff sitting out on my front seat in plain view, do you? Course, I might have patted that pile of stuff I had the junk hidden under, just to be sure it was nice and safe.

Public Defender: You didn't go to reach under it?

Arthur: Nope, I just kind of patted it, you know.

Public Defender: Well, O.K., I'll get back to you in a few days, let you know what's going on.

As Arthur hears about the various steps necessary to fully process his case, a duplicate file is being reviewed by people in the District Attorney's office. A governing principle of the District Attorney's office for determining the effort put into a case is what might be called the "probable win test." Attorneys in this office want to assess the probability of winning a case and expend their effort accordingly. Review the rules enunciated by the prosecuting attorney at the beginning of this chapter. Note that many of them specify how to assess the chances of winning. But, there are considerations other than winning. The District Attorney must take into account the desires of the Police Department in particular cases and, at the same time, take into consideration the political implication of either pursuing or not pursuing the matter. The predilections of the judges are also an important factor in determining the future steps to be taken in a particular case. All of these factors will become clearer as the case proceeds to the stage of the preliminary hearing.

The preliminary hearing serves a number of functions. First and foremost, it is a screening device, designed to insure that only the most important cases get to the trial stage. Second, it acts as a check to insure that the officials meet the appropriate standards of evidence in presenting a case. As the case proceeds from the time of arrest to the time of the trial, the standards for evidence become more exacting. What is considered probable cause for a police officer who has to make a decision in a brief period of time may not be considered probable cause when a case is reviewed at the various stages of the judicial process. Thus, the quality of evidence and probable cause have to be well established for the case to proceed from the preliminary hearing to the arraignment. Likewise, for the case to proceed from arraignment to trial also requires an exact standard of probable cause and evidence. In practice, this means that before a case reaches trial it has a great likelihood of being handled at a lower level of the judicial process. Only a small percentage of all the cases filed ever reach the trial stage. Thus, it is not surprising to find that most cases that come to trial result in the person's being found guilty. Weak cases are generally filtered out before they reach that stage, or the person pleads guilty to a lesser charge. If the case gets to trial, it generally means that the state has fairly strong evidence to convince either a judge or a jury that the person being tried is, in fact, guilty. A third function of the preliminary hearing is to give the defense attorney a chance to ascertain the strength of the case presented by the state against his client. While in theory, this particular function of disclosure is central to the concept of a preliminary hearing, in practice the preliminary hearing provides a very poor stage for reviewing the state's case. This is because, in general, the state will only present the minimum amount of evidence necessary to convince a lower court magistrate that the case should be allowed to proceed to the next step. Obviously, the prosecutor is not going to show the defense all his cards unless it is absolutely necessary.

The preliminary hearing took less than fifteen minutes. An assistant district attorney called the police officers to the stand, asked them to reiterate the circumstances of the arrest, and then requested that Arthur Johnson be held for arraignment. The public defender did not cross-examine the officer witnesses but simply moved for a dismissal on the grounds that evidence obtained was sullied and could not be introduced at trial. The magistrate waived aside the objection to the evidence and asked the defense to save his arguments for the arraignment. The public defender responded that Arthur Johnson was going to plead "not guilty" at that time. With that, the magistrate bound Arthur over for arraignment. The public defender had another case pending, so after the proceedings he hurriedly told Arthur he would try to see him that afternoon. Before he went off, however, he managed a few words with the assistant prosecutor:

> Public Defender: This case looks like simple possession, not possession with intent to sell.

> Assistant Prosecutor: Well, he was caught with enough marijuana so that intent to sell is presumed by the statute. And those officers were pretty good witnesses, and the Police Department is starting to push on some of these narcotics cases.

> Public Defender: Yeah, I know. But that search and seizure is a little iffy, and you know a jury is going to look real close at that in this kind of case.

> Assistant Prosecutor: Well, see what your guy is willing to take and let me know.

That afternoon, the public defender talked to his client.

> Public Defender: Listen, those guys got a pretty good case. Those cops were very professional on the stand, and a judge or jury is likely to believe them. Now, I know you said you just patted a pile of clothes, but they sure make it sound like you were going for a weapon. Let's

see. The arraignment is in three weeks. If you go to trial, like I told you, that will be three to five months. Then if they find you guilty, with your record they might put you away for a while. Maybe I can get you a deal.

Arthur: What kind of deal?

Public Defender: Well, if you plead guilty to simple possession, we might be able to get the D.A. to handle it as a third-class felony rather than a first-class felony. Maybe even get it down to some kind of a misdemeanor. So maybe you'll get sentenced to a couple of years probation plus time already served. Hell, you could be out on the streets in three or four weeks, rather than facing ten years. Even if you get two or three years, they'll give you credit for time already served while awaiting your day in court; plus good time you should be out at the most in a year and a half.

Arthur: Still, what kind of deal is that?

Public Defender: Listen, don't give me that. I'm doing what I can for you. If you want, I'll take it to trial. But that means you'll sit in here for at least three more months before it gets on the docket. Then a two-day trial. Then if they find you guilty, another couple of weeks before you get sentenced. And when you get to that point, you can expect them to throw the book at you, since you got a prior record and you wasted everybody's time going through the motions. You're good for maybe ten years on this. Take your pick. It's your roll of the dice. But I'm telling you justice delayed is justice denied. By the time you get to trial, you'll have been locked up for pretty near four months or more with a good chance of them throwing away the key if you lose. I think you should take the best deal I can get for you.

Arthur: Okay, man, let's see what they offer.

Although it may not be clear in the foregoing scenario, it is safe to assume that all of the people representing officialdom (the prosecuting attorney, the defense attorney, and later on, the judges and the probation officers) have all worked together before. Each probably has a fair idea of what the other actors will and will not accept as a definition of the situation in this particular circumstance. As noted previously, these understandings result in what some authors have called the courthouse subculture. The subculture of the courthouse is simply the agreed-upon definitions, norms, and values that any work group arrives at from spending time, day-in and day-out, handling a work product. In the courthouse, the work product is literally "the case." And all the actors have an idea of how individual cases will be viewed by the various other actors on the judicial stage. It is these understandings that allow attorneys to predict what various judges will do in particular instances and allow attorneys to also predict the reactions of each other to particular strategies and moves in the game. Put another way, all participants generally agree on what rules govern the construction of reality. This agreement significantly circumscribes the adversarial relationship existing between the prosecuting attorney and the defense attorney. If each were to act as out-and-out adversaries (that is, if each were to invoke different rules for the construction of reality), too much time and energy would be wasted and the efficient handling of cases impaired. Like the police, the attorneys, particularly those employed by public agencies, must be able to show their superiors that they are competent craftsmen. In order to do this, a case must be handled efficiently. Thus, efficiency, the probability of winning measured against the cost both in time and money of pursuing a matter to the fullest, becomes the hallmark of a successful bureaucrat. Within this type of framework, the interests of the individual client, whether the accused or the state, is only one factor among many which needs to be considered. Making it in the bureaucracy requires knowing when to cooperate. Therefore, much of the initial contact between prosecutors and defenders appears to be a matter of posturing. Each attempts to ascertain what the other will settle for and what the other will consider unreasonable. Actually, the process is one of making sure that "typical" rules for social world construction will be invoked in a particular case. As noted previously, in most instances this mutual understanding of how the world is to be put together allows for relatively quick agreement on appropriate case disposition, limiting the need for trials. But, as the scenario showed, such understandings are themselves subject to influences outside the control of the courthouse subculture. Thus, the feelings of the police or, for that matter, citizens expressed through their political representatives, can influence how a particular case will be handled (that is, what rules will be invoked for structuring the meaning of the case). This is true most especially in those cases where there is little agreement on the nature and the extent of the problem.

A narcotics case such as Arthur's is a good illustration of the point. On the one hand, such cases often present to prosecutors special difficulties because of probable cause requirements and search-and-seizure guidelines. Cases of this type often require the cooperation of informants or the police officer's catching the individual in the act. It is unlikely that drug users will report themselves. Therefore, the behavior is hidden, and special police methods are used to uncover violations. However, we have seen in previous chapters that sometimes such methods violate standards of procedural law. The courts have shown an awareness of this tendency. Therefore, a number of decisions, most notably *Mapp vs. Ohio,* have developed what is known as the exclusionary rule. In brief, evidence obtained illegally by police cannot be used by the government in the course of the trial and is suppressed or excluded from consideration. Before a trial, there is generally a series of evidentiary hearings to determine what evidence will be allowed to be considered by the court or the jury. Questionable evidence has a good chance of being excluded, and, in some cases (Arthur's is probably one of them), the exclusion of evidence means the state is left without any evidence at all. It is clear, then, that narcotics cases can sometimes present special problems to prosecutors. On the other hand, such cases are generally received favorably by jurors. The juror's image of the narcotics pusher and narcotics user (an example of an unconventional person being subject to law) is extremely negative. Therefore, some studies have found that in narcotics cases, if the prosecution can survive the preliminary hearings and the evidentiary hearings, the case stands a very good chance of being won before a jury. This is true even if the evidence is fairly weak.[7] The prosecutor at the beginning of the chapter noted the same point, except that, in his experience, jurors tended to exclude marijuana from the category of dangerous drugs. But in "hard" drug cases, the evidence could be "sloppy" and the case would still have jury appeal.

Given the nature of the case at hand, it appears that both the prosecutor and the defense will decide to settle this case with a plea. From the prosecutor's standpoint this is the kind of case that a jury would hold to an exacting standard of evidence. From the point of view of the defense a lesser plea gives the defendant the most gain with the least risk. As long as the prosecutor agrees to charging a lesser degree of criminal involvement, it is clearly in the client's best interest to waive a trial.

Arthur's arraignment will be a cut-and-dried affair.

References

1. See for example Abraham S. Blumberg, "Lawyers with Convictions," in *The Scales of Justice,* ed. Abraham S. Blumberg (Transaction, Inc., 1970), pp. 51–67, and Paul B. Wise, *Criminal Lawyers* (Beverly Hills, Ca.: Sage Publications, Inc., 1978), particularly Chapter Four.
2. ROBERT C. WELCH. "Investigating and Marshalling the Facts Other Than Formal Discovery," in *Missouri Criminal Practice* (Jefferson City, Mo.: The Missouri Bar, 1978), I, 4.4.
3. BLUMBERG. "Lawyers with Convictions," p. 55.
4. WELCH. "Investigating and Marshalling the Facts," p. 4.5.
5. LYNN M. MATHER. "Some Determinants of the Method of Case Disposition: Decision-Making by Public Defenders in Los Angeles," in *Law and Society Review,* Vol. 8, (1975), pp. 187–216.
6. *Ibid.*
7. See for example John Kaplan, "How It Works in a Federal Prosecutor's Office," in *Criminal Justice: Introductory Cases and Materials,* 2nd ed. ed. John Kaplan (Mineola, N.Y.: The Foundation Press, Inc., 1978), pp. 239–47. This excerpt also provides an example of a set rule invoked by federal prosecutors when deciding whether to pursue a case.

chapter nine

The Judge and His Helpers

The Ritual of Public Justice

At precisely ten o'clock A.M., Judge Julius Sweeney entered his court-room to the sound of the bailif's cry, "All rise." Arthur, the public defender, and the assistant prosecutor sat at tables facing the raised bench and highbacked chair where Judge Sweeney seated himself. Arthur and his lawyer were on Judge Sweeney's right, the pros-ecutor on his left. A lectern with a microphone attached to it was in the center between the two tables for opposing counsel. The two attorneys and the judge each had copies of Arthur's case before them. At this point in the proceedings, the processing of Arthur's case became part of a ritual that portrayed to the few spectators in the court "the doing of justice." The judge banged his gavel, the attorneys recited their lines, Arthur mumbled the appropriate re-sponses, and in less than ten minutes the case had been further processed and, at the same time, further separated from the person whose name it bore. After the first bang of the gavel, the ritual began with the prosecutor approaching the lectern and saying, "Your Honor, with the leave of the court, the people move that the Infor-mation in this case be deemed amended by charging the defendant with simple possession of a controlled substance, Twelve-dash-Twenty-Two-dash-Three-O-Two, a misdemeanor."

The public defender then approached the lectern and stated, "Your Honor, the defendant consents to the amendment as proffered by the Assistant District Attorney and hereby enters a plea of guilty to this charge, the misdemeanor offense of simple possession of a controlled substance. Further, Your Honor, it is my understanding that the Assistant District Attorney will move to withdraw all the other charges at the time the sentence is imposed on this charge."

Judge Sweeney turned to the prosecutor and asked, "The District Attorney agrees to this procedure?"

She replied, "That is correct, Your Honor."

The judge then turned directly to Arthur, "Mr. Johnson, do you understand what was just said?" Arthur mumbled that he did. Judge Sweeney continued, "Have you been given a copy of the information and discussed the charges contained in it with your lawyer?" Arthur indicated that he had. Again, the judge addressed him, "Do you understand that you are now charged with simple possession of marijuana, a controlled substance?" Arthur responded that he did understand the charge.

"The Fifth Amendment to the Constitution provides you with the privilege against compulsory self-incrimination. You may remain silent at all times, and your silence may not be commented upon or used against you. Do you understand that?" Arthur responded, "Yes, sir."

"Do you understand that under the Sixth Amendment you are also entitled to confront your accusers, to require that they testify in open court at a public trial and to cross-examine the witnesses against you, and to call witnesses on your own behalf by the order of this court?" There was another mumbled, "Yes, sir," from Arthur.

"Finally, do you understand that by your plea of guilty you are giving up all of these rights and subjecting yourself to sentence and punishment without a trial?" Again a mumbled, "Yes."

"Were any threats, promises, or inducements made to cause you to offer this plea?" Here there was a slight pause on Arthur's part, before he responded, "No, sir."

Finally, Judge Sweeney concluded, "O.K. I'll accept the plea, but will require a presentence investigation. Sentencing is set for two weeks from today. The defendant is remanded to jail pending sentencing. Next case."

The ritual that constituted Arthur's arraignment served a variety of purposes. The questions directed to Arthur by Judge Sweeney and Arthur's mumbled responses met the constitutional requirement that judges ascertain whether a plea is voluntary. Of course, voluntary is in the eye of the beholder. Some might argue that the threat of increased punishment for going to trial and being found guilty reduces the voluntariness of any plea bargaining arrangement. The courts, however, have held that increased penalties associated with going to trial do not really constitute coercion, in part because there is always a chance that a person could be set free.[1] If an individual chooses to roll the dice and go to trial, he or she must accept the consequences of the gamble, win or lose. Thus, a voluntary plea is defined as one in which the ritual of voluntariness, that is, *pro forma* judicial questions and equally *pro forma* answers by defendants, has been followed.

Besides meeting the legal requirement of determining voluntariness, the ritual also allows for a portrayal of justice, a making visible of that elusive quality the system is supposedly enhancing. At its best, this function of ritual is educative. The social system represents to itself its goals and its ideals and, in the process, recommits and reconfirms its image of itself as good, decent, and so forth. In short, the ritual of the court is a minicivic lesson, portraying to all who see it the type of society we think of ourselves as being. If you have ever seen a grammar school class on a field trip to a courtroom to observe the process of justice, you can gain a sense of the educative function of such a proceeding. After such encounters with the rituals of justice, the young students often express a very deep commitment to the process of government and a desire to avoid legal infractions which go against the ideals of our society. After such encounters, the commitment to law is at a peak. Unfortunately, the ritual of justice often only works in such a way for the occasional, naïve spectator. For those who are part of the process, either as legal functionaries or as defendants, the ritual indexes either bureaucratic efficiency or another example of the system's discriminating against those it considers losers. Thus, many people found guilty of crimes deny their culpability, in part because the ritual has little to do with their actual circumstances. As indicated, the case and the individual are two separate entities. The ritual most often deals with the case and ignores the individual.

Finally, the ritual serves a function for the professionals involved in the process. In those cases where a private attorney is retained to defend an individual, the ritual arraignment allows counsel to publicly plea for mercy for his client (even if a deal has been previously worked out), thereby showing those who pay his bill that he is, in fact, worth the fee being charged. At the same time, prosecutors get a chance to publicly show that they are convicting those guilty of crimes. It appears, then, that many people are served by the ritual that took place during Arthur's arraignment. Arthur, however, may not be one of them. What services and/or benefits Arthur will receive are the questions to be pondered by the social service component of the criminal justice process.

Doing Probation and Parole Work

Arthur's case temporarily moves out of the courthouse and on to a new set of case processors. In the state where Arthur lives, the Probation and Parole Department is administratively independent of the courthouse. It is part of the State Department of Social Services. Probation/parole officers (p.o.'s) are assigned by supervisors of their agency to all felony courts and certain misdemeanor courts throughout the state. Each officer with a caseload will supervise both probationers and parolees. Unlike some states, p.o.'s in Arthur's state work within and are responsible to their own bureaucratic chain of command. They are not hired by, nor are they responsible to, judges of a particular court.

The first step in case processing within this new bureaucracy is the presentence investigation. Arthur's case ends up on the desk of a presentence writer. Presentence writers, like police officers, have rules for structuring their written accounts. A key rule concerns the decision on how deeply the client's background should be investigated. A probation officer talks about this decision:

> He [the p.o.] will interview the client, both at the office and at home.
> He may or may not interview the family members, friends, or what we

call significant others, which may be anything from a former employer to his pastor to anybody who just seems important. A psychiatrist who treated him. Whomever it may be. Typically though, what happens is that it's just the client and some family members at the office and at the guy's home. Or jail.

If you have a client who—well, there are some cases that it looks very obvious that the person will make probation, should be on probation, there's really no question. It's a lesser offense generally. Like down in a rural county we get a lot of driving while intoxicated from the associate circuit court down there. Well, ninety-nine times out of a hundred that person is gonna make probation. So I think the officer is more inclined to put a case like that on the back burner and not spend a whole lot of time on it and just interview the client and get a record check on him and check out his past work history and pretty much leave it at that and figure, well, if he's got a number of DWI's let's put him in an alcohol education program or send him to AA or whatever. Let's not invest too much time. On the other hand, at the other end of the spectrum there's a much smaller group who have very serious kinds of crimes and in some of those cases that person is really—the judge may not even be seriously considering the person for probation but he's using our report more as an aid in sentencing. You know, you have a guy who's pled to an arson and a robbery and, you know, one or two other relatively serious felonies. Well he doesn't have any idea of putting him on probation but he thinks, well, I want to know some more about him. I want to know what kind of egg this is that I'm gonna be sending to the penitentiary. So I want to know am I gonna sentence him to five years or twenty-five years or fifty years. O.K. So that's what our report is for. And in those cases I think because of the seriousness of the charge I think the officer takes the case a lot more seriously and I think he's inclined to really delve into a case like that. Now there does come a point where the charge becomes so serious that we think— what the heck—it should be obvious to everybody that this guy's a—you know—oughta be gettin' about fifty or seventy-five years and I'm not gonna strain myself to find out a bunch of goodies about this when they're really not gonna be used. So then I guess the difficult decisions are those that fall somewhere in the middle. You know, the guy who's pled to, you know, he's previously had a burglary charge and he did a little time for that and now he's graduated to a robbery, you know. And the question is, how much are we gonna look into all this. I think a lot of—I'm really at a loss to give you any further insight into how that decision is made to go further. I think beyond that the individual case is gonna dictate a lot of what happens. If a guy is—oftentimes I think what happens is you get a client who's very open about what's been goin' on and gives you a lot of information to check out, you'll go ahead and pursue it because you see it as being a serious enough matter that you're gonna look into it further. You're gonna send letters to people. You're gonna go out and interview people. And so on and so forth. A lot of times I don't think some probationers and parolees are aware of it but there would probably be a lot less dirt drawn from them if they would simply keep quiet and not tell us anything.

In Arthur's case, the decision on who to interview would be a relatively easy one. Arthur pleaded guilty to a misdemeanor and was going to be put on probation. Therefore, Arthur would probably be the only one interviewed. The sentencing decision was already made. What was left to be done was to provide a rationale for it.

Probation/parole officers, like new attorneys, police recruits, and everyone else concerned with the doing of justice, have to learn rules for structuring meaning that will be relevant in their social world. The p.o. quoted above describes the learning process:

> . . . I think it's just an experiential thing. You see people sentenced enough that you finally, through osmosis or however the heck it is, you find out that this guy in this county who commits a burglary and is a first offender is not going to the penitentiary come hell or high water. That just doesn't happen. In the same way, if you plead to a multiple felony, you're not gonna make probation, no matter what—with maybe one or two unusual exceptions. One or two very liberal judges that we have in some counties. But it's, yeah, it's just an experiential thing. You find out after a while, you come to know what the judges see a case as being worth and you kind of tune into that.

Obviously, tuning into what the judge is likely to do in a case also provides a guideline for making recommendations in those cases where likely sentences are not so readily apparent. Nevertheless, in jurisdictions where the probation/parole staff operates with a fair amount of autonomy because it is not administratively tied to the courthouse, the judge's desires may not be the most important influence in the structuring of a presentence recommendation. A variety of personal world views, organizational pressures, and necessities of the moment influence the rules for making a particular recommendation:

> Again, I'm just speaking for our agency. I think it may be different elsewhere. I think the only tensions that may arise with our agency are

tensions from within, that a particular guy may have certain prejudices about a certain client and he may be aware that he has those prejudices and he goes ahead and adjusts for those and recommends probation where he thinks the guy really, you know, that sex pervert ought to be in the penitentiary but my supervisor doesn't see it that way and most of society feels that he needs treatment so I'll give him treatment. I think that happens, but for us, I think largely because of being an autonomous state agency, we're not really obligated to recommend anything in particular. We can recommend whatever the heck we want to recommend. And I think that happens most times.

P.o.'s, like everybody else, regardless of how much freedom and flexibility they have, tend to establish certain recognizable, predictable patterns. Judges then take such patterns into account when they consider a given recommendation.

—I think most presentence writers are fairly predictable. Just like the judge, they have a certain conception of what a particular case is worth and the kind of person they like to see on probation and, you know, if you were keeping stats, you would find that certain probation officers recommend that a person be sent to the penitentiary ten times more than other officers do. Which makes you wonder how much of a science all of this is—but what I was gonna say was, that officer that constantly recommends that people be sent to the penitentiary, it's my perception that the judges eventually attach a presentence writer's name with a particular outlook and discount that.

The language of social work, psychology, and other casework-oriented disciplines is sufficiently flexible to allow for the structuring of a report in a way that does not seriously violate either professional sensibilities or courthouse realities. Terms like "socially maladjusted," "inadequate personality development," "dysfunctional behavior," and a variety of other similar terms allow for a making over of the defendant/client into an image that would appear logical to a variety of world views. Such flexible images can then be used to justify a variety of case dispositions. A person who is "socially maladjusted" can be recommended for prison or probation with equally plausible justification. In the following account, notice that, despite the use of such concrete-sounding terms as "evidence" and "factual," there is considerable room for interpretation and negotiation when "facts" are part of a social history:

> As long as the presentence writer can support his recommendation with factual evidence, the supervisor will let him recommend anything he wants with that caveat that he has to have factual evidence to support it. You know, if you're recommending that a person be sent to the penitentiary, you have to be able to give me, as supervisor, some reason to believe that, yeah, he ought to be sent to the penitentiary. You know, he's got a lengthy prior record. He's got a history of drug addiction or alcohol addiction. You know, whatever the case may be. He's irresponsible in that he screwed up a probation before so what leads us to believe that he's gonna be successful on a second one. Any of those kinds of rationales, if you can give me those, I'll let you do what you want to do. I'll respect your professional decision and I won't go over your head and change it . . . in our agency that is a fairly accepted rule.

> [There is still] an extreme amount [of variability in individual recommendations]. For example, a person who's a drug addict . . . my rationale for placing him on probation is that he has a drug problem and that needs treatment and, on the other hand, this other guy's rationale for sending him to the penitentiary is that this guy's got a serious drug problem. He'll never succeed on probation. You know how they are. They never make it. They're losers.

At this point, you may be inclined to view the whole criminal justice enterprise as somewhat chaotic. The process appears to be a piling of discretion upon discretion upon discretion. Despite the seemingly random nature of criminal justice processing, various actors do agree, however tenuously, on certain rules, vague and flexible though they may be, for constructing accounts. The rules can change, agreements can disintegrate, but, generally, the acceptance of the rules among various builders of crime accounts allows them to convince each other of the "facts" of the case. Thus, routine processing is possible, expected, and engaged in most of the time. Even idiosyncratic individuals can be taken into account when establishing a routine pattern, such as when a judge automatically discounts a sentence recommendation from a particular presentence writer. Again, though, who convinces whom of what? While it seems clear that attorneys, judges, and probation and parole people can all agree on what a case is worth, thus establishing routine patterns that allow for plea bargaining and efficient case disposition, it is less clear that the defendant experiences a logical, rational system. In fact, when the presentence investigator interviews the client for the first time, the client (who probably still sees himself as the defendant) may well wonder what happened to the bargain he struck in exchange for a plea. Having a presentence investigation suggests that one's imminent release is not at all as certain as the public defender indicated. For the defendant the criminal justice process may begin to look like a crap shoot, with all the players following different rule books.

When Arthur actually experiences being supervised in the community, his perception of the criminal justice enterprise as a crap shoot will be reinforced. Had Arthur been exposed to ethnomethodology, he would, however, have had a better understanding of this dynamic. People are not playing by different rule books, but are instead invoking different rules for different occasions to index and create different patterns. A probation/parole officer, for example, must respond to and cope with a variety of pressures. These, in turn, will influence his invoking of rules to account for and make sense of his clients and his relationship to them. Sometimes, the rules invoked will emphasize the p.o.'s role as a support agent, available to help the individual work through his problems. At other times, rules will be invoked emphasizing the client's need for control and the agent's power as a rule enforcer. Often, the set of rules invoked will be determined by the client's perceived willingness to structure his life within a probation/parole framework. The following comments by a probation/parole officer illustrate the point:

> Now of course we would say that we're not structuring it [a treatment program] for the person. We would be doing it *with* the person. There's a subtle little difference there. Yeah, we would say, coming from the background that we're coming from, that we're working with the client in developing a particular plan for rehabilitation. . . . We're coming much more from a background of what are that person's needs and let's try to tailor the program to those needs. If a person doesn't want to be structured—well, ultimately the option is you either get with the program or get over to jail. That doesn't really have to be used too often . . . a decision has to be made by the officer. Is this a serious enough problem that I am going to force this person into treatment, which is frequently done. Or is this a problem that I'm willing to work with the guy a while and try to get his, get some motivation from him to deal with the problem—most of us feeling like that is generally the more successful way. . . . You know, you have to

realize—I, as a probation officer, have to realize that sometimes the amount of unspoken authority there is in that relationship between myself and the probationer—if I suggest to you, you know, I think for people who drink, AA is really a good resource. And you may be taking me to say, get your keester over to AA if you want to stay in my good graces. Or you may just take it as a word of wisdom or a word of advice or whatever.

The relationship between the p.o. and his clients forms a fulcrum for balancing the competing demands of treatment and control. The agent perceives himself as attempting to strike a balance that will be in the client's best interest. The client, however, is part of a different social world. For him, the distinction between treatment and control is a subtle one at best. More often, he sees no distinction at all. Thus, as the probation officer above notes, control often becomes the dominant motif in the client's perspective of the relationship. Clients, then, must themselves learn how to do probation or parole. In other words, if they are to be successful they must learn two sets of hidden rules.

The first set of rules involves the norms of enforcement his p.o. will invoke concerning revocation for various types of legal infractions. Such rules however, vary according to the particular agent:

Revocation really again is a very subjective kind of thing . . . there are some officers who have a very strict policy—if you commit a new felony while you're on probation, you're going to the penitentiary. I don't care who you are or what you've done. You can be in ninety-six treatment programs, you're still going to the penitentiary. That's one fairly well-accepted general guideline. In a lot of cases, misdemeanors are pretty much up for grabs depending on what kind of mis- demeanor it is. Technical violations you really get into an extreme amount of discretion. The first question is, do I even write it up to begin with? Guy misses a couple of appointments. I got a lot of things to do. I'm busy. I don't have a lot of time to be writing this up. It's Mickey Mouse. Nothing is gonna happen about it anyway so I'll bawl the guy out and that'll be it. You know, the guy not only misses a couple appointments but he also misses an AA meeting. What do you do then? Well, it's gonna depend on who's the probation officer. A guy moves without telling you. How much time are you gonna give him to tell you about it or are you gonna issue a warrant. Technically, our definition of an absconder is anybody who you don't know where they're currently living. Well, you know, you may have been out of

touch with the guy for a day. Do I call him an absconder then or do I
wait for two weeks? Do I give him a grace period? How do I work that?
There is a tremendous amount of discretion.

The probationer or parolee must not only learn the rules to be used
by his officer in applying the formal criteria for supervision in the
community, he must also learn the rules for acting middle-class. As
the p.o. below emphasizes, many of the factors used in judging the
success of a client are based on a middle-class view of what the world
should look like:

> . . . it's a very middle-class type of theory. The middle-class client—
> the one who has a decent job, the supportive family, the so on and so
> forth is recommended for probation and the one who doesn't have
> those things is recommended for the penitentiary. [In judging prog-
> ress while on probation], . . . if we can document that a person is
> working steady, is attending regularly whatever treatment program
> they have, be it AA or a drug program or a financial management
> course or an intake group or whatever the heck they're doing, O.K.,
> they're doing that. That they are, that things seem to be going well at
> home—defined as the wife will give me a good report about him or she
> at least won't give me a bad report about him . . . he's not being
> dunned by creditors and we're not getting calls from creditors, you
> know, why isn't this deadbeat paying and if all of those major areas of
> his life seem to be in pretty good stead, we're inclined to think that he's
> doing a good job. And he's not being arrested—that kind of thing.

> The troublesome client is not necessarily the guy who's a parolee on
> for second degree murder, you know, who kind of stares at you when
> he looks at you, and you begin to think whoa—what's going on with
> this guy? A more troublesome client may be the seventeen-year-old
> kid who is placed on probation and doesn't understand how the game
> is played. He doesn't know that you don't come in here, into the office
> with no shirt and no shoes on and say, "Hey, man, you know every-
> thing's cool. Hey listen I, really man, I smoke a little dope but that's all
> I do. Hey." He just doesn't understand, you know, you don't neces-
> sarily say that kind of thing. You want to be a little cool about that. Or
> the kid that is continually being caught at street festivals smokin' dope.
> Or he gets kicked out of his house for being hard to get along with,
> with the parents and all that. At that point the probation officer has
> the proverbial hot potato. You know. I am in some way responsible for
> this kid. And he has no place to stay. And it's not really kosher for him
> to be living out in the streets. That's not acceptable behavior so, you
> know, any port in a storm I guess, so we want to, you know, where can
> we get this guy some temporary housing and I think that you have to

keep in mind that we're talking about maybe one hundred cases and this is going on, there are small brush fires everywhere. This guy's just been kicked out of his house and this one's just been kicked out of the halfway house and now I'm obligated to write up some violation reports on this guy because we can't just let this behavior go by unnoticed. So, I think those kinds of clients may be the more troublesome ones for the officer rather than the guy who comes in and reports to you—I just got arrested for armed robbery, you know, I'll be honest with you, I did it—well, we'll take his statement and write it up for the court and, you know, we'll see you in court or whatever. It's fairly straightforward, fairly clean type of violation.

Trouble. The word defines for the p.o. what course his rule-invoking behavior will take. Rules will be invoked to avoid trouble and to enable the officer to convince others that his behavior forms a logical, coherent pattern. The awareness that others may need to be convinced of the "rightness" of a probation/parole officer's handling of a case causes some agents to "bank" violations. John Irwin, in his book *The Felon,* notes that by keeping track of violations, p.o.'s can retroactively draw upon the necessary legal criteria in the event a case "has to be made" for revocation.[2] The need to make a case for revocation can arise from a number of circumstances. In some instances, the reason for revocation is clear-cut, as when a client commits a felony. Other times, the reasons are clear to the agent but need to be structured in a way that is acceptable to others. In these instances, drawing on past violations, retroactively moving from a lenient to a strict interpretation of the rules of parole or probation, provides the officer with the rationale he needs for incarcerating an individual. The following provides two such examples of situations where a case needs to be made. In the first, the officer accounts for a troublesome client based on the perceived desires of the community. In the second instance, the officer relates how probation or parole revocation serves the needs of criminal justice agencies other than the Department of Probation and Parole.

Oh. I don't know [if people get revoked for being troublesome]. I think they do. I don't think they get . . . it's never written down that they're troublesome. It may be that they left their place of residence without notifying the probation officer within forty-eight hours and that sounds a lot nicer than [saying the guy is a] shitbum. Yeah. I think they do. Yeah. And I think at various times probation officers feel uncomfortable about that fact. That's a fact. We're kind of a, you know, I was reading somewhere we're doing some of society's dirty work and the fact of the matter is that society doesn't want these young kids out in the streets with no supervision at all and living in cars or, you know, living in derelict buildings or whatever. So they wind up in the penitentiary.

So often the decision whether or not to revoke has very little to do with what the alleged violations are. I think that's really a significant point. You know, legally the judge needs something to hang his hat on to revoke this guy. [The judge will say to me] 'I need a missed appointment which is clearly a violation or I need him to have moved and not notified you within forty-eight hours of that change of address or I need something that you as a probation officer can come in and tell me this guy did very clearly—it's a very clear violation even if it's minor.' . . . Then I can revoke him on that in spite of the fact that maybe what we're really revoking is over what police officers gave us—certain information that was not wholly substantiated but that indicates that this guy is dealing drugs. And in fact that's why he's being revoked and it has nothing to do with the fact that he missed an appointment and missed his appointment at the drug treatment facility.

Of course, cases need to be built not only within the context of cooperation but also within the context of competition. Judges, probation/parole officers, the police, and attorneys can find themselves disagreeing over the nature of a case and the need for revocation. The p.o. is more vulnerable to the social world constructions of others when the issue is the revocation of probation, a status over which the court has direct control. The granting or revoking of parole is more firmly in the hands of the Probation and Parole Department. The need to draw on stored violations may thus be greater when the officer seeks to justify certain instances of probation revocation. In the following comments, the probation/parole officer explains the difference between the two procedures and the greater difficulty posed for the officer by a probation revocation hearing:

> Parolees go before the parole board. That's kind of an interesting thing too in that the parolee will be taken into custody and he'll be given a preliminary hearing in front of an officer of our agency and,

assuming probable cause is found, he's held in jail until he's returned to the penitentiary. Now he's given his probation [parole] revocation hearing at that point . . . at the penitentiary. However . . . that's a very perfunctory kind of hearing and the parole board acts as if the actual fact-finding hearing was back at the preliminary stage and all they do is basically review the hearing officer's report and if he's in line, then the guy is revoked. It even goes a step further than that. When they receive that hearing officer's report and the guy is still back at county jail, they're basically making the decision then. If they send their order of arrest and return to bring the guy back, we're not spending money to get this guy back up here so that we can cut him loose again.

I think that the parole board is much more likely to back us up on revocation recommendations, to actually take the guy back than the court is. The court, I think, in a lot of cases has different priorities than we do. I think sometimes we get hung up on certain aspects of whether or not the guy is progressing in his "rehabilitation," and the court, some courts feel like as long as he's not out there committing felonies, I don't really give a damn whether he goes to AA or stands on his head or what he does.

As you reflect on the doing of probation and parole work, the irony of the process may become apparent. Ideally, the role of the p.o. as described by one practitioner involves imposing "restraint, supervision, and order upon an erratic lifestyle, and to this adding an essential element, namely, guidance." And yet, the rules for guiding are often hidden, changeable, and subject to the influences of the moment. A process designed to provide order presents an image of disorder. Concerns with practicality, neatness, and steady habits, therefore, appear as scams for the maintenance of control, rather than as agreed-upon rules for living practiced by those who preach them. The image of life as a crap shoot is often reinforced.

Like most individuals on probation and parole, Arthur will not be revoked for a technical violation, nor will he be accused of any other crime. The reasons for "successful" completion of probation, though, will remain unclear. Some will assume that Arthur refrained from committing either further legal infractions or from violating the conditions of his supervised release in the community. This interpretation must remain at the level of an assumption, since data on Arthur's case will be of the same quality as the data on most probation/parole experiences. Such data is often sketchy and incomplete. After his release from probation, no effort will be made to follow up Arthur's future progress, and, thus, no information will be gathered on whether the probation experience had any long-term effect.

What seems likely, however, is that the overworked p.o. will come to an understanding with Arthur that technical violations will be ignored as long as Arthur does not get caught in any serious drug infractions or other types of crime. The term "serious" will be subject to negotiation, based in part on how the p.o. resolves the central dilemma of his role, whether to be primarily a support agent or a law enforcer. The probation/parole officer previously interviewed underscores the dynamic Arthur will become sensitive to as he uncovers the hidden rules of the game:

> I don't think it's [the dilemma between being a law enforcer and a support agent] necessarily something that's resolved once and for all at one particular time. It keeps cropping up. We feel comfortable with a particular resolution to that problem at one point for a time but then new information that we learn or new things that we're exposed to . . . you begin to say well—gee—I don't know if I really like that role that I'm playing right now or not. I think a fairly common resolution to it is . . . as long as the guy's not out committing serious crimes, I'm willing to go with him. I'm willing to give him the benefit of the doubt and keep working with him treatment-wise but that at a certain point, namely where he commits that felony crime and it's very obvious he did it, then the treatment options have pretty much run out. And I think in some cases there may be something of an unspoken agreement between the officer and the client that that's what . . . that there are these rules here but in fact what's going on is if you commit a new felony, I'm gonna lock you up and you're going to go to the penitentiary. But anything short of that we'll work it out. I may not be happy about it but well, we can live with it.

The final irony of the probation/parole relationship appears to be that the p.o. invokes rules that allow him to see himself as balancing the scales of treatment and control in the best interest of the client. Arthur will invoke rules for constructing the meaning of the relationship so that he sees himself as a victim, controlled by the balancing of the treatment/control scale to serve the needs of the officer rather than himself. Each builds different worlds.

Before such buildings can be undertaken, a construction project in the courthouse must be completed. Arthur and his case are once again rejoined for the final courthouse ritual.

Sentence Is Passed

Arthur's sentencing ceremony took less than five minutes. The prosecutor spoke first: "Your Honor, the people at this time have no furthur recommendation or comment to make. Since you have the presentence investigation report before you, the people will abide by your decision, Your Honor." She sat down, knowing that the presentence writer had been around long enough to know how the game is supposed to be played. Arthur's probation report would confirm the deal already made.

The public defender was the next one to approach the podium. His statement was longer, much longer than Arthur felt was needed, given the fact that the deal was already made. Again, Arthur felt somewhat uncomfortable. "I would simply like to remind the court, Your Honor, that this defendant is more misguided than he is criminal. I feel that with an appropriate probation period, and with appropriate treatment, the court can go a long way towards helping this young man become a productive citizen of this society. I might also remind the court that my client has already spent a considerable amount of time in jail. If he is to be restored to the community as a productive citizen, he needs to be in that community of which he will become a part. We agree, Your Honor, that at this point my client may not be quite ready to assume the responsibilities of citizenship without help. Therefore, Your Honor, I sincerely hope that the court will grant probation in this case, a sentence that would be both just for the community and just for my client. Thank you, Your Honor."

Chapter 6 noted that the decisions of judges are greatly influenced by a variety of individual beliefs and values. Despite being final arbitrators of official legal accounts, however, judges are limited in their ability to enforce idiosyncratic world views. They are constrained by the patterns and common understandings that emerge from the subculture of the courthouse.

Judge Sweeney sentenced Arthur to time served plus one year on probation. Arthur and his case had completed the typical processing that defendants and papers about defendants go through in our criminal justice system.

References

1. ARTHUR ROSETT and DONALD R. CRESSEY. *Justice by Consent* (Philadelphia, Pa.: J.B. Lippincott Company, 1976), pp. 29–31 and 58–65.
2. JOHN IRWIN. *The Felon* (Englewood Cliffs, N.J.: Prentice-Hall, Inc., 1970), p. 162.

chapter ten

Being In Prison

John Swetowski was thirty years old and a senior correctional officer at the state's maximum security prison. He had worked at the prison for seven years. When he began, there was no formal training program for guards. There was just a warning from his shift lieutenant:

> When you walk on the tiers, walk close to the railing. Whatever you do, don't let those guys get you so they can pull you with your back against a cell. They'll start to choke you, so don't let them grab you. Now if you get something thrown at you, food, urine, or shit, and I mean shit, you know, excrement, that's pretty normal on this shift in this cell block, so don't lose your cool. If you stay cool you'll be O.K. If something happens, and for some reason those guys get loose, and sometimes the automatic locks fail, and you get taken hostage, we're coming in there. If it's your life or getting those guys back in the cell, I hope your affairs are in order.

After that first night, John did not think he would last the week. Not that such a short tenure would be so unusual. He knew that the annual turnover rate of correctional officers in the state was close to 30 percent.[1] He also knew that his state was one of the better ones, both in terms of employee turnover and in terms of pay. Mississippi had a 54 percent turnover rate, and in Maine in 1976 correctional officers started at $6,240.[2] Many guards held two jobs, the one at the prison and another, with the guard job being considered the second job. If a person stuck it out, though, there was job security and a steady, if meager, paycheck. However, you had to live to collect, a condition that the lieutenant had made clear was at times problematic.

It was hard to maintain a desire to help people when there was such a pervasive concern with safety and a not-too-subtle message that guards were expendable. Another guard told him during his first week, when he asked a question about handling a certain situation:

> You're expected to think for yourself when something happens. If it turns out fine, all's well and good. If you make a decision they expect of you and it doesn't turn out right, even if it might not have been the wrong decision but it just didn't turn out right, then you're an asshole. After a while, if you're called an asshole enough by inmates, and you're called an asshole enough by the brass, and the public thinks you're a jerk, you know, just a fat, dumb hillbilly, chewin' a cigar and beatin' heads, well after awhile you begin to feel like an asshole, you even begin to act like one.[3]

The physical surroundings also mitigated against a helping orientation on the part of guards. The constant hum of convicts, the clicking of locks and banging of doors, the seemingly disembodied arms of inmates in maximum security holding mirrors so that any activity in the corridor was reflected back into the cells, all added to the oppressive atmosphere.

On some cell blocks, inmates were reduced to a very basic level. Guards had been assaulted in an attempt on the part of some convicts to get extra cookies. The cookies were a kind of prison currency that could be used to buy a variety of commodities, from cigarettes to homosexual liasons. Cookies with raisins were particularly valued, since the raisins could be used to make "hootch," a kind of prison booze.[4]

Guards reacted in a variety of ways to prison conditions. During the second week on the job, the lieutenant told John:

> Listen, you've only been here two weeks, but you can see that guys in here are under a lot of pressure. I mean the guards. You're locked up

in here just like the inmates. You eat the same things they do, and you've got some of the same concerns they have about physical safety. You know the worst thing about being in prison? The worst thing about it is having to associate and live with murderers, rapists, child molesters, and so on. Prisoners are concerned with their safety, and obviously we're concerned with our own and with theirs. Inmates have different ways of coping with the pressures. Some of the young ones, the ones who aren't too tough, when they're put into the general population, the hardened cons think of them as fresh meat. They're gang raped. Some decide to hook up with a protector. The young fellow lets himself be used sexually in exchange for protection. Others can't cope with that. If they're tough, they try and establish their rep as a tough guy. It's almost like they have to become exploiters, in order to avoid being exploited themselves. Some of these guys obviously can't play the tough guy role. And they don't want to sell themselves for protection, so they look for another way out. Some try suicide, and if they're lucky, and don't die and get a sympathetic shrink they'll get sent to the mental ward. Of course, some think of being lucky as succeeding at a suicide. Others will try and get a serious infraction on their record so they'll be sent here. These guys are locked up most of the time, but they're safe. Sometimes, I've had guys scheduled to move back to the general population and they've refused. No use sending them back if they don't want to go. They'll just get another infraction and be back here.

But you see, guards have fewer options open to them. Some guys try and deal with their situation by being mean and tough. But that can just make the situation worse. Other guards figure that if you treat the inmates with respect they'll treat you with respect. If you're firm but fair, you'll avoid trouble.

Another way of avoiding trouble was to overlook certain infractions. John remembered seeing an inmate with a steel pipe and asked why he was allowed to have it in his cell. What the lieutenant said boiled down to a strategy of live-and-let-live.

Who's going to go in there and take it away from him? Since all of these doors work on one lock, we'd have to unlock all of the cells, get all decked out in our riot gear, and then decide who's going to be first going in. Some things you just have to overlook. Hell, I know that some of the politicians and the fine citizens get upset that the inmates make hootch. They use raisins or potato peelings or whatever. Some guys even get a buzz on by drinking mouthwash. But, if it keeps the place calm, and it isn't blatant, it makes our job easier. Now, obviously, if it gets out of hand you've got to do something just to cover your own ass. But sometimes it's better to look the other way. Besides, the prison administration is legally doping up some of them guys, and the reason is to keep the place under control. We give out medication on this block four times a day. Over half the inmates in this block get something. Sedative, tranquilizers, sleeping pills. Almost everybody gets something at one time or another. Five milligrams of Valium four times a day plus a sleeping pill at night is not unusual. Hell, and people get worried about a little homemade hootch. You can't run a cell block by the book. You've got to improvise. They got a rule book, but sometimes the rules aren't too clear. You know, it says not to fraternize with the inmates, but what does that mean. Where is the line between friendly or at least civil and fraternization? If you do a favor for a guy, I mean go the commissary for him or let him make a phone call or something like that, is that fraternization? Now some guys go too far. You know, smuggle stuff in like marijuana or something. I think we got rid of most of those guys. You know what they'd do is supplement their income. But I mean, if you can do a good turn for some of these guys your payoff will be a smooth-running cell block.[5]

Seven years ago. The time went fast, and John learned the doing of corrections. He learned when to ignore violations and when to write an inmate up. He learned, too, that inmates exerted their own form of social control on their fellows. The night he learned about inmate social control, he had the assignment of phone rounds. Each night, a certain number of inmates were allowed ten-minute phone conversations. It was in the middle of the third telephone call that trouble began. An inmate began to yell that he was supposed to get a call. John's list showed him to be ineligible for phone privileges. "You get me my phone call or I'll blind you." With that the inmate began mixing a brew of cleanser and water, a combination that, properly aimed, could cause temporary loss of sight. John did not have to think twice about what to do. He yanked the phone plug out of the jack, cutting off the inmate who was talking in mid-sentence. The plea to let him finish his call was drowned out by the yell of the inmate with the lethal mixture, "I'm going to blind you, you son of a bitch." By that time, John was off the tier.[6]

He felt bad about depriving an inmate of his full phone privilege because of the actions of another inmate, and expressed as much to the sergeant on duty. "Don't worry about it," said the sergeant. "Everyone on that tier knows why the phone was cut off and they'll deal with that guy themselves." Sure enough, the next night when John came on duty, the inmate who had caused the commotion was lying in his bunk with one eye swollen shut and a puffed lip. Yet, there was no report of any violence on the block from the previous shift.

When John worked in the general population, he learned more about prison life, both as experienced by guards and by inmates. He discovered that there was more than one prison within those iron-gray walls. Depending on the specific cell block worked and the shift one was assigned, a tour of duty could either present an image of a fairly normal environment or one of an extremely depraved atmosphere. He learned quickly not to judge a man by the official categories describing the crime an inmate committed. After a while he did not even bother to find out why a person was in prison. The information he needed to do his job required different categories than the legal ones provided by the system that brought him his charges. It did little good to label a man a burglar or a robber or a murderer. Those were categories that might be helpful to other criminal justice personnel, but they were not helpful to John. An old sergeant that John once worked for summarized the need for different categories rather precisely:

> You see, the cop on the beat, he's got to know who the dirt balls are, who the hypes are, who the snitches are, and so on. Then the lawyers and the judges, they've got to figure out whether someone's guilty of first degree murder, second degree murder, manslaughter, or is innocent by reason of insanity. See, but that stuff don't mean nothing to us in here. For us, we've got to know who the gorillas are, who the punks are, and the politicians. We've got to know who the hoosiers are and the right guys and the square johns. Those are the guys we live with, not that legal crap.

As John worked in the general population, he learned to process information in ways that allowed him to recognize the denizens of the prison world, and he soon learned the inapplicability of the legal labels people came in with. "Square johns," inmates who eschewed prison values and identified with guards and the nonconvict world, were often used as trusties, no matter what crime they had committed on the outside. And some had committed very vicious crimes, including multiple homicide. But on the inside, the square john was often the only source of help for a guard trying to run a cell block. Being a trusty meant that the individual was trusted enough by the correctional staff and the administration to have a job that allowed him considerable freedom of movement within the institution. Such individuals would sometimes report infractions, and the information they gave could prevent outbreaks of serious disturbances in the cell blocks.

Of course, they could also mean trouble. If they were too loud about their contempt for fellow inmates and too indiscreet about passing along information, they could easily become victims of a "shanking." Shanks were makeshift steel blades, used for protection or enforcement of the inmate code. Square johns were sometimes easy prey for "gorillas," those inmates who sought power and status within the inmate world by force and toughness, or for "punks," the weak inmates who, for protection, let themselves be sexually exploited by gorillas and carried out their bidding. This sometimes included the disciplining of square johns.

Even gorillas and "hoosiers" had their uses. In many prisons, because they were so shorthanded, it was the former who taught the new guards how to use the keys and where things were kept.[7] Also, they could keep a cell block under control, and, in so doing, make the guard look good with his superiors. The hoosiers were useful because they'd give information away unintentionally, just by their bungling behavior. The illicit exchange of goods, prison hootch, or in some cases dope, could almost always be detected if a hoosier were involved. He would just look suspicious by being overly cautious or overly nervous. If you knew who the hoosiers were, you could find out if something forbidden was going to "go down" just by watching them closely. And those inmates who did their own time, kept quiet, did not bother other inmates, and, in turn, would not let other inmates hassle or bother them, the "right guys," were perhaps the easiest group to deal with. Not that they cooperated with guards to the extent that they would pass on information or anything like that. The right guys, or, as some called them, the guys with heart, were the pros. They looked at prison as simply one of the hazards of their job, and their job was crime. Their only goal was to do "easy time," not hassle anybody and not be hassled. They were committed to the inmate code of never squealing on a fellow inmate, but they would not go out of their way to bait or harass the guards. In many ways they were probably the least reformable group in the prison. They would go to group therapy meetings or to classes, but their participation was obviously perfunctory. The classes or the therapy sessions were simply ways of passing time and breaking the monotony of the prison routine. Yet, this group that was the least open to reform presented the fewest problems for the custodial staff. Both shared, to an extent, in the live-and-let-live philosophy. John Irwin in his book *The Felon* quotes from an inmate interview that captures the essence of the live-and-let-live philosophy from the convict's standpoint:

> The convict code isn't any different than stuff we all learned as kids. You know, nobody likes a stool pigeon. Well, here in the joint you got all kinds of guys living jammed together, two to a cell. You got nuts walking the yard, you got every kind of dingbat in the world here. Well, we got to have some rules among ourselves. The rule is "do your own number." In other words, keep off your neighbor's toes. Like if the guy next to me is making brew in his cell, well, this is none of my business. I got no business running to the man and telling him that Joe Blow is making brew in his cell. Unless Joe Blow is fucking over me, then I can't say nothing. And when he is fucking over me, then I got to stop him myself. If I can't then I deserve to get fucked over.[8]

John Swetowski was constantly amazed at the complexity of prison life. The people he guarded were supposed to be deprived of their freedom and of many things that individuals on the outside took for granted. Yet, within the physically confining space of prison, and despite the obvious deprivations of confinement, a complex social pattern was created.

Erving Goffman's *Asylums* is helpful in understanding this observation. The book, a study of the social life of a mental hospital, points out that every institution has two faces. There is the public face, the official goals and practices of the organization, and the private face, or the underlife of the institution. Both are real, and institutional life is a constant movement between the two faces. Thus, in the prison, there are the "make do's" talked about by Goffman, those things that substitute for things not available on the inside.[9] Prison hootch is an example. But to make the institution come close to some of its formal goals, it is necessary to overlook certain kinds of make do's. As a result, in John's prison, inmates were able to work the system. The con politicans and the hustlers got the good jobs and, in so doing, were able to supply the goods and sometimes the services that help create a viable system of economic exchange. In the general population, tobacco was the major medium of exchange, and extra cigarettes could be gotten by those working in the commissary. Those working the kitchen could get extra food, and even extra cookies that would find their way to the maximum security wards. For all of this to happen, John understood that there had to be "free places," places that guards would ordinarily ignore on their rounds. As with any economic system, there were also those who tried to get the commodities of the system through exploitation, rather than work or fair exchange. These were the "low-riders," who would steal and hijack from other inmates. Symbols of social status were also evident within the confines of the prison. Groups or individuals would stake out their territory in the T.V. room, those with high status near the front where they could control programming and command the best view, and those with lower status toward the rear. Goffman had found a parallel situation in the mental hospital.[10] Prison, like the mental hospital, creates a dynamic that in some ways defeats their mutual, official purpose of reform. The deprivations of imprisonment lead to make do's that are clearly deviant. In prison, the most obvious make do within this category is the exploitive homosexuality that goes on. Less obvious is the way the institution creates a gulf between the watched and the watchers, so that identification of the former with the latter (and, therefore, presumably with the values of conventional society) make one a traitor to one's inmate group. Thus, status often tends to be based on criteria at odds with assimilation into nondeviant culture. A comment from Claude Brown's book, *Manchild in the Promised Land*, made by an inmate who had "graduated" from the state reformatory into a maximum security prison underscores this process:

> Yeah. The time I did in Woodburn, the times I did on the Rock, that was college, man. Believe me, it was college. I did four years in Woodburn. And I guess I've done a total of about two years on the Rock in about the last six years. Every time I went there, I learned a little more. When I go to jail now, I live, man. I'm right at home. That's the odd part about it. If you look at it, a cat like me is just cut out to be

in jail. It could never hurt me, 'cause I never had what the good folks call a home and all that kind of shit to begin with. So when I went to jail, the first time I went away, when I went to Warwick, I made my own home. It was all right. Shit, I learned how to live. Now when I go back to the joint, anywhere I go, I know some people. If I go to any of the jails in New York, or if I go to a slam in Jersey, I still run into a lot of cats I know. It's almost like a family.[11]

Of course, the guards have make do's, too, since as the lieutenant who broke John in said, it was "impossible to run a block by the rule book." In some instances the make do's are humane ones, like letting a brother visit his sibling, even in maximum security where it is strictly forbidden. On the other hand, some make do's are clearly to the prisoners' detriment, as when a guard engages in some physical punishment of an inmate or purposely spills most of the inmate's food in maximum security to "teach a lesson." Where John worked such make do's were used only in response to the more assaultive make do's of the prisoners, such as the mixing of water or urine with kitchen cleanser to temporarily blind a guard. John knew, however, that the dehumanizing conditions of the environment, particularly in the maximum security wing of the institution, could quickly reduce both guard and prisoner to extremely violent make do's as both sought to exert control over their environment.

Goffman also comments upon the "looping effect" found in total institutions. A total institution provides a single stage on which a person lives out his entire life, including recreation, work, sleeping, and eating.[12] Such a setting allows for institutional access to and control of the most intimate details of an individual's life. Inmates of both the mental hospital and of the prison often defend themselves against the assaults of the institution on personal integrity—the loss of identity occasioned by having to wear a uniform indistinct from that worn by everyone else, the loss of privacy, the invasion of physical space, and so forth. The inmates' reactions to such deprivations are then used by the institution to justify further intrusion into an individual's life. This is the looping effect. In prison, such intrusions are either formal, such as putting an individual in maximum security or insisting on "treatment," or informal, such as a guard teaching a prisoner a lesson. The prison would also justify activity aimed primarily at easing the administrative burden of the institution as being necessary for the reform of the inmate. Thus, inmates who file, sweep, serve food, cut hair, and do the hundreds of mundane tasks necessary for the smooth functioning of the prison are viewed by staff, particularly staff involved in treatment, as being trained in the development of "work-ready attitudes." If the tasks are performed well, the inmate would be considered well on the road to reform. Guards, however, had their doubts. They knew that a lot of the things justified as therapeutic were really necessary, both from the point of view of maintaining the daily functioning of the institution and from the point of view of maintaining control. John felt that the large number of pills given out, even though justified as therapeutic, were really aimed more at control.

Despite the tremendous effort to control, the dynamics of the total institution, as both John Swetowski and Erving Goffman discovered, allowed for human ingenuity to create an oasis of freedom within a desert of deprivation. Gresham Sykes, whose book, *Society of Captives,* written more than twenty years ago, underscored the point specifically as it relates to prison life:

> . . . Indeed, the glaring conclusion is that despite the guns and the surveillance, the searches and the precautions of the custodians, the actual behavior of the inmate population differs markedly from that which is called for by official commands and decrees. Violence, fraud, theft, aberrant sexual behavior—all are commonplace occurrences in the daily round of institutional existence in spite of the fact that the maximum security prison is conceived of by society as the ultimate weapon for the control of the criminal and his deviant actions. Far from being omnipotent rulers who have crushed all signs of rebellion against their regime, the custodians are engaged in a continuous struggle to maintain order—and it is a struggle in which the custodians frequently fail. Offenses committed by one inmate against another occur often, as do offenses committed by inmates against the officials and their rules. And the number of undetected offenses is, by universal agreement of both officials and inmates, far larger than the number of offenses which are discovered.[13]

Sykes also illustrated the influence of reciprocity on guard–inmate relationships. As John learned early in the job, a mean "screw" (the inmate term for a guard), was a marked man. Further, in the words of Sykes:

> The custodians . . . far from being converted into brutal tyrants, are under strong pressure to compromise with their captives, for it is a paradox that they can insure their dominance only by allowing it to be corrupted. Only by tolerating violations of "minor" rules and regulations can the guard secure compliance in the "major" areas of the custodial regime. Ill-equipped to maintain the social distance which in theory separates the world of officials and the world of the inmates, their suspicions eroded by long familiarity, the custodians are led into a *modus vivendi* with their captives which bears little resemblance to the stereotypical picture of guards and their prisoners.[14]

Both guards and prisoners, then, undergo what Clemmer has called prisonization.[15] Unfortunately, in John's view, Clemmer overlooked the prisonization process as it applied to the former group. Clemmer noted that inmates go through stages that eventually lead to acceptance of the norms and values of prison life. They make sense of their current environment by constructing a world view compatible with their current circumstances. But guards do the same. They, too, use strategies that allow them to make sense out of their situation, and one such strategy is that of compromise, so that captors and captives together build a unique kind of social world.

Not that the social world of prison is simply a function of unique relationships and strategies that develop as a result of deprivation. True, prisoners are deprived by the functioning of the institution. So, too, are guards. They wear uniforms, have their movements restricted, and are subject to violations of personal space and privacy. John, for example, reacted very negatively when a rule went into effect mandating that guards themselves be thoroughly searched, both upon entering and leaving the establishment. But the prison community is also affected by the larger outside community.

Stanton Wheeler's article, "Socialization in Correctional Institutions," nicely summarizes the various factors affecting the development of the prison subculture.[16] Wheeler discovered a U-shaped pattern of prisonization. Inmates were least integrated into the inmate subculture at the beginning of their sentence. By roughly the midpoint of their sentence they were most integrated into the subculture. Surprisingly, however, as the time of release neared, many inmates again began to express values more in keeping with the outside community. In other words, commitment to the inmate subculture appeared transitory. Wheeler's findings, though, clearly supported the notion of a unique inmate social world. He probed this phenomenon further by comparing United States prisons with those in Scandinavian countries. He reasoned that if the inmate subculture was purely the result of deprivation, a finding clearly in line with the arguments of Gresham Sykes, the inmate subculture should be the same, regardless of the differing cultures of the countries. His findings, however, did not support this view. There were distinct differences between the inmate subcultures in the United States and Scandinavian countries, and such differences seemed to be related to the differences between the larger cultures of the countries. For example, Scandinavian prisons were far less violent than American ones, reflecting the differing levels of violence within the two cultures. Further support for this interpretation is found in the writings of Rose Giallombardo and her study of women's prisons in the United States.[17] There was much less violence and exploitive sex in women's prisons when compared to institutions housing men. Sex in women's facilities was institutionalized into family patterns, with women taking on the roles of father, mother, and even siblings. Such patterns were in keeping with the cultural values at the time Giallombardo wrote (1966). Women, particularly lower-class women, tended to make the family their central concern.

John knew from personal experience that prison life was influenced by values outside the iron-gray walls. Thus, the street gangs that operated on the outside continued to operate inside the walls, with status in the prison sometimes related to the gang affiliation of the inmate. Racial tensions in prison were also obviously related to outside cultural values. The fact that they were in prison did little to change the attitudes of black, Chicano, and white inmates toward one another. Finally, inmates also had status based on the crimes they had committed on the outside, with child molesters and rapists having the lowest status among inmates.

John had seen a variety of prisoners go through the prisonization process. Many would be difficult to handle initially, but then eventually they would settle into the routine of prison life. As their time approached for release, however, some would again create discipline problems, exhibiting the stress involved in once more entering the outside world.

In many ways, it seemed to John that there were parallels

between the experiences of inmates and those of guards. The first exposure to prison life made new guards very upset. John remembered when he was finished with his first night and he met another new officer who had just come from working the general population. The man was upset because somebody tried to throw some water on him. Nevertheless, he vowed to stick it out. He was gone before the week was out. John knew others, however, himself included, that settled in and developed a sense of self and job that allowed them to function reasonably well. But for the professional guard, the frustration would build, and, indeed, much of the frustration emanated from outside the cell block. Just as the outside culture seemed to influence segments of the prison subculture, so that deprivation interacted with larger cultural factors to create the inmate view of reality, so, too, did the larger culture affect the guard and his view of reality. John thought that the problems of guards could be summarized into three categories.

The first was public image. Correctional officers were stereotyped as overweight, overbearing, and undereducated. Such a view influenced many public decisions about corrections. The negative view of the prison environment, which included guards as well as inmates, meant that, for most of the public, corrections was a last priority. Public awareness, public concern, and public funding were all adversely affected. Further, such an attitude had an impact on the way guards were treated by both the prison administration and the treatment staff. Both groups often viewed correctional officers as "only guards." From the administrator's standpoint, that often seemed to mean that they were expendable. Such an attitude contributed to a second major problem (or really a set of problems) facing guards, namely, high turnover, low wages, and very little formal training. If the guards were dumb, brutal, and so forth, there would really be little reason to improve their working conditions. To John, the stereotype contained a good bit of urban prejudice toward the rural working class. Guards could come and go because there was always a pool of farm boys to draw from, farm boys for whom formal training would be a waste of time.

Ironically, the urban-rural prejudice reversed itself when the relationship was between guards and inmates, rather than administrators and custodial staff. Most of the inmates were from the city, most of the guards were from rural areas. This pattern was the same nationally. Maximum security prisons tended to be built in rural communities. Such communities often welcomed the prison as a source of employment. Moreover, John felt that those built in the nineteenth century were built in the country because of the philosophy that the city was a breeding ground for crime and, to reform criminals, it was necessary to remove them from such an evil environment. Finally, if the reaction of many urban dwellers to the location of halfway houses in their neighborhoods is indicative, most did not want prisons in their midst. The "ship of fools" might now be anchored, but it was going to be anchored as far away as possible from the population centers.[18] And yet, the removal of the inmate from his environment and the recruiting of his keeper from groups outside the city created some needless tension in the prison community, both between the custodial staff and their superiors and between the guards and those that they were charged with guarding. The latter problem, however, could be overcome with training. Indeed, guards who stayed learned through on-the-job experience to come to terms with their charges, even though both often came from radically different backgrounds. The point was that training could lessen the frustration involved in such a coming to terms with one's reality and, by so doing, perhaps bring a bit of stability into the ranks of guards. But again, if guards were seen as just dumb country boys, the attitude would be, "Why bother?"

From John's point of view, the term "expendable" also took on a more sinister meaning. He remembered the Attica uprising of 1971, where a number of guards were taken hostage by the inmates. After four days of protracted negotiations between inmates and authorities, those in charge decided to storm the prison. This, despite the threat of inmates to kill hostages if this happened. The result was predictable, ten hostages and twenty-nine inmates dead. None of the hostages were killed by inmates. All were killed by bullet wounds inflicted by the authorities when the prison was stormed. John wondered whether the order to storm the prison would have been given if the governor had been the one held hostage. Probably not. Guards are expendable, unlike governors.

Attica, in many ways, represented what was and is wrong with many prisons. Rural guards with black and Puerto Rican inmates.

Age disparity between guards and inmates. Overcrowded conditions. On and on. Fortunately, at John's prison there had not been the type of violent outbreak that Attica and other prisons had experienced. But there had been a number of skirmishes. Again, better training would help lessen tension, but, as always, prisons were the last in line for tax dollars, and within prisons, guards were the last to be considered when it came to allocating the meager resources for improvement. It was a vicious circle. A bad public image contributed to the lack of interest in improving the guards' lot in life, and such lack of concern contributed to high turnover and enough incidents of guard brutality to reinforce the stereotype.

Besides the problem of bad images and the complex of problems that included low salaries, lack of training, and high turnover, there was a third set of problems that had to do with the contradictory expectations facing guards. No one was quite sure what they wanted guards to do. In simplistic terms, the pendulum swung between demands that guards be purely custodial workers to demands that they be part of a treatment team. Such a dichotomy was oversimplified for a number of reasons. First, guards were never and could never be simply either custodians or correctional personnel. The nature of the job required that somehow they be both. Anybody who tried to be solely a keeper, emphasizing only security, adherence to the rules, and discipline, was going to find himself having trouble with the inmates and trouble remembering that the inmates were more than just things to be controlled. On the other hand, if a guard forgot that his basic job was to maintain security (and sometimes one had to overlook certain rule violations to do it) and became too wrapped up in the lives of inmates, such a guard was likely to either become corrupt or get himself hurt. John liked to help the inmates as much as he could. He would give advice when asked for it and would sometimes even go to the commissary to pick up items for an inmate who was on twenty-four-hour lockup. At the same time, however, he would not hesitate to write up an inmate for a serious rule violation. Firm but fair. That was John's approach. He had seen guards get taken advantage of by inmates and then become embittered. Once that happened, they would either act brutally or they would only help inmates for a price. For the right price, such help could include bringing narcotics into the prison. Also, young guards had gotten hurt because they were not conscious of security and had overlooked potential weapons when processing an inmate they thought they had won over.

The contradictory demands placed on guards made them vulnerable to any kind of criticism from any quarter. Inmates could complain to their counselors that guards were thwarting treatment. Wardens would get pressure from the public because of so-called "security problems." Psychologists and social workers would complain that guards never considered what was best for a person from a treatment perspective, and yet, at the same time, they would exclude guards from any discussion of an inmate's case with the words, "They wouldn't understand what we're trying to do."

The guards' dilemma was a kind of microcosm of the cross-pressures and contradictions that pervaded the whole correctional field. Society simply did not know what it wanted. As a result, corrections seemed subject to fad innovations that moved along a continuum from a "get tough" stance to a "get easy" one. And always, correctional innovations seemed to occur without any thought given to the people who worked inside the prison. John thought of recent suggestions for reform that could make his job more difficult. One was the move to sentence people for flat time, five years or ten years or whatever, with the abolition of parole. Some people even wanted to do away with good time, whereby an inmate would get released so many days early for each day he served his sentence without causing trouble within the walls. What people on the outside did not understand was that, by removing parole and, worse, by removing good time provisions from existing penal programs, the incentive for an individual to obey prison regulations was also removed. If a guy was sentenced to ten years, and he knew he wasn't going to get out any sooner, he could raise hell inside almost with impunity. Guards threatening to write a person up for such behavior would have little impact. What control tools would be left? Increased use of solitary, which many people thought bordered on the inhuman, or physical force, a tool that most guards and most inmates would prefer to have the guard use infrequently. Such repressive instruments of control would also further reduce the likelihood of any successful treatment within the prison.

Not that coerced treatment could be of much benefit. John

knew that many inmates went to various so-called "treatment" sessions just to get out of their cells. Moreover, even if one adjusted to prison life, it did not mean that the same individual would be successful out in the community. For that reason, John applauded the increased use of both minimum security institutions and halfway houses. The closer inmates could get to the community they would eventually have to live in (and around 70 percent get back into the community within three years of confinement), the better their chances of making it.

Ironically, however, the move toward community corrections created another serious difficulty for guards in a maximum security prison. "Creaming" was occurring so that, in some states, maximum security prisons contained a far greater proportion of inmates sentenced for assaultive behavior than was formerly the case. John could see the trend in his own prison. Those prisoners who contributed to a relatively nonviolent atmosphere, thieves, check forgers, and so on, were becoming a smaller proportion of the population. The best-behaved inmates would be transferred elsewhere, with the result that the maximum security prison was getting a heavier concentration of more recalcitrant prisoners. As one of John's fellows put it:

> Instead of having 1 or 2 percent of the population made up of crazies, you might get 10 or 20 percent. And you don't have time to separate them out so they're always getting to where they can cluster together and coming up with some crazy idea like let's punch this guard or grab this guy and rape him or whatever the insanity of the moment.[19]

Unfortunately, dispersing the prison population to a variety of correctional institutions did not seem to be having an immediately beneficial effect on the problem of overcrowding. The proportion of crazies seemed to be getting larger, as did the absolute number of prisoners. The resultant overcrowding created havoc. Serious disturbances increased, and any treatment was undermined. A model prisoner who previously could look forward to being put on an honor wing with far more privileges could now be told by his counselor that there were one hundred people ahead of him waiting for one of the forty honor cells to open up.

The growth of a conservative "lock 'em up" philosophy was

partly responsible for the dramatic increase in prison populations. Difficult economic times further added to the burgeoning prison rolls. As the economy faltered, some people turned to crime, which ultimately put greater pressure on prison facilities. Some officials estimated that for every percentage point rise in unemployment, the prison population increased by 1,300.[20] This, combined with increasing citizen demand for a get-tough policy with criminals, meant that, in some industrialized states (Illinois was an example), a new prison would have to be built every fifteen months just to stay at capacity.[21] John knew that the trend was a national one. California's prison population was, at one time during the mid-to-late '70s, rising at a rate of 1,000 prisoners a month.[22]

Unfortunately, a conservative penal philosophy often existed simultaneously with a conservative approach to government spending and an ardent desire to cut taxes. But corrections were expensive. The average national cost per jail inmate per year was $7,041. For adult prisoners in a state prison, the average yearly cost per inmate was $9,439.[23] Of course, John knew that there were rather wide variations by location for these figures. In New York City, it cost $26,000 a year to keep an individual in jail.[24] In Illinois, the cost for corrections rose 150 percent over a five-year period (1975–1980). Now the state budget for corrections was nearing $250 million, with costs guaranteed to rise even more dramatically as a new determinate sentencing law took effect.[25] If people wanted a lock 'em up approach to crime, they would have to pay for it. Either that or the guards working in overcrowded prisons would have to pay for it with increased threats to their physical safety. When people were stacked three and four in a cell originally built for only one, the result was going to be trouble for those working on the inside. It might mean trouble for those on the outside as well. The cost/benefit ratio for corrections was high, with a recidivism rate of between 30 and 66 percent. While nobody was quite sure what the rate was, it was almost certain to get worse if conditions inside got worse. People coming out of prison would be even more bitter and less committed to the norms of society. It would be both cheaper and perhaps more effective to follow the example of the Dutch. They imprison approximately eighteen people per 100,000, whereas in the United States the rate is 230 per 100,000.[26] John knew of a final irony in the

United States' policy of incarceration for solving the crime problem—its almost total lack of relevance for the world of the victim. The money spent on correction apparently did little for those subject to the process, and nothing for those for whom the whole system, at least ideally, was designed to give justice to.

There had to be a better way. But what it was, John did not know.

References

1. "National Survey of State Correctional Officers," *Corrections Magazine*, (December 1976), 35.
2. Ibid.
3. For an excellent discussion of the dilemmas faced by a prison guard see Edgar May, "Prison Guards in America," *Corrections Magazine* (December 1976). This conversation and some of those that follow are based on information in this article.
4. Another excellent source for a description of the life of a prison guard is William Rechtenwald, "I Was a Guard in Pontiac Prison," a series of articles which appeared in the *Chicago Tribune,* October 29, 1978 through October 31, 1978. This incident is based on these articles.
5. For a good ethnographic description of a typical working day in a guard's life, and for a discussion of medication procedures see Edgar May, "A Day on the Job in Prison," *Corrections Magazine* (December 1976), 6–11.
6. This incident is based on the *Chicago Tribune* articles cited above.
7. May, "Prison Guards in America," p. 44.
8. IRWIN. *The Felon,* p. 83.
9. ERVING GOFFMAN. *Asylums* (Garden City, N.Y.: Anchor Books, 1961), p. 207.
10. Ibid., pp. 48–60.
11. CLAUDE BROWN. *Manchild In The Promised Land* (New York: Mac Millan, 1965), p. 412. Also quoted in Irwin, *The Felon,* p. 75.
12. GOFFMAN. *Asylums,* p. 35.
13. GRESHAM M. SYKES. *The Society of Captives* (Princeton, N.J.: Princeton University Press, 1958), pp. 42–43.

14. GRESHAM M. SYKES. *Crime and Society* (New York: Random House, 1956).
15. DONALD CLEMMER. *The Prison Community* (New York: Holt, Rinehart and Company, Inc., 1958), pp. 298–301.
16. STANTON WHEELER. "Socialization in Correctional Institutions," *American Sociological Review*, 26 (1961), 697–712.
17. ROSE GIALLOMBARDO. *Society of Women* (New York: John Wiley and Sons, Inc., 1966).
18. MICHAEL FOUCAULT. *Madness and Civilization* (New York: Pantheon Books, 1967).
19. Quoted in *Corrections Magazine* (September 1978), 70.
20. W. PAUL ZEMITZSCH. "Illinois' Badly Overcrowded Prisons," *The St. Louis Globe-Democrat*, July 19–20, 1980, p. 3E.
21. Ibid.
22. Ibid.
23. NEIL M. SINGER and VIRGINIA B. WRIGHT. *Cost Analysis of Correctional Standards: Institutional-Based Programs and Parole* (Washington, D.C.: American Bar Association, Correctional Economic Center, U.S. Government Printing Office, 1976), I.
24. COOPERS and LYBRAND. *The Cost of Incarceration in New York City* (Hackensack, N.J.: National Council on Crime and Delinquency, 1978).
25. ZEMITZSCH. "Illinois' Overcrowded Prisons."
26. POLLY D. SMITH. *Mildness Breeds Mildness: A Look at the Dutch Penal System and Attitudes* (Philadelphia, Pa.: American Foundation, 1977).

chapter eleven

The Forgotten Role in Criminal Justice: The Victim

Who Is the Victim?

Mrs. Joanne Lemay is a thirty-five-year-old, white, middle-class suburban housewife. She is currently sitting on her living room couch, wearing only an old, soiled housedress. She is in a fetal position. Her husband will come home and find her like this. Her house is in disarray. Her two children are on the second floor watching television and eating cupcakes washed down with cherry sodas. That will be their dinner. Since Mommy has been taking her medicine more often, anything more substantial than cupcakes and soda has been increasingly rare. When Daddy comes home, he will just yell. Mommy's medicine consists of a variety of pills. She began her regime of pill-taking three years ago by taking one of the amphetamines for help in dieting. After a period of time these pills began to make her feel extremely nervous and upset. To counteract this she took one of the minor tranquilizers, diazepam, and over time increased her dosage substantially. She also found that she needed help sleeping. Secobarbital was the drug taken for this problem. All of the drugs being taken by Mrs. Lemay are the result of prescriptions given her by her physician.

Willie Evans is a sixteen-year-old, black youth. He lives with his mother and five brothers and sisters in a two-room flat in a deteriorating city neighborhood. Today he decided to skip school. He earned some extra money helping old man Bailey clean out his candy shop, and he is now walking down the street deciding how he wants to spend his extra time and money. Two youths, whom he vaguely recognizes as dudes from the neighborhood, approach from the opposite direction. As they pass, Willie hears one youth say, "Let's pop him." It is the last thing Willie hears before a sharp pain rips at his shoulder blades, convulses his body, and doubles him up on the sidewalk. He blacks out. His assailants get six dollars. Willie will die in the ambulance on his way to the hospital.

Mr. and Mr. John Wydown are on their way to a combination Christmas party and family reunion at Mrs. Wydown's mother's house. Mrs. Wydown has been looking forward to this day for a long time. She has not seen her two older sisters for a number of years, since each moved with their husbands to opposite coasts. They are within five miles of their destination on a two-lane, secondary highway. A car crosses over into their lane. Mr. Wydown reacts a second too late to avoid a head-on crash. His head goes through the windshield. He is killed instantly. Mrs. Wydown survives the crash with multiple injuries. She will require extensive hospitalization and a year of physical therapy. The driver of the other vehicle is not injured. His blood alcohol level is .12. In the state in which the accident occurred, a blood alcohol level of .10 is considered legally intoxicated.

Mr. and Mrs. John Smyth are a middle-aged, professional couple with no children. Mr. Smyth is a CPA. Mrs. Smyth is an instructor at a local junior college. They have been married twenty years. On the day in question, Mr. Smyth arrived home before his wife and discovered that the house had been burglarized. A back door window had been broken and the thumbturn twisted to release the lock bolt. The loss was fairly extensive and included a portable color television set, a good quality fur coat, a number of men's and women's suits, and two guns that Mr. Smyth kept to protect his property in the event of a burglary.

The government lost twenty-five billion dollars last year because of income tax evasion.[1] Major retail outlets lose more through employee theft than through shoplifting.[2] In the construction industry it is estimated that between 1 and 6 percent of the net worth of a contractor's equipment is stolen each year.[3]

A large midwestern city's downtown area is deserted in the evening, as its daytime residents flee to the safety of suburban homes. Increasingly, large businesses are following their employees out of the central city areas to shopping and business malls in outer suburban rings. As a result, the rate of abandoned commercial property in the city is steadily increasing. Many families living in outer-ring suburban areas consider the core suburbs and the city unsafe. Indeed, a sizable number have not been to the city's downtown area in a number of years, and in certain families even older children have never been to the central city business district.

To this point, we have explored the implications of saying that the term "criminal" is conditional. The term is part of the construction material used to put together a logical, coherent social world. It will have different meanings and implications depending upon the building project of which it is a part. Police officers, prosecuting attorneys, defense lawyers, and prison guards all build somewhat different social worlds, and so their uses and applications of the term "criminal" are somewhat different from one another. If the term "criminal" is conditional, so, too, is the term "victim." Who is seen as the victim is in part dependent upon who is doing the seeing. The above cases are illustrative. Each portrays the plight of a potential victim or set of victims. They are potential victims in the sense that their victim status depends on how their plights are judged and by whom.

Creating Victims and Nonvictims

Consider the case of Mrs. Lemay. She is a victim, but of what? Her own weaknesses that cause her to abuse drugs? Medical malpractice? Ignorance of pharmacology and drug interaction? An unscrupulous drug pusher? Recall our discussion in Chapter 1 on the prescribing habits of physicians. Is the doctor in Mrs. Lemay's case just part of the American medical culture that is simply responding to the American insistence on a pill for every illness? Clearly, Mrs. Lemay is a victim of some kind, but is she a crime victim?

We have already seen that one of the conditions influencing whether the term "criminal" is applied to an individual is the individual's status. Chapter 6's discussion of Black's propositions about the amount and direction of law noted that, among people of low socioeconomic status, there was less law than among people of higher status but that, in terms of direction, law was greater as it moved from those of higher status toward those of lower status than when it moved in the reverse direction. Concepts concerning the amount and direction of law might also help us understand the likelihood of the designation "criminal victim" being applied to a person. It may be that an upper-class person is more likely to gain this status when involved in a confrontation with a lower-class person than the reverse. Moreover, when people of the same status are involved in an altercation, those of higher status are more likely to be seen as innocent victims, but of noncriminal activity, while those of lower status are likely to be seen as criminal victims, but victims who are somehow culpable. If Mrs. Lemay's case above were to gain some kind of official notice, we might predict therefore, that it would be handled through noncriminal channels, since when higher-class people come into conflict, there is less chance of the conflict being defined as criminal. The person seen as the cause of the problem will likely be treated through an administrative, rather than criminal, process, and the person victimized will be viewed as something other than a criminal victim.

The Smyths, on the other hand, will probably be viewed as wholly innocent victims of a burglary. Few are likely to ask why an inadequate lock was securing the back door or whether all appropriate target-hardening and security procedures were utilized. Fewer still will suggest that contractors, development planners, and so on need to pay as much attention to security needs as to fire safety codes. Finally, many people will say that at least Mr. Smyth had the foresight to keep a weapon handy in case of a break-in. Of course, burglars generally try to break in when nobody is at home. As one burglar said, "If I wanted to meet people I would have been a mugger." This means that most weapons kept for household defense are not only not used for the purposes intended but will often end up in the illicit gun market.

The lack of culpability on the part of the Smyths will be matched with the supposed obviousness of their victimization. However, on closer examination, even the extent of victimization is unclear. Middle- and upper middle-income people will likely have their losses reimbursed at least partially by insurance. Moreover, as Herbert Jacob notes in his book, *Crime and Justice in Urban America,* people of middle- and upper middle-income circumstances often enjoy the opportunity to replace objects lost through burglary with new items. This is because they are immersed in the disposable culture pervading American consumer habits.[4] In such circumstances, the loss is often psychic rather than material. There is a feeling on the part of the victim that a private territory has been sullied by the intrusion of a stranger. It may be stretching a point to term most property thefts as "happy crime," as some New York City police officers call automobile theft, but it is clear that in certain types of thefts, automobile theft perhaps being the most notable, nobody seems to lose.[5] Victims are recompensed by insurance, burglars get a return for their effort, and consumers of stolen property get a good price on an item.

When we talk about different kinds of victimization, particularly in terms of the culpability dimension, we are talking about a matter of degree. A police officer responding to the Smyth's house to take a report on the burglary might tell them that their back door lock was inadequate and that they should get it replaced with a double-cylinder deadbolt, but that would probably be the extent of the implied criticism of the Smyths and their culpability in the burglary. Compare that with what up until quite recently was the response of the criminal justice system to the crime of rape. Historically in our culture, there was a clear status distinction between men and women, with the former having a higher status. Thus, the crime of rape was a crime between people of unequal status. The perpetrator had the higher standing. The response of the system was to blame the victim for her own victimization. The way the victim dressed, the way she walked, and so on, were factors presumed to have enticed the rapist. If the case went to trial, a highly unusual circumstance, the victim's previous sex life was also considered relevant to her present plight. The whole system, generally, seemed to react in a way that would discourage official criminalization of the event. Police questioning would at times be crude and insensitive, prosecutors would be reluctant to pursue prosecution, and even the judicial response to the event would seem to favor the defendant. This is illustrated by the Lord Hale instruction, a cautionary statement that judges were required to deliver to juries considering evidence in sexual assault cases. It advised juries that while the charge of rape was easy to make, it was difficult to prove.

The above discussion is in keeping with Black's proposition about the behavior of law in the face of status inequality. Figures showing that, in the day-to-day operations of the justice system, such status considerations regularly affect the outcome of case processing are rather difficult to come by, however. Most of the defendants dealt with by urban criminal courts are the lower class/status members of the community. So, too, are most of the victims. Thus, there is often not enough status or class variation to show whether status of victim is correlated with case outcome. Nevertheless, there are certainly indications that status of victim contributes to the judgment of criminality and victim culpability in such events. The discussion of rape provides an illustration of the point when the status inequality favors the defendant. Further, data analyzed on 960 victims and 968 defendants in Indianapolis showed that, generally, the victim's credibility as a witness, culpability as an injured party, and status affected case dispositions.[6] Thus, for example, among defendants whose cases proceeded to trial, those who committed crimes against persons employed in high-status occupations were more likely to be convicted.[7] As indicated, however, most crime is between persons of equal status or class, with the stratum of participants likely to be the lower stratum. Again, this means that most victims are at or near the bottom of the social heap. Violent crime is far more likely to be visited upon the young, the black, and the poor. Even for certain property crimes, those least able to afford the loss bear more than their share of the burden. Burglaries, for example, are greatest for the lowest and highest income groups. Those in the middle are relatively safe. The rate of theft from blacks is higher than would be expected based on the size of their population, and homes of blacks are burglarized more often than are those of whites.[8]

The case of Willie Evans is an empirically accurate portrayal of whom the violent crime victim is likely to be. And yet, the response from the larger community and from its criminal justice representatives to this event might be only minimally sympathetic. As noted previously, such events might be seen as routine for the area. Clearly, available evidence indicates that those most likely to be crime victims are also the most dissatisfied with police response to their plight.[9]

Willie Evans was black, young, and a member of a lower-income group. What happened to him was tragic, and, because of the seriousness of the events, the matter will be treated criminally.

But how will the status/class attributes possessed by him and his antagonists affect the processing of the case? Again, evidence is difficult to obtain, but based on previously collected data concerning factors affecting the imposition of capital punishment, we might expect that Willie's killers will be treated more leniently than they would have been had they killed somebody of higher standing in the larger community. Garfinkel, for example, in a 1949 article, reports that blacks convicted of first-degree murder were more likely to be executed when the victim was white than when the victim was of the same race. Further, blacks who killed whites were more likely to be executed than whites who killed blacks.[10] In the most complete study of how interracial differences between defendant and victim affect the imposition of capital punishment, Wolfgang and Riedel found that in rape cases in southern states, black defendants were eighteen times more likely to receive the death penalty when the victim was white than when the victim and defendant were part of any other racial combination.[11] Black has implied that if the behavior of the defendants, rather than the legal charge, was the focus of comparison, the influence of status differences (whether measured by race or by income) on the likelihood of execution would be even more pronounced.[12] This is so because the legal charge itself is a variable property of law, and, therefore, lower-status people, according to Black, will be charged with a more serious legal infraction than higher-status people, even if their conduct is the same. In brief, then, both the perceived degree of criminality and the perceived degree of victimization attaching to the circumstances of an individual are conditioned by factors other than simple involvement in a particular empirical event. The notion that the degree of victimization is variable can be underscored by discussing the remaining cases presented at the beginning of this chapter.

The ambivalence of people toward certain victims is most clearly apparent when the victim is a large corporation or government entity. Although such organizations may be successful when they pursue legal claims against individuals or smaller organized entities and, in general, do better than such entities when using or avoiding law, the general culture contains a host of rationalizations that justify the victimization of such entities. In a sense, they are viewed as highly culpable in any untoward action that occurs against them. Thus, "ripping off" the government is O.K. because (a) everybody does it, and (b) the government is wasteful, corrupt, unfeeling, or fill in your own adjective. Big businesses, similarly, are seen as "nonvictims" if actions taken against a particular corporation are either (a) involving only money or goods, and/or (b) carried off with a certain panache. There are many examples from America's past in which the thief was raised to the status of a folk hero and a hapless corporation was lowered to the status of villain. Bonnie and Clyde, who robbed banks for a living during the 1930s, Billy the Kid, who did the same thing earlier, and D. B. Cooper, the famous modern-day plane hijacker, are examples of this phenomenon. Many of us, even the most law abiding, develop a vocabulary that permits a restructuring of the organization we are about to victimize, so that our actions can be justified and our prey made culpable. A favorite restructuring is the oft-heard verbalization that hotels and motels expect guests to take towels, ash trays, and so on. A single hotel chain reports an annual loss of $3 million in towels alone![13] Similarly, justifications are verbalized when people "borrow" office equipment from their place of employment. The belief that contractors leave things unguarded so that people can help themselves is perhaps the most blatant example of restructuring an event so that the perpetrator is blameless and the victim is culpable.

The fact that impersonal entities are easily devictimized by those about to exploit them does not negate the legal advantages such groups have when they decide to pursue a course that will result in the official recognition of their victimization. Legally, they are treated as nonculpable victims. Culturally, however, they often times gain little sympathy for their plight. Again, this appears to be so because many of us can easily invoke rules to justify their victimization. In this respect we are not unlike delinquents. Frank E. Hartung has shown that there exists in the public domain a set of rationalizations used by delinquents to neutralize the moral opprobrium of their conduct.[14] In other words, delinquents, by using what Hartung calls a vocabulary of motives, restructure the world so that their activities appear acceptable and right. As we have seen, everybody is engaged in structuring and restructuring the world so that one's actions appear logical, right, called for, and so on. We sometimes even use the same building strategy as delinquents for devictimizing our prey. Denial of responsibility, denial of injury, denial of victim, condemnation of the condemners, and appeals to higher loyalty are building techniques appropriate for justifying either purse snatching or income tax evasion, and, in the latter case, such rationalizations are more easily applied by a broader segment of society. Actions perceived as immediately beneficial to our self-interest can be and are made permissible, regardless of the short-term consequences for the receivers of our actions or the long-term effects on society and ourselves. The view generally taken toward drunken driving illustrates the point.

Certainly Mr. and Mrs. Wydown are victims, but what kind of victims? Most probably they will be categorized as victims of a tragic accident, not as victims of criminal conduct. The perpetrator could be charged with vehicular homicide, a criminal offense, but such cases are routinely handled in ways that lessen criminal stigmatization and, consequently, the punishment attached to the act. We feel sympathy for the victim but might also feel it for the perpetrator since, as has been suggested, the perpetrator can be more easily seen as like us, a "we" rather than a "they."

Finally, our cities can be categorized as victims of crime. Historically, cities have been viewed as hotbeds of vice and corruption. It is this image that led early reformers in a movement to rescue youth from adult criminal processes and to establish reformatories in rural settings. The growth of suburbia is, in part, a response to this cultural urge to seek the good life in an environment at some distance from the city. While many other factors have contributed to the outward migration of both people and industry from the city, such movement has done little to dispel the notion of the city as dangerous. It is in this sense that the city, too, is a victim of both crime and the fear of crime. The risk of crime victimization has been shown to be generally higher in cities. The risk decreases as one moves to the suburbs and is lowest for nonmetropolitan areas.[15] However, crime is not equally distributed throughout the urban environment. As the data presented earlier suggest, crime tends to be concentrated in central cities, the slums, and the downtown business section.[16] Obviously, the city is more than just its central business district and the deteriorating neighborhoods surrounding it. Further, crime is not directly related to city size. The rate of assault, for example, is lower in cities of one million or more residents than in cities between 50,000 and one million.[17] Thus, while there is some empirical indication that risk of victimization is greater in urban areas than it is in nonmetropolitan locations, the data suggesting this differential must be carefully interpreted.

When attempting to understand the meaning of urban crime, reporting habits of the population must also be considered. Certain studies have shown, for example, that inner-city residents turn to the police or other official agencies more readily for help in family matters than do residents of affluent areas. Therefore, a large number of the assaults reported to the city police are the result of intrafamily violence. A study of case dismissals in the Criminal Court of the District of Columbia showed that 75 percent of homicides and assaults involved prior relationships. Further, assaults accounted for over one-half of all the violent criminal cases. Ninety percent of these were dropped, in most instances because the assault involved either family members or people previously acquainted with one another. Overall, the study indicated that 60 percent of violent crime cases referred by the police ended up being dismissed.[18] The various statistics, taken out of context, can be used to argue that either (a) cities are dangerous, or (b) city courts are extremely inefficient. However, once the nature of most cases is understood, it appears that city courts are not inefficient, nor are cities dangerous in the way that term is typically understood. As has been indicated elsewhere in this book, the enemy is often not the stranger out there, but, instead, is ourselves and the people with whom we are acquainted. Moreover, individuals involved in such personal confrontations vary in their desires for official recognition as victims and, as will be discussed later, also vary in their propensity to keep and maintain their victim role. All of these variations, however, are seldom recognized when the city is defined as a dangerous place.

Given the above discussion, the fear of crime is perhaps a greater detriment to the quality of life in the city than is the actual empirical likelihood of victimization. Clearly, the two constitute different phenomena, with no necessary relationship between fear and the chances of becoming a victim. Women and the elderly fear crime more than do men and youth.[19] As we have seen, however, it is precisely the latter two groups that have a far higher risk of actual victimization. Despite a popular misconception to the contrary, as people get older their chance of victimization decreases. Yet, fear of crime can and does affect how people relate to the urban environment.[20] The abandonment of some of our downtown areas in the evening suggests that central business districts can be considered further casualties of the crime problem, and specifically the fear of crime. If cities are viewed as victims, it is clear that they are also viewed as culpable victims. Hence, there is little interest expressed in helping cities. They once again become defined as the place where vice, crime, and corruption reign, and the road to salvation is seen as the highway that leads to suburbia and beyond.

Obviously, how victims are perceived affects the policies society adopts toward those victimized and those viewed as the cause of the victimization. The social role construction processes of criminal justice personnel, then, control more than just the criminal or noncriminal status of individuals. Such social building also provides categories in which to place victims and either validates or negates their claims to special consideration. As indicated previously, victims are not a part of this process of validation (and, in most instances, neither are defendants). Victims, like defendants, are on the receiving end of a process they have little input into. They, too, are made over into an image more in keeping with the needs of criminal justice professionals rather than into an image in keeping with their own self-concepts.

Therefore, a number of questions arise. How do victims reconstruct their world after victimization? What does the criminal justice system contribute to this reconstruction process? Does it serve to reintegrate an individual into a world where beams do not fall, or does it confirm the world as an essentially unfeeling, uncaring place of random events? It is to these questions that we now turn.

Rules for Being a Victim

The preceding analysis suggests that there are different ways that the role of victim can be patterned. Available evidence seems to indicate that not all types of victimization produce a drastic alteration in one's social world.[21] In assessing the impact of victimization on various groups, William E. Berg and Robert Johnson conclude that elderly and female victims are more likely to see their victim role as self-defining.[22] These two groups tend to experience both greater lifestyle changes and have higher levels of anxiety than do younger or male groups of victims. The authors hypothesize that both the aged and women are more predisposed to the victim's role since, in their other relationships, they also experience a relative lack of power. Thus, the elderly experience less mastery of the world around them than they did when they were younger and, consequently, have greater feelings of vulnerability. Victimization simply adds to the construction material already available to see the world as essentially hostile and containing external threats. Women have similarly found themselves in situations of vulnerability, to which victimization simply adds a confirming note. The authors hypothesized that blacks, too, would be more likely to embrace the victim role than would their white counterparts. However, this proved not to be the case. The authors suggested that the discrepancy may be due to the fact that, after a point, victimization becomes an accepted way of life. Adjustments are made in the form of simply accepting one's fate or pretending, in spite of evidence to the contrary, mastery over the world (the "cool" role).

It appears that victims differentially construct their social worlds based both on what they bring to crime encounters and on the degree and type of victimization. Further, some types of victims adjust better than others, making the victim role a transitory one. For those who make the role a predominant one, the adjustments engaged in can sometimes be self-defeating. The elderly person who refuses to leave his or her apartment may be safer, but sacrifices the social contacts needed to maintain a healthy view of the world and one's place in it. Those who adjust to victimization by simply accepting their fate may not be able or willing to take the action necessary to lessen the likelihood of future victimization.

Victims' differing responses to their plight is in part due to the fact that, unlike court personnel, police officers, and other criminal justice functionaries, they do not work together to form a uniform view of the world. Thus, each relates to his or her new circumstances somewhat differently. Yet, there is a thread that seems to unite many victims. While the differences are not great, victims, regardless of age, sex, race, and other demographic variables, consistently rate police officers less highly than do nonvictims.[23] This small but consistent difference raises the issue of whether the criminal justice system itself contributes to certain victims' feelings of isolation and estrangement from society.

Research on this question has been relatively sparse. Nevertheless, that which exists is not encouraging. For example, satisfaction with the police decreases as the criminal justice process continues. Moreover, the later stages of criminal case processing result in increasing problems for the victim. Loss of both time and income escalate when the victim enters the criminal justice system, and these continue to escalate in subsequent stages.[24] Unfortunately, while the victim's losses in both time and money appear to increase as the case penetrates the various levels of the system, the victim's influence on the eventual outcome seems to decrease. In an analysis of 5,042 cases of violent crime screened by prosecutors in the Washington, D.C. Superior Court (1973), it was found that victim characteristics or victim behavior exerted the most influence at the time of initial case screening by the prosecutor. After that initial decision point, the victim had less and less impact on the process.[25] In a study dealing exclusively with the female victim's perception of the criminal justice system, it was found that both victims and a control group of nonvictims felt the system was fairly ineffective in handling a wide variety of crimes but that perceptions of ineffectiveness were heightened by the experience of victimization.[26] This feeling seems confirmed by Morton Bard who, with his colleague Dawn Sangrey, wrote *The Crime Victim's Book.* When asked in an interview what was the most pervasive complaint victims had, Bard responded, "The most prevalent thing we heard was disappointment with the criminal justice system, whether at the police level, the court, or the prosecutor's office. The victims had no sense of anyone in the system working for them. They believed the system was directed toward the criminal."[27] Based on the research available, it appears that the justice system does not do a great deal to reintegrate the victim into the view that life is essentially a routine, rational, controllable experience. In this regard, it presents both the victim and the defendant with a common experience. Instead of confirming the world as a place where falling beams are the exception, experiencing the doing of justice becomes a building block in the perception of life as a crap shoot. Ironically, then, the criminal justice system, for both the victim and the defendant, is status-confirming and world-confirming in a way that perpetuates an alienated, hostile view of life. It is in this sense that the system creates and perpetuates the very problem it is supposedly structured to solve.

Whether and how this all might be altered is the subject of the next and last chapter.

References

1. JOSEPH F. SHELEY. *Understanding Crime—Concepts, Issues, Decisions* (Belmont, Ca.: Wadsworth Publishing Company, Inc., 1979), pp. 37–38.
2. GWYNN NETTLES. *Explaining Crime*, 2nd ed. (New York: McGraw-Hill Book Company, 1978), p. 79.
3. Ibid.
4. HERBERT JACOB. *Crime and Justice in Urban America* (Englewood Cliffs, N.J.: Prentice-Hall, Inc., 1980), p. 18.
5. NETTLES. *Explaining Crime*, pp. 5–6.
6. MARTHA A. MYERS. *The Effects of Victim Characteristics on the Prosecution, Conviction, and Sentencing of Criminal Defendants* (Ann Arbor, Mich.: University Microfilm International, 1977). This dissertation from Indiana University is summarized in *Criminal Justice Abstracts*, September 1978, pp. 293–94.
7. The study did not always support the notion that culturally disreputable victims contribute to leniency toward the defendant. Victim characteristics did not invariably operate in a straightforward manner. Hence, the need to consider relative status differences between victim and defendant.
8. See Jacob, *Crime and Justice in Urban America*, pp. 21–24. Also, the U.S. Department of Justice, *Criminal Victimization Surveys in Eight American Cities* (Washington, D.C.: Government Printing Office, 1976) and *Criminal Victimization Surveys in Thirteen American Cities* (Washington, D.C.: Government Printing Office, 1975).
9. JAMES GAROFALO. *Public Opinion About Crime: The Attitudes of*

Victims and Nonvictims in Selected Cities (Washington, D.C.: U.S. Department of Justice, Law Enforcement Assistance Administration, 1977), pp. 28–29.

10. HAROLD GARFINKEL. "Research Note on Inter- and Intra-Racial Homicides," *Social Forces,* 27 (1949), 369.

11. MARVIN E. WOLFGANG and MARC RIEDEL. "Race, Judicial Discretion, and the Death Penalty," *The Annals of the American Academy of Political and Social Science* (May 1973), 119–33.

12. DONALD BLACK. *The Behavior of Law* (New York: Academic Press, Inc., 1976), p. 24.

13. "People, etc." *St. Louis Globe-Democrat,* March 8–9, 1980, p. 12.

14. FRANK E. HARTUNG. "A Vocabulary of Motives for Law Violations," in *Delinquency, Crime, and Social Process,* eds. Donald R. Cressey and David A. Ward (New York: Harper & Row, Publishers, Incorporated, 1969), pp. 454–73.

15. See U.S. Department of Justice, *Criminal Victimization in the United States, 1975* (Washington, D.C.: Law Enforcement Assistance Administration, 1976), p. 6.

16. JACOB. *Crime and Justice in Urban America,* pp. 24–25.

17. Ibid., pp. 20–21.

18. KRISTEN WILLIAMS. *The Role of the Victim in the Prosecution of Violent Crimes* (Washington, D.C.: Institute for Law and Social Research, 1979).

19. GAROFALO. *Public Opinion About Crime,* p. 19.

20. Ibid., p. 24.

21. Ibid.

22. WILLIAM E. BERG and ROBERT JOHNSON. "Assessing the Impact of Victimization: Acquisition of the Victim Role among Elderly and Female Victims," in *Perspectives on Victimology,* ed. William H. Parsonage (Beverly Hills, Ca.: Sage Publications, Inc., 1979), pp. 58–71.

23. GAROFALO. *Public Opinion About Crime,* p. 29.

24. RICHARD D. KNUDTEN, et al., *Victims and Witnesses: The Impact of Crime and Their Experience with the Criminal Justice System,* 2 vol. (Milwaukee, Wis.: Marquette University, Center for Criminal Justice and Social Policy, 1976), reviewed in *Criminal Justice Abstracts,* 9, no. 2 (June 1977), 135–36.

25. WILLIAMS. *The Role of the Victim in the Prosecution of Violent Crimes.*

26. CLARK D. ASHWORTH and SHIRLEY FELDMAN-SUMMERS. "Perceptions of the Effectiveness of the Criminal Justice System: the Female Victim's Perspective," *Criminal Justice and Behavior,* 5 (1978), 227–40.
27. Interview with Morton Bard by Robert Enstand, "What It Means to Be a Crime Victim," *St. Louis Globe-Democrat Chicago Tribune News Service,* 1980.

chapter twelve

Some Modest Policy Suggestions: A Summary

Never Trust a Guru

Public policy is a funny thing. The attempts of significant groups in society—legislators, urban administrators, community organizations, professional associations, and a myriad of others—to construct and apply strategies for societal improvement often have mixed results. Public policies designed to ease the lot of certain handicapped groups in our communities provided an illustration of the point. Groups whose constituencies are confined to wheelchairs lobbied for changes in the design of street corner curbs, building accesses, and the placement of elevator buttons. One result of this effort was the leveling of curbs at the intersections of sidewalks and streets. In some communities, urban designers replaced the hump between street and sidewalk with a smooth incline. This ramplike continuation of the sidewalk made it easier for people in wheelchairs to negotiate getting from one side of the street to the other. Children on bicycles also found the new design much more convenient. But, as with many public policies, there was an unintended consequence of the change. Seeing Eye dogs are trained to stop before leading their masters across the street. How do they know where the sidewalk ends and the street begins? Never having reflected on this question before, you might assume that the dog knows what a sidewalk is and what a street is, having learned the conceptual categories necessary for making such a distinction. Reflecting on it further, however, you will probably conclude that dogs, no matter how bright, generally do not construct their worlds with such conceptual building blocks as sidewalks and streets. A Seeing Eye dog stops at a street corner not because he says to himself, "Aha, a street. I must be careful crossing." He stops because he has been trained to stop at the abrupt demarcation between street and sidewalk. If the one just flows smoothly into the other, the concrete, material cue that the dog has been trained to recognize as a signal for stopping is missing, and, so, the dog continues on his merry way. A public policy designed to help those handicapped confined to wheelchairs had the unanticipated consequence of complicating the life of the blind, who rely on Seeing Eye dogs to negotiate cities' thoroughfares.

The criminal justice enterprise is replete with examples of failed policies and of policies that had unintended consequences. While it may seem obvious that there are no simple solutions to the complex problems associated with the phenomenon called crime, criminal justice remains one area of the public domain that appears to constantly embrace simple solutions. It is a field in which gurus are easily accepted. Pass a law, increase a penalty, substitute a treatment, spend more money, get tough, be lenient, do less, do more, do something. Underlying all of the reforms is the notion that the crime problem is soluble. During the 1970s, public expenditures for criminal justice rose dramatically, so that by the end of the decade, government at all levels was spending a total of over $20 billion a year for a system that employed well over a million people.[1] Despite the rise in both expenditures and personnel during the decade, however, there was not a correspondingly dramatic alteration in crime patterns. Yet, the notion persists that crime patterns can be dramatically altered in a short period of time. When somebody builds a prison there is the temptation to think that, finally, the community will be safe from crime. Why is it that nobody thinks the community will be free of disease if a hospital is built? Instead, the public feels that better health care has been achieved and, with it, a better chance of postponing the inevitable. We need not go to our reward prematurely because of inadequate health care. But again, hospitals connote only a postponement, not a reprieve. Such expectations regarding the effects of health care policy are realistic. This realism needs to be transferred to the domain of criminal justice policy.

At this point, it should be apparent why various criminal justice policies were not the panaceas promised. Everybody builds his or her own unique social world, and so nobody sees problems in exactly the same way. Further, what may be a problem for one individual or set of individuals might be perceived as an absolutely necessary element in the social world of another individual or group. Curbs are either a problem or a necessity, depending upon whose social world you are in. This means that, by structuring a problem and a solution in a particular way, one risks interfering with the construction processes of somebody else. People do not take kindly to having their view of the world challenged. Moreover, individuals are extremely creative in overcoming the challenges posed by others to their view of things. There are examples throughout this book attesting to the ingenuity and creativity of criminal justice professionals in maintaining and actualizing their view of the world, despite challenges from others.

The above discussion contains a moral for those concerned with change in society generally and with change in criminal justice specifically. The moral is, "Do not become a true believer, either in your own plans for change or in the plans of others." Nobody has *the* answer, *the* public policy that will solve all, or even most, of society's ills. Even you (or, in this case, me). The sentiment was captured in the title of a book, *If You Meet the Buddha on the Road, Kill Him.*[2] Despite the title, the book is not about violence, but rather about the need to be cautious in accepting uncritically the sayings, strategies, and directions of gurus. People actively participate in and create their social worlds, often at variance with what scientists and policymakers say they will or should do.

If No Gurus, Then What?

My impression is that the gurus of social science have lost favor with those who formulate and implement the public policies of criminal justice. Paradoxically, the types of policies flowing from the traditional theories discussed in Chapter 4 are both too complex and too simple to be of major importance to those seeking strategies for dealing with crime. This is not to say that the theories are unimportant in formulating a view of crime. As noted, such theories provide some of the background assumptions about who the criminal is and what to do about him. They do not provide, however, clearly defined strategies which the policymaker can utilize as part of a cost-effective crime control program with easily verifiable results. Traditional theories tend to concentrate on ultimate causes, and, as James Q. Wilson has remarked, the delineation of such complex causal factors usually has little relevance for policymakers.[3] The busy city administrator who is told that changing the family structure is the way to lessen delinquency is likely to say, "Thanks a lot," and shelve the report. Ultimate cause is not easily manipulated by public policy. And yet, the concern with ultimate cause found in traditional explanations of crime illustrate the point that the short-term prognosis for a radical alteration of the crime pattern is bleak. Those factors that are manipulable by public policy are the same ones that can only be expected to incrementally alter the overall crime picture. Thus, training the police in better investigating techniques or training citizens in crime prevention strategies might help alter the crime pattern for one category of crime or in one geographic locale, but, overall, the crime picture can be expected to remain fairly consistent in the short run. In the long run, as people begin to adopt different family styles, different educational delivery systems, and maybe even different economic structures, crime and crime patterns can be expected to shift. But, barring a sudden violent upheaval in the society, such changes will be a long time in coming. The historical review of various accounts in Chapter 1 suggests that crime and crime rates are intimately tied up with the values and social structure of a society. As has already been suggested, crime may be part of the price we pay for the cultural values and the economic structure that make up our modern, technologically sophisticated, corporate, capitalistic society.

Ironically, while many of the traditional theories about crime deal with complex ultimate causes that are often beyond the control of policymakers, the language imagery of such theories presents an oversimplified picture of crime, thus encouraging the belief in oversimplified solutions. Most of the explanations for crime and criminal conduct can be compared to still photography. A snapshot captures the moment. But, in a way, a snapshot is always false. It holds still an instant of time and freezes it. Life, however, goes on in a continuous stream. A still photograph is unable to capture process, and is therefore unable to illuminate change. Photographs allow for comparison, for example, Aunt Matilda when she was twenty and Aunt Matilda when she was fifty. But the movement from one point to the other, the process of going from twenty to fifty, is something that can only be inferred, not imprinted on a negative. Similarly, many of the theories that were discussed tend to use language in a way that suggests rigid, nonfluid, absolute categories. The sense of law as a process, the sense of criminal behavior as being a moment in time rather than an immutable definition of self, the sense of judgments about such behavior being flexible and responsive to a variety of circumstances, is lost. Most theories attempt to take a snapshot and freeze one moment or instant, which then serves as the foundation for a particular explanatory structure. In freezing the instant and ignoring the process of which the instant is just a fraction, the theories oversimplify. As Chapter 4 noted, our concept of crime gets trapped by the mechanistic language categories we use to talk about the phenomenon. We miss certain of the processing complexities. The policymaker's subsequent disenchantment with theory is akin to the disgruntled feeling of a customer taken in by a sharp salesperson. Traditional criminological theory provides a come-on of simplicity. Its language and background assumptions assure a simple, efficient "fix" for the problem. The unwary succumb to the pitch, only to find that there are no simple, short-term strategies for eliminating crime.

Policymakers have replaced the guru of social science with action strategies based on the practical. Theory has been supplanted by a desire for practicality and a belief in the value of utilitarianism. The cry is, "Let's do something. Let's see what works. Leave the theories to the professors." The pragmatic approach seems particularly popular with community groups. The result has been a number of programs that lack a general theoretical foundation. Rather than being based on social science theory, they are based on theories of everyday life, theories such as those used by the police officer and the narcotics agent in Chapter 7. Such citizen incursions into criminal justice have, however, resulted in some exciting programs. Some of these are discussed below.

In certain communities of the United Stages, groups of citizens have organized to observe the process of justice as it is transacted daily in urban criminal courts. These groups are called court watchers. They perform a variety of services. Once they become familiar with the system, they act as guides and sources of information for people facing for the first time the labyrinth of a typical big-city criminal courts building. Court watchers are more than just criminal justice travelers' aides, however. A citizen's presence in the halls of justice serves to keep attorneys and judges aware of community concern with their daily processing activity. Thus, citizens act as a check on the tendency to let bureaucratic concerns overshadow the legitimate interests of the community, both for its own safety and for the fair treatment of its citizens before the wheels of justice.

The elderly in a community can be a source for developing community guardians, since they are present in a neighborhood when many others are away. In some communities, the role of neighborhood guardian is formalized into a program of block watchers. People are trained to recognize what constitutes suspicious activity in their area and are given special instructions for contacting the police department.

Historically, citizen's groups have also been involved in certain specialized areas of criminal justice, particularly prison reform and community corrections. More recently, groups of citizens have helped establish victim assistance programs, victim self-help groups, and community education forums. One such group has established an effective antifencing program that includes citizen and merchant education on the distribution mechanisms for ill-gotten goods.

As you review some of these practical programs, your immediate reaction might well be, "See, who needs social science theory?" But recall some of the problems associated with everyday-life theories as discussed in Chapter 7. Such theories tend to be narrow in focus and fairly unresponsive to needed changes in perception and/or problem-solving strategies. True, traditional theory can fall prey to some of the same problems. Thus, to avoid such pitfalls, theory and practice need each other. Practice can correct some of the faulty mythology that citizens have about how criminal justice works, while theory can keep such experience grounded in a broad, self-critical base, preventing an atrophy of perception. Theory wedded to practice constitutes the Marxian ideal of praxis. Theory applied and lived contributes both to further theory and to community betterment. An enumeration of some of the problems associated with practical programs can illuminate the need for praxis.

First, there is a danger that citizens naïve about the process of justice may, as a result of their involvement, become converted to the idiosyncratic viewpoints of the practitioners with whom they work. Hence, some citizens who work with the police begin to argue that the police can do no wrong, and that it is the rest of the system that is totally at fault. Such total identification with a particular viewpoint has been carried to an extreme in some community patrol programs. Citizens have been known to respond to calls over the police radio and to administer curbstone justice before officers arrive on the scene! This type of conversion, however, need not always be so dramatic. Groups of involved participants, particularly those informed about the practicalities of criminal justice (with little, if any, theoretical base) can develop into what might best be termed "professional citizens." In effect, they discourage broad-based community involvement and act as experts, that is, the only people who possess secret knowledge capable of solving a particular problem. These comments are in no way meant to denigrate the need for *informed* citizen participation in the process of justice. Instead, they are meant to suggest a need for theoretical, as well as practical, training for such volunteers.

There is a second difficulty with too great a reliance on the practical. Programs and individuals immersed in the day-to-day doing of justice are likely to miss crucial elements in the process, unless some mechanism is available that allows them to maintain a broad view of the overall system. Prison reformers, for example, often talk only to prisoners and administrators. Thus, there is little understanding of the world of the prison guard, an oversight that causes this group to blunt the effects of suggested correctional innovations.

There is a final problem with programs based only on practical, utilitarian, everyday-life theories. Sometimes they get trapped in the search for practical results. "How much money has your program saved the system?" "How many cases have you diverted to lighten the administrative burden of case processing?" and "How many crimes have you or your group prevented?" are the types of queries that assault innovative community and governmental programs. The phrases "How much" and "How many" have often sounded a death knell for such efforts. Either that, or the questions have forced programs into rather grandiose interpretations of limited data, which argue the benefits of particular strategies far beyond what can be empirically demonstrated. There is a need to ask different kinds of questions, questions based not on a desire to unequivocally show practical results, but on an interpretive understanding of how people construct meaning. We turn now to the potential contribution such an understanding can make to the process of justice.

Conflict, Involvement, and Language: Some Nonutilitarian Policy Suggestions

The policy suggestions flowing from an interpretive view of social life can be conveniently summarized under three key terms. These three terms are "conflict," "involvement," and "language." Each highlights policy strategies in keeping with the notion that individuals construct their social worlds by invoking rules and indexing patterns to weave a logical, coherent framework for their activities. From this perspective, social order exists because people are able to convince themselves and each other that it exists. Therefore, the policy issues highlighted deal with certain of the convincing mechanisms available in the community.

It may seem strange to suggest that interpretive sociology (symbolic interactionism and ethnomethodology, but most particularly the latter) is capable of and/or interested in policy-relevant issues. After all, the perspective specifically cautions against having high hopes for systematically altering the construction processes of individuals through the rational application of any given set of policy principles. People will simply account for a new policy, a new disturbance in their social world, in ways that will allow them to perceive their world as still essentially intact. In the course of this "fitting in" of a policy, the policy and its intended effects can become considerably altered. Again, individuals resist acting in a way the policymaker conceives as rational and coordinated. From this perspective, it might be more accurate to talk about the criminal justice arena rather than the criminal justice system. Within the arena, different social worlds struggle for recognition and legitimacy, so that the process of justice results in a number of decisions about whose world view will prevail. The description of justice emerging from an interpretive framework seems to leave little room for policy-relevant statements. And yet, there is an irony in the interpretive view of social life. On the one hand, the view seems to argue that policy is of little value, since it will be accounted for and changed in its application. On the other hand, it is only through disturbances in a social world that creative, change-oriented processes are activated. The analogy of the oyster in Chapter 2 suggests that it is only through disturbances that pearls are created. In the same way, forcing accounts of taken-for-granted activity can produce changes in the way people structure their world. Policy interventions, while destined to only be incrementally successful, are, therefore, the necessary grains of sand for producing pearls of change. A second insight can be gleaned from this perspective. Since disturbing taken-for-granted activity is necessary to foster change, conflict becomes an important factor in fostering creativity in daily life. Policies that foster particular kinds of conflict can be part of a powerful dynamic for changing the perceptions of crime and community. In brief, the criminal justice enterprise must expand its arena for conflict so that a variety of accounts can be heard and argued, and so the rules for indexing and creating particular social worlds can be articulated. An expanded arena of conflict directly addresses two problems endemic to our system of justice. First, the mythology that surrounds the system is faulty. The language of the mythology (law and social science) seems to suggest clear demarcations between the good guys and the bad guys, the winners and the losers, them and us. Yet, the process of justice seldom results in an unambiguous demarcation between the forces of good and the forces of evil. The system is a system of compromising the various definitions of reality, so that a definition of a situation emerges that can be agreed to, more or less. Being more or less a victim, more or less a criminal, more or less right in the decision to arrest, prosecute, and so on, is at variance with the mythology surrounding criminal justice. What happens to individuals raised in the good guy-bad guy view of the world when they actually see how the criminal justice process equivocates these definitions? Most seem to become alienated from the process, doubting, questioning, and challenging the motives and viewpoints of those who are a part of the doing of justice. Police recruits look upon others in the system as morally unworthy opponents out to subvert justice. If justice is to be done, it is up to the cop on the beat. Attorneys, both prosecutors and defenders, look at police officers, judges, and each other as hindrances in getting their own jobs done. One's own career can be negatively affected by these others. Defendants go through the system, often unsure of exactly what is happening and feeling as the defendant portrayed in *Justice by Consent* commented, that the whole system is just a ". . . phony fucking game."[4] As noted in the last chapter, the victim ironically often ends his or her own criminal justice odyssey feeling the same way as the defendant does about the system. The low status given criminal justice personnel—police officers, prison guards, even criminal lawyers—attests to the general community's feeling about criminal justice. Everybody questions the system, seldom the mythology. Expanding the arena for criminal justice conflict can allow for improved mythology about what the system does or should do. Citizens need to be exposed to how criminal justice actors actually account for criminal behavior, and, alternatively, criminal justice people need to hear the accounts of citizens as they attempt to structure and explain the phenomenon of crime. The meeting and clash of accounts can begin the process of rebuilding the mythology surrounding the doing of justice.

Improved mythology is only one benefit of expanding the arena of conflict. A second benefit can be in the form of alleviating some of the alienation felt by those subject to the process of justice. Again, such alienation is felt by both the professional doers of justice and those subject to their doings. The alienation results, in part, from being left out of much of the process that results in a final account of a criminal event. The arena of the courthouse operates so that only a relatively few accounts are heard. Thus, the rules for deciding a case one way or another remain hidden from many intimately involved with a case, including, oftentimes, the victim and the defendant. Expanding the arena of justice so that more voices are heard can force an articulation of hidden rules, giving people the opportunity to at least understand what has taken place and to feel a sense of having been a part of some kind of community accounting mechanism.

Those concerned with criminal justice policy may be saying to themselves, "Well, that is all very interesting, but so what? At this point, I still don't see any specific policy implications flowing from an interpretive framework." Describing two specific programs might lessen the fear that "it's all just theory," and at the same time illustrate the usefulness of allowing for a broad-based conflict of accounts.

Community meetings about the problems of justice have been underrated by many in the criminal justice community. Such gatherings are sometimes seen by professionals as only speech contests or revival meetings. Everyone attempts to give his or her testimony about the state of the world, the state of the nation, the state of the state, and the state of the neighborhood. It seems that people like to argue about crime, much as they like to argue about the weather. These arguments seldom end in utilitarian, pragmatic action, however. The professional doers of justice who attend such meetings end up simply being flack-catchers. They catch all the flack, all the gripes and complaints, but they do not seem to catch solutions to the very real problems they face. Yet, such nonpragmatic, nonutilitarian activity serves an important function. It allows people an opportunity to express what they would like to see the world become. Individuals need such opportunities, because it is through them that common articulations of what the social order should look like can be forged. Again, social order exists because people are able to convince each other that it exists. The more opportunities for such convincing, the more isolated social worlds can be broken down and a sense of community emerge. Originally, the formal rituals of justice performed such a function. The process could serve to remind people of community ideals and of the kind of world individuals were seeking to create. The ambiance of the courtroom expresses this ritual function of justice. Raised benches, high ceilings, formal clothes, and even a robe for the overseer of the process are all symbols of the majesty of justice or, put another way, the majesty of the values we as a community would like to be identified with. As we have seen, however, the full carrying out of the justice ritual seldom takes place. Those rituals that are engaged in by court personnel are attenuated, and in the attenuation point only to one community value, efficiency. Where, then, can the average citizen testify to his or her ideals? Seemingly nonpragmatic community meetings, with people vying to be heard, may be the substitute ritual for expressing concerns of justice. The overconcern with pragmatism and verifiable results sometimes causes criminal justice professionals to overlook this important point. You might, though, at this juncture be tempted to ask a pragmatic question. What about the problem of crime? Such meetings do not seem to result in many solutions. That may be only partly true. These meetings can give their participants a sense of having been part of an important community activity. Thus, the problem of how to actualize justice in their lives, together with the problem of how to feel part of a community, has been dealt with. This, in turn, may stimulate more community involvement, and even if it is of the ritualistic variety, individuals are out and about in their communities, increasing the activity within their neighborhoods, thereby hopefully decreasing one of the opportunity factors associated with some criminal occurrences, the absence of an alert, visible citizenry.[5] Thus, to broaden the arena for constructive conflict, policymakers should encourage community meetings, regardless of the apparent lack of concrete, pragmatic results. Justice, or more correctly the sense of justice, does not simply result from a process for establishing concrete, empirical fact. It comes about when a community can give expression to the values and ideals it would like to uphold, a need provided for in the context of the nonpragmatic community meeting.

The methods of actual case processing can also be altered to expand the base of meaningful conflict, thereby expanding the sense of participation in structuring various case outcomes. Neighborhood justice centers provide an example of an expanded building site for putting together the meaning of an event. Neighborhood justice centers are defined as "facilities . . . designed to make available a variety of methods of processing disputes, including arbitration, mediation, referral to small claims courts as well as referral to courts of general jurisdiction."[6] Within the definition, two types of third-party intervention in a dispute (besides referral to the legal system) can be distinguished. Arbitration refers to those situations in which the party hearing the dispute makes a decision regarding its resolution. Such decisions are usually binding on the disputants. Often, arbitration is considered a last resort and is preceded by a period of mediation where the third party helps the individual disputants work out their own solution to the problem. In both procedures, however, the individuals bringing their dispute to the neighborhood justice center have ample opportunity to get their particular stories heard. The importance of being able to tell your story is noted by a probation/parole officer:

> I sometimes think that the biggest thing that we need to do as probation officers is listen to the client and hear what the heck he's saying and treat him as an individual, because there's a hell of a lot of resentment among probationers after going through that whole criminal justice system. . . .
>
> Everybody's got their own story about what happened and I think a lot of times the probation officer is the first one to actually hear what the real story is. . . . the more I do this, the more I think that's really what needs to happen. You know, we need to listen to what the heck the client is saying and not necessarily agree with it but just hear what he's saying.

Mediation and arbitration allow an individual to tell his or her story at the beginning rather than at the end of the criminal justice process.

The idea of mediating or arbitrating disputes outside of the formal legal system has a long history. Various religious and ethnic communities have often avoided the civil or criminal system for dispute settlement, choosing to rely instead on their own community mechanisms. Orthodox Jewish communities still maintain their own form of courts for working out disputes among their members. Less formally, certain Hispanic and Italian communities rely on their neighborhood church for third-party adjudication in a family or community altercation. Of course, the success of this type of dispute settlement depends upon an individual's commitment to a community, either religious or ethnic. Nevertheless, as the discussion of community meetings above pointed out, such activities can be a harbinger of community, as well as a symbol of an already existent common bond.

Mediation and arbitration also better fit the empirical nature of most disputes. They avoid the tendency sometimes found in formal, legal case processing to base a decision on a snapshot of an event, on that point in time when a dispute gains some sort of official recognition. Lon Fuller has argued that, often, disputes categorized as criminal, and thus disputes perceived of as having clearly delineated good guys and bad guys, are really polycentric. That is, they contain complex webs of cause and effect and complex rules for creating, indexing, and manipulating social patterns. This view is in line with the ethnomethodological perspective that argues that a current offense can only be understood in light of prior relationships of the disputants, the world views that they index, and the meanings they attach to particular events in their lives. Further, when such disputes are officially recognized, their ultimate categorization can only be understood when one understands the relationships of the criminal justice processors, both to the particular case and to their own bureaucracies and social milieus. Thus, while official case determinations at times take into account the background factors of those involved, such factors are filtered through the eyes of officials who have their own reasons for constructing events in particular ways. Mediation and arbitration allow for the articulation of complex webs of circumstance, while at the same time actively involving those individuals most intimately connected to the events portrayed. The stories told are accounts of the disputants, not accounts of criminal justice personnel who, as we have seen, provide an account of an account. Therefore, participants feel that they are more than just observers to a process, the outcome of which has little to do with them. In mediation and arbitration procedures, individuals are not simply cases processed, but are themselves the processors.

Neighborhood justice centers have, unfortunately, been plagued by a problem common to those community efforts that fail to articulate certain of their theoretical premises. Their success as judged by the pragmatic dimensions of cost, time, and the ability to relieve the burden of the court system has not always been clear.[7] On nonpragmatic dimensions, however, the success of such centers is less ambiguous. In a recent evaluation of three centers (Atlanta, Georgia; Kansas City, Missouri; and Los Angeles, California), it was found that nearly 90 percent of the disputants said they were satisfied with their experience in the centers. Moreover, in a six-month follow-up, 80 percent of the agreements arrived at were working well.[8] Alternatively, there are programs that are pragmatic successes but, on the dimensions of meaning and participation, are absolute failures. Indeed, typical statistics kept by prosecutor's offices concerning the number of cases handled, the number of people adjudged guilty, and so on, exemplify the point. The pragmatic statistics only seem to be indicators of success. Questions about the meaning of the process for defendants, victims, and even criminal justice professionals yield answers that suggest the impressions of success are illusory. In evaluation, then, errors are often committed by overemphasizing the pragmatic dimensions of the program being analyzed. When programs are analyzed along nonpragmatic dimensions as well, those programs that are less than clear-cut successes, pragmatically speaking, can appear much more worthwhile. Policymakers should, therefore, begin to ask different kinds of questions about the nature and benefits of programs seeking to foster community involvement in justice processes.

Different kinds of questions can also yield different strategies for reform of the legal system and its method for processing cases. As has been described in Chapters 8 and 9, the procedures of the courthouse are designed to enhance administrative efficiency, rather than a sense of community participation. The administrative nature of the process is particularly apparent in most misdemeanor cases, where rapid-fire, assembly-line justice is the norm. Professor Malcolm Feeley, in his book *The Process Is Punishment,* asks why, then, in most misdemeanor cases, should we even bother with the trappings of an adversarial procedure?[9] He suggests that, like Sweden and West Germany, American courts could rely on penal orders to control troublesome behavior (brawls, domestic altercations, petty theft, and the like). The order would describe the allegations against the defendant, summarize the evidence, and specify a punishment, in most instances, a fine. The individual accused could either accept the order or request a hearing. Feeley argues that such a procedure would more closely index the true nature of most misdemeanor case processing. By emphasizing its administrative nature and using judicial power only as a backup procedure, the rules of misdemeanor case processing are made more apparent to everyone. Obviously, such a procedure does not enhance community participation in the process of justice (nor does it really lessen it to any appreciable degree, since courthouse professionals control the present process), but, as Feeley points out, many people want to get their interaction with the legal system terminated as quickly as possible. Both defendants and victims often feel that a given incident is not ripe for protracted adjudication or mediation. In such instances, their wishes should be respected and the patterns of processing efficiency clearly enunciated and followed, thereby avoiding burdening participants with the sham of adversarial procedures.

Throughout this book, the importance of language in the building of social worlds has been emphasized. Thus, another policy-relevant area flowing from interpretive sociology is in terms of the language used to talk about crime and criminals in our society. At first glance, it may appear that a concern with language is like a concern with ultimate cause, that is, it is beyond the control of the policymaker. Yet, in an era of rapid technological innovation and mass media, policymakers adopt and disseminate new language imagery rather rapidly. We clearly need a new language imagery to describe the doing of justice. Language that portrays both the fluid nature of criminal violations and the legal processing of such infractions can increase public understanding. At the same time, a different language can provide criminal justice personnel with a rationale for carrying out their discretionary activity in a humane, consistent manner designed to convince individuals of the worthwhileness of the social order. Donald Cressey, in a review of Charles E. Silberman's book *Criminal Violence, Criminal Justice*, has argued that we are, at this point in the history of criminal justice, between rhetorics.[10] For a time, we talked about the doing of justice with a treatment rhetoric that allowed for the humane treatment of those subject to the process. This rhetoric has now fallen into disfavor. Increasingly, a prevention-deterrence rhetoric is being adopted which, according to Cressey, allows for barbarism toward those caught in the web of crime. He suggests that alternative language is therfore needed.

Programs of stress training, family life counseling, and crisis intervention in police academies provide an illustration of how a new language imagery can be introduced into justice circles and some possible benefits of such language changes. Officers learn a new set of supportive rather than punitive terms for describing their world, terms that help them articulate *their* personal problems and needs as well as the problems and needs of those whom they serve.

New images and new accounts are needed throughout the criminal justice system if we are to avoid creating the very problem we wish to solve. We are not being inundated by crime. We can experiment with different images, accounts, and accounting mechanisms. Consider that, in any given year, approximately 99.8 percent of people in the United States will not be victims of theft, 99.6 percent will not be victims of robbery, 99 percent will not be victims of car theft, 95.5 percent will not be victims of a burglary, and 86.1 percent will not be victims of larceny.[11] Most of those crimes that will be committed will be relatively minor and confined to a fairly limited geographic area. The criminal justice community and concerned citizens can afford to give time and attention to the nonpragmatic, symbolic, and ritual dimensions of justice. By doing so, understanding will increase and, more accurately, beneficial accounts will emerge, accounts that help both the community and those charged with its protection.

This book has, I hope, been one step in that direction.

References

1. See for example *Expenditure and Employment Data for the Criminal Justice System, 1978* (National Criminal Justice Reference Service).
2. SHELDON B. KOPP. *If You Meet the Buddha on the Road, Kill Him* (Ben Lomond, Ca.: Science and Behavior Books, 1972).
3. JAMES Q. WILSON. *Thinking About Crime* (New York: Basic Books, Inc., 1975), pp. 58–63.
4. ARTHUR ROSETT and DONALD R. CRESSEY. *Justice by Consent, Plea Bargains in the American Courthouse* (Philadelphia, Pa.: J. B. Lippincott Company, 1976), p. 46.

5. LAWRENCE E. COHEN and MARCUS FELSON. "Social Change and Crime Rate Trends: A Routine Activity Approach," *American Sociological Review*, 44 (August 1979), 588–608.

6. DANIEL MCGILLIS and JOAN MULLEN. *Neighborhood Justice Centers, An Analysis of Potential Models* (Washington, D.C.: U.S. Government Printing Office, 1977), p. i.

7. U.S. Department of Justice, *Neighborhood Justice Centers Field Test: Final Evaluation Report* (Rockville, Md.: National Criminal Justice Reference Service, 1980).

8. Ibid.

9. MALCOLM FEELEY. *The Process Is Punishment* (New York: Russell Sage Foundation, 1979).

10. DONALD R. CRESSEY. "The Scientist and the Writer," *Contemporary Sociology, A Journal of Reviews*, 9, no. 3 (May 1980), 341–47.

11. WESLEY G. SKOGAN quoted in Herbert Jacob, *Crime and Justice in Urban America* (Englewood Cliffs, N.J.: Prentice-Hall, 1980), p. 16.

Index